The World and Its People

CALIFORNIA YESTERDAY AND TODAY

THE GREAT SEAL OF THE STATE OF CALIFORNIA

EUREKA

SERIES AUTHORS

CALIFORNIA

Durlynn C. Anema, Director of Lifelong Learning,
University of the Pacific, Stockton, California

Val E. Arnsdorf, Professor,
College of Education, University of Delaware,
Newark, Delaware

Ronald A. Banaszak, Director,
Center for the Development of Economics
Education, School of Education,
University of the Pacific, Stockton, California

Dennis C. Brennan, Associate Director,
Center for the Development of Economics
Education, School of Education,
University of the Pacific, Stockton, California

Carolyn S. Brown, Late Principal,
Robertson Academy School, Nashville, Tennessee

Kenneth S. Cooper, Professor of History, Emeritus,
George Peabody College for Teachers, Vanderbilt
University, Nashville, Tennessee

Alvis T. Harthern, Professor of Education,
University of Montevallo, Montevallo, Alabama

Timothy M. Helmus, Classroom Teacher,
City Middle and High School, Grand Rapids,
Michigan

Bobbie P. Hyder, Elementary Education Coordinator,
Madison County School System, Huntsville,
Alabama

Theodore Kaltsounis, Professor and Associate Dean,
College of Education, University of Washington,
Seattle, Washington

Richard H. Loftin, Director of Curriculum and Staff
Development,
Aldine Independent School District, Houston,
Texas

Norman J.G. Pounds, Former University Professor of
Geography,
Indiana University, Bloomington, Indiana

Edgar A. Toppin, Professor of History and Dean of
the Graduate School,
Virginia State University, Petersburg, Virginia

GRADE–LEVEL CONTRIBUTORS

Jane Boston, Teacher,
San Ramon Valley Unified School District, San Ramon
Valley, California

Stephen Clark, Teacher,
Horton Elementary School, San Diego, California

Kimchele Lim, Teacher,
Robert Hill Lane Elementary School, Monterey Park,
California

Lydia Sarmiento, Bilingual Teacher,
Greenwood Elementary School, Montebello, California

Barbara Todd, Educational Consultant,
Former Teacher, Los Angeles Unified School District,
Los Angeles, California

Map chapter by Stan Christodlous, Executive Editor,
Social Studies, Silver Burdett Company

YESTERDAY AND TODAY

DURLYNN C. ANEMA, Director of Lifelong Learning,
University of the Pacific, Stockton, California

RONALD A. BANASZAK, Director,
Center for the Development of Economics Education, School of Education,
University of the Pacific, Stockton, California

DENNIS C. BRENNAN, Associate Director,
Center for the Development of Economics Education, School of Education,
University of the Pacific, Stockton, California

SILVER BURDETT COMPANY Morristown, New Jersey
Glenview, Ill. • San Carlos, Calif. • Dallas • Atlanta • Agincourt, Ontario

ACKNOWLEDGMENTS

Page 157: Excerpt from CALIFORNIA GOLD DAYS by Helen Bauer, published by Doubleday and Company, Inc.

CONTENTS

MAPS

ATLAS

GRAPHS

GRAPH APPENDIX

TIME LINES

DIAGRAMS AND TABLES

TABLES IN APPENDIX

SPECIAL INTEREST MATERIALS

END-OF-CHAPTER SKILLS DEVELOPMENT

CALIFORNIA

The land of California has wonderful variety. It has tall mountains and deep valleys. It has forests with the tallest trees in the world. It has hot deserts with some of the driest weather in the world. It has a rugged coastline and roaring waterfalls. It is not surprising that many people come to visit or to live in California every year. Let's take a look at California.

I LOVE YOU, CALIFORNIA

Words by
F. B. Silverwood

Music by
A. F. Frankenstein

I love you,___ Cal - i - forn - ia,___ ___ you're the great - est state of all.___ ___ I love you___ in the win - ter, sum - mer, spring, and in the fall.___ ___ I love your fer - tile val - leys; your dear moun - tains I a - dore.___ ___ I love your grand old o - cean and I love her rug - ged shore.___

Mount Whitney is the second highest mountain in the United States. It is 14,494 feet (4,418 m) high.

11

The Central Valley is one of the most important farming areas in the United States. A large variety of fruits and vegetables are grown here.

Death Valley is the lowest, driest, and hottest place in the United States. Once in a while it rains. The water dries up quickly, leaving miles of salt flats. Salt flats are made up of dried mud mixed with white salt.

The Making of Death Valley

California is known for its beautiful coastline. Every year many people from all over the United States drive along the Big Sur.

California redwoods are the tallest living trees in the world. The tallest of the redwoods is about 368 feet (112 m) high.

Some of the highest
waterfalls in the United
States are in Yosemite
National Park in
California. Nevada Falls
is shown here. The
Indians called it
Yo-wipe, or The Twisted
Fall, because it is
so wild.

Many people live in our beautiful state of California. In fact, more people live in California than in any other state. The people who live in our state are called Californians. Their ancestors, or family members of long ago, came to California from many places in the United States and from other countries. Even some present-day Californians were born in another state or another country. Where were you born?

18

These fourth-grade students are Californians. They told us about their families.

I was born in New York. When I was 4 years old, my father sold his vineyard in New York. We moved to California, and dad bought another vineyard in the Napa Valley.

LOUIS

GRETCHEN

My grandparents came to the United States from Germany in 1938. First they settled in South Dakota. Then they heard about the fine farmland in California. They moved here. I love to visit their farm.

GAIL

My grandfather was born in China in 1917. He learned how to draw plans for bridges in China. When he came to California in 1950, he was asked to draw plans for several California bridges and waterways.

My grandparents were farmers in Oklahoma in the 1930s. They had some years with very little rain. The good soil turned to dust. In 1937 they packed up all their belongings and moved to California.

SANDY

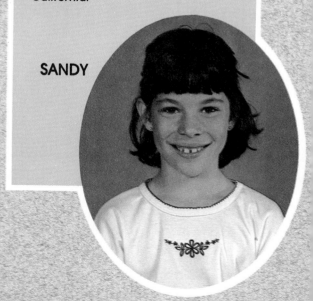

My mother was born in Japan. She visited Hawaii when she was 23 years old. She liked it so much, she decided to stay. I was born in Hawaii. Last year my dad's company moved to San Francisco. It was hard for my mom to leave Hawaii, but we like California very much.

TOSHIKI

RICHARD

My mom said our family has been living in California for a long, long time. They lived here when California was still part of Mexico.

My ancestors came to California from Alabama in the 1840s. They helped Darius Stokes, a black minister, to start 14 churches here.

MARIAN

MANUEL

I was born in Mexico. Two years ago my dad came to California for a good job. After he started working, he found a home for my mom, my brother, my sisters, and me. I am glad we moved to California. A lot of our neighbors are from Mexico, too.

MONNA

My mother's ancestors were among the first Californians. They lived here long before the Spanish, Mexican, and English people first arrived. My mother has taught me the music and dances of the Mojave tribe. She learned them from her mother.

21

Californians have many different kinds of jobs. The work they do makes California a healthy and growing state. Their work also helps people and businesses all over the United States. Here are some of the many jobs that Californians have.

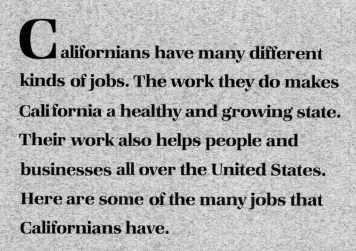

Oil has been found in or near California. It has been found on land and under the ocean floor. Some Californians are flown from the mainland to work on offshore oil wells like this one.

Many southern Californians build airplanes. In fact, southern California is the largest center in the United States for building airplanes.

Do you play video games or learn with computers? Video-game and computer businesses have grown fast in California. Here some Californians put together the tiny parts that make a video game work.

These Californians are working on their tuna nets. California is the second leading state in fishing. Tuna is the most valuable part of each year's catch.

About 30 million people visit California every year. They come to see the national parks, amusement parks, movie studios, and other interesting places. Many Californians have jobs guiding and helping visitors.

Most Californians love recreation. Recreation means all the things people like to do after their work is done. There are many different things Californians can do for fun. In fact, some people move to California because of all the different kinds of recreation here.

The Pacific Ocean and California's many large and small lakes offer people all kinds of water sports.

Californians have built special places for both Californians and visitors to our state to see and enjoy.

Zoological Society of San Diego

29

Hiking, camping, horseback riding, and skiing are some of the favorite activities in California's mountains, forests, and fields.

Californians like to cheer for their favorite teams. Some of the best sports teams in the nation are here in California. Can you name a well-known sports player from a California team?

31

Dear Student,

Our state of California is a special place. The pictures that you have just seen show that it is a beautiful state with many beautiful places to live in and visit. Our state has mountains, deserts, beaches, and the huge Central Valley. Our state has hot weather, cold weather, and mild weather. As you know, California has national parks, like Yosemite, and big cities, like Los Angeles, San Francisco, and San Diego.

We can find many different things to do here in California. We can surf and we can ski. We can visit famous museums and amusement parks. We can study at some of the best colleges and universities in the world. We can work in a factory, on a farm, or on a ranch. We can watch championship football, basketball, and baseball teams.

As you continue to read this book, you will learn more about the many different people living in California. You will see that Californians are very interesting people who face and solve many different problems.

You will also learn more about California's history and geography. Learning all about our state will be fun. When you finish this book, you will understand why California is such a special place to live.

Sincerely,

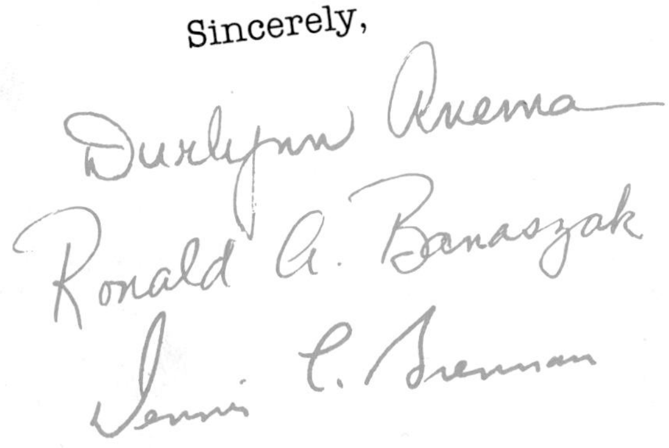

Durlynn Anema

Ronald A. Banaszak

Dennis C. Brennan

California—Our Home

Tools for Learning About California

Learning About the Earth

┌─VOCABULARY─────────────┐
astronauts	continents
sphere	history
globe	events
oceans	geography
└────────────────────────┘

Where do you live?   How would you answer if someone asked you where you live? Would you give the name of the street on which you live? Or would you simply say that you live on the earth? Of course, both answers would be correct. Your street is part of the earth. You do live on the earth. In fact, the earth is the home of all people. Only **astronauts**, or pilots who journey in outer space, can leave the earth for a long stretch of time. And even they must return. (Words in heavy type are in the Glossary at the end of the book.)

High above the earth   Have you ever dreamed about being an astronaut? Would you like to fly in a spaceship high above the earth? The first picture on the next page shows what the earth looks like from space.

The earth is a **sphere**. That means it is round like a ball. If you look at a ball, you can see only half of it at a time. Therefore you can see only half of the earth at one time.

A model of the earth   As the picture shows, the earth is made up of land and water. The picture of the **globe** at the top of page 35 will help you to see more clearly the difference between land and water. A globe is a model of the earth. It shows the shapes of the earth's land and water.

Oceans and continents   About two thirds of the earth is made up of water. The largest bodies of water are called **oceans**. There are four oceans. They are the Atlantic, Pacific, Indian, and Arctic oceans.

Only about one third of the earth is made up of land. This land is divided into **continents**. A continent is a very large body of land. There are seven continents. They are Asia, Australia, Africa, Europe, Antarctica, South America, and North America. Asia is the largest continent. Australia is the smallest.

The photographs at the top of the page and the map below them show that the surface of the earth is made up of land and water.

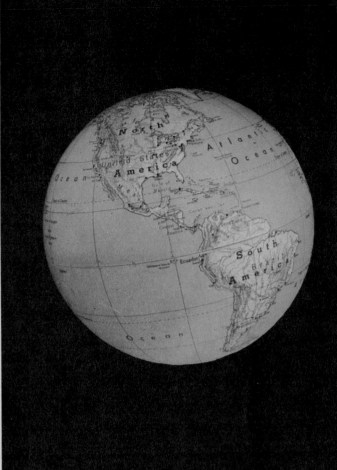

THE EARTH'S OCEANS AND CONTINENTS

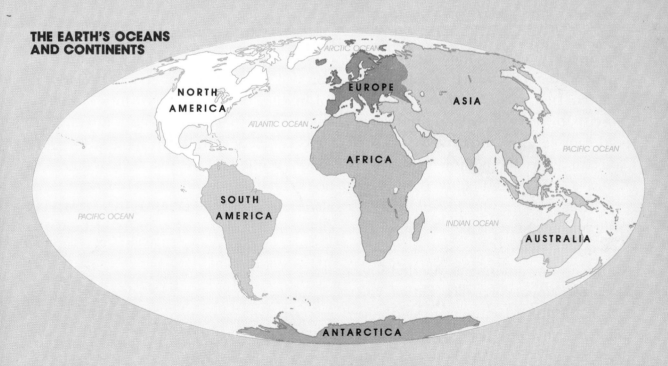

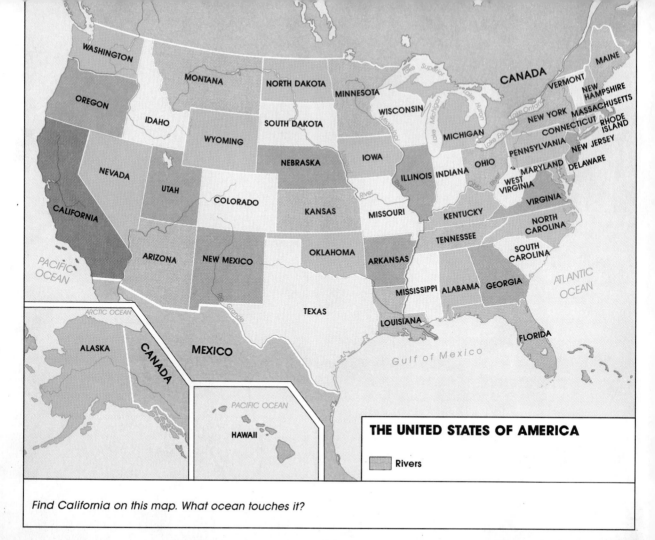

Find California on this map. What ocean touches it?

Countries   For us the most important continent is most likely North America. Do you know why? There are more than 130 countries on the earth's land. Our country, the United States of America, is on the continent of North America. The United States is the second largest country in North America. Only our neighbor Canada is larger.

States   Our country is divided into 50 parts. Each part is called a state. You live in the third largest state—California. This year you are going to learn more about your state. You will learn about its people. You will find out where they live and how they make a living. You will learn about the rich and colorful **history** of your state. History is the study of the past. The history of your state is filled with interesting stories about people and **events**. People's actions can make events happen. You will also learn about the **geography** of your state. Geography is the study of how people use the earth.

CHECKUP
1. What is a globe?
2. Name the four oceans.
3. What is a continent?
4. How many states are in the United States?

36

Finding Your Way on a Map

<table>
<tr><td colspan="2">VOCABULARY</td></tr>
<tr><td>maps</td><td>east</td></tr>
<tr><td>boundary</td><td>west</td></tr>
<tr><td>border</td><td>North Pole</td></tr>
<tr><td>north</td><td>South Pole</td></tr>
<tr><td>south</td><td>compass rose</td></tr>
</table>

Boundary lines There are many tools that will help you to learn about your state. **Maps** are among the most important tools you can use. A map is a special kind of drawing. Look at the map at the bottom of page 35. It shows the earth's continents and oceans. Which oceans touch North America? Now look at the map on page 36. What is the title of this map? What does it show?

A **boundary** is a line that separates one state or country from another. States and countries **border**, or touch, one another at the boundary. Sometimes the boundary is called the border. Name the three states that share a boundary with California. What country shares a boundary with your state?

This map shows a part of Sea World in Mission Bay, San Diego. Which sea animals would you visit first at Sea World?

The language of maps   Have you ever been lost? Have you ever wanted to go somewhere but did not know how to get there? Have you ever been in an amusement park, looking for a special ride? Or have you ever been at a zoo, looking for the animals you most wanted to see? If so, maps could have been a big help to you. Maps show you where things are. They also can tell you how far places are from one another. Maps can give you important and interesting facts. To find these facts on maps, you must first learn the language of maps. It is a simple language.

Directions   Before learning where things are on a map, you must first learn about directions. There are many ways to tell where something is. You could say that something is *up* or *down*. You might say it is *above* or *below*. You might also say it is to the *left* or to the *right*. Or it might be *in* something else or *on* something else. You have probably used these direction words many times. There are four other special direction words you should learn. They describe the main directions on a map. They are **north**, **south**, **east**, and **west**.

North is the direction toward the **North Pole**. The North Pole is the most northern place on the earth. The boy in the picture below is pointing to the North Pole on the globe. Look at the second picture on this page. The girl in this picture is pointing to the **South Pole**. The South Pole is the most southern place on the earth. It is at the opposite end of the earth from the North Pole.

The North Pole and the South Pole are opposite each other.

If you face north, south is behind you.

South is the direction toward the South Pole. North and south are opposite one another.

East and west are the other two main directions. They too are opposite one another. If you face north, east will be on your right. West will be on your left.

Sometimes a drawing like the one below is used to show where north, south, east, and west are on a map. This drawing is called a **compass rose**. It is also called a direction finder. The letters *N*,

The letters SE stand for southeast. What does SW stand for? NE? NW?

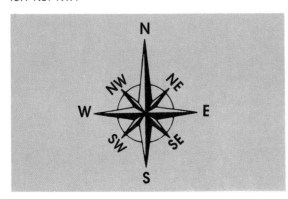

The North Pole is the most northern place on the earth.

E, S, and *W* stand for north, east, south, and west. Sometimes we need to find places that are somewhere in between two of the four main directions. The other letters on the drawing show us where these in-between directions are. *NE* stands for northeast. Northeast is between north and east. What do you think the other letters stand for? What direction is between north and west? Find all the in-between directions on the map above.

CHECKUP

1. How can maps help you?
2. Name the four main directions.
3. What is a compass rose?

Using Latitude and Longitude

┌─VOCABULARY─────────────────┐
│ **Equator**   **Prime** │
│ **hemisphere**   **Meridian** │
│ **latitude**   **grid** │
│ **longitude**   **estimate** │
└───────────────────────────┘

The Equator   Halfway between the North Pole and the South Pole is a special line. It circles the entire earth. This line is called the **Equator**. A half of the earth is called a **hemisphere** (hem′ ə sfir). The land and water north of the Equator is called the Northern Hemisphere. The land and water south of the Equator is called the Southern Hemisphere. The continent on which we live is in the Northern Hemisphere. Find both the Northern Hemisphere and our continent on the map below.

Latitude   The Equator is a line of **latitude**. All the lines that run *across* the map are called lines of latitude. Those between the Equator and the North Pole are called lines of north latitude. Those between the Equator and the South Pole are called lines of south latitude.

The Equator is numbered 0°. It is the most important line of latitude. All other lines of latitude measure distances north

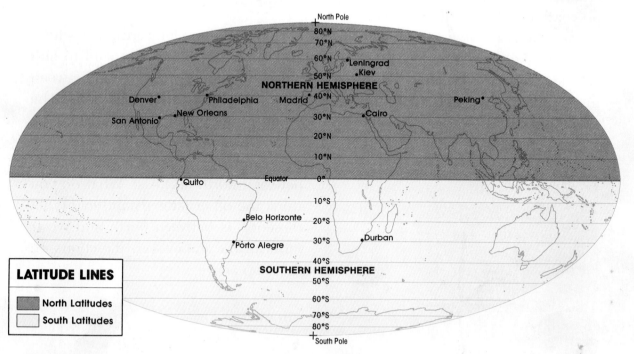

Philadelphia and Peking are both at 40° north latitude. What is the latitude of Cairo? Madrid? Kiev?

40

or south of the Equator. These distances are measured in degrees. The symbol for degrees is °. By using these lines it is easier to find places.

Prime Meridian   Lines of **longitude** are another set of lines drawn on maps. These lines run from the North Pole to the South Pole. There is one special longitude line. It is called the **Prime Meridian** (mə rid′ ē ən). It is numbered 0°. All other longitude lines measure distances east or west of the Prime Meridian. The Prime Meridian passes through Greenwich, England.

The Prime Meridian divides the earth in half from east to west. The land and water west of the Prime Meridian is called the Western Hemisphere. The land and water east of the Prime Meridian is called the Eastern Hemisphere.

Look at the map below. Put your finger on the line marked 30°E. Move it until you come to Leningrad. You will see that Leningrad is found at 30° east longitude. Look back at the map on page 40. You will see that Leningrad is also found at 60° north latitude. To tell someone where Leningrad is, you would say that it is at 60° north latitude and 30° east longitude. Philadelphia is also shown on both maps. How would you tell someone where Philadelphia is found?

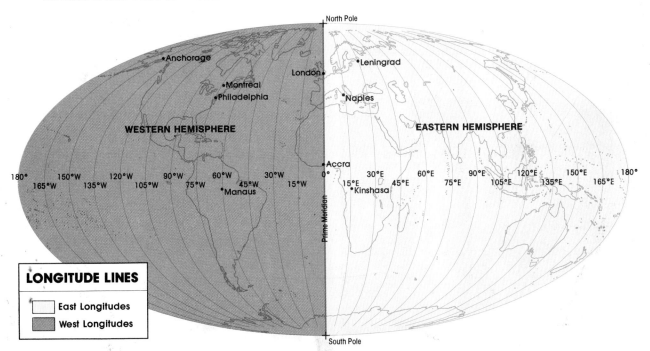

North America and South America are both in the Western Hemisphere. Europe, Asia, Australia, and most of Africa are in the Eastern Hemisphere.

41

Using a grid   If you know the latitude and longitude of a place, you can find it on a map by using the **grid**. A grid is a system of crossing lines or boxes. Crossing latitude and longitude lines are a grid. But sometimes the places you are looking for are not found exactly at the point where the two lines cross. When this happens, you have to **estimate**, or figure out *about*, where those places are. Look at the map of California on the next page. You will see that Los Angeles is found at exactly 34° north latitude. It also is located very close to

118° west longitude. Now find Barstow. It is not found exactly on any line of latitude or longitude. Therefore you have to estimate its latitude and longitude. Barstow is almost halfway between 34° north latitude and 36° north latitude. So it would be close enough to say that it is at 35° north latitude. It is also about halfway between 116° west longitude and 118° west longitude. So you would be close enough if you said it was at 117° west longitude. Figure out the latitude and longitude for San Jose, San Francisco, and Sacramento.

Notice that the crossing lines of latitude and longitude form boxes. At the top of the map you will see the numbers *1, 2, 3, 4, 5,* and *6*. Along the right-hand side of the map you will see the letters *A, B, C, D,* and *E*. Put a finger on the *C*. Put a finger of your other hand on the *4*. Now move both fingers, one across and one down, until they meet. You have now found box C-4. You will see that Mount Whitney, Sequoia National Park, and Fresno are all in box C-4. This is another way of finding places on maps. Road maps often help you find places in this way. What national park is in box A-3?

Sequoia National Park in central California is the second oldest national park in the United States.

CHECKUP

1. What do latitude lines measure?
2. What do longitude lines measure?
3. What is the Prime Meridian?
4. What is a grid?

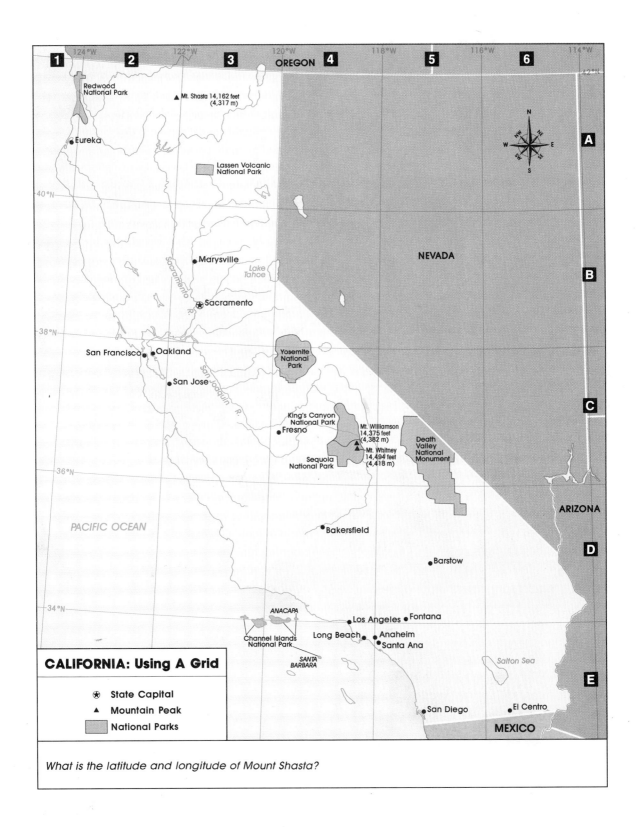

CALIFORNIA: Using A Grid

- ⊛ State Capital
- ▲ Mountain Peak
- ▨ National Parks

What is the latitude and longitude of Mount Shasta?

Symbols and Scale

Symbols   A map can show where any place or thing on the earth is found. Maps use **symbols** to stand for real things and places. The part of the map that tells what the symbols stand for is called the **key**.

There are many symbols that can stand for the real things and places on earth. The table on the next page shows only a few of the symbols that might be used on a map.

Scale   Maps cannot show places and things in their real size. To do that, you would need a piece of paper as large as the place being mapped. So maps are drawn to **scale**. This means that the places and distances shown on maps are many times smaller than their real size on the earth.

A certain number of inches on a map stands for a certain number of feet or miles on the earth. When we show size or distance this way, we say the map is drawn to scale. The map scale in the key box tells the real size or distance from one place to another.

Scale is also used to make copies of people or things. Have you ever played with dolls or model trains or model airplanes? Then you have a good idea of what scale is. The dolls you may have played with were much smaller than real people. The models you may have

THE METRIC SYSTEM

On page 47 you will find the words *1 inch stands for about 200 miles. (One centimeter stands for about 125 kilometers.)* Centimeters and kilometers are units of measure in the metric system.

The metric system is a way of measuring area, distance, weight, capacity, and temperature. This system is used in all major countries except the United States. Plans are being made to "go metric" here also.

To get you ready for this change, both American and metric measurements are given in this book. Each measurement used in our country is followed by the metric measurement that is about equal to it. Miles are changed to kilometers (km), inches to centimeters (cm), feet or yards to meters (m), acres to hectares (ha), pounds to kilograms (kg), and degrees Fahrenheit (°F) to degrees Celsius (°C).

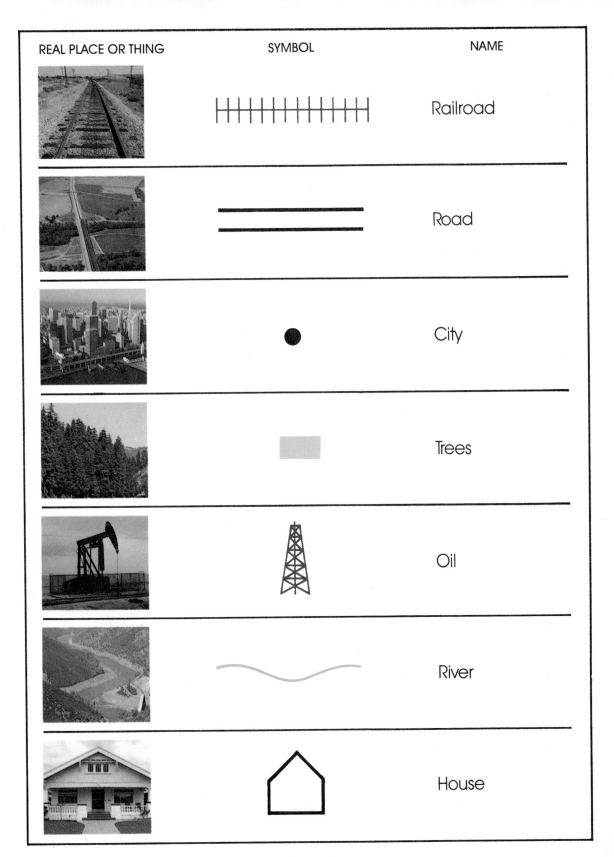

REAL PLACE OR THING	SYMBOL	NAME
	⊢⊢⊢⊢⊢⊢⊢⊢⊢⊢⊢⊢	Railroad
	══════	Road
	●	City
	▭	Trees
	🛢	Oil
	⌒	River
	⌂	House

Map symbols stand for real things and places on the earth.

built were much smaller than real trains or airplanes. Many model airplanes are built to a scale of about 50 to 1. This means that if you built a 1-foot-long model, you would know that the length of the real airplane was 50 times 1 foot, or 50 feet.

Make believe you are in an airplane flying over a football field. The football field would probably look like the drawing below. This drawing was made to a scale in which 1 inch stands for 20 yards. The drawing is 6 inches long. So the total length of a real football field is 120 yards, or 6 groups of 20 yards (20 + 20 + 20 + 20 + 20 + 20 = 120). How wide is a real football field?

Have you ever made a model of a real ship?

Have you ever played football on a field like this?

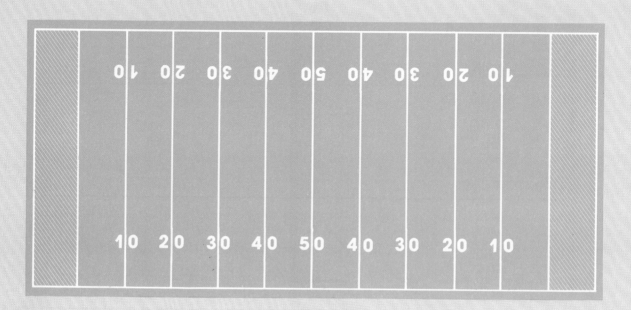

California and scale   The scale line on a map shows how much an inch (or centimeter) on the map stands for in real distance on the earth. A map can be drawn to many different scales. Look at the three maps below. Each map shows the state of California. But each map is drawn to a different scale.

Put a ruler under the scale line of the map on the left. You will see that 1 inch stands for about 200 miles. (One centimeter stands for about 125 kilometers.) On this map, how many inches (cm) is it in a straight line from San Francisco to San Diego? If you measured correctly, your answer should be about 2¼ inches (6 cm). To find out how many miles (km) it is from San Francisco to San Diego, you should have multiplied 2¼ × 200 (6 × 125).

Go through the same steps with the other two maps of California. You will find that the number of inches (cm) to miles (km) changes from map to map. However, when you use the scale for each map to figure miles (km) on the earth's surface, the distance from San Francisco to San Diego stays the same.

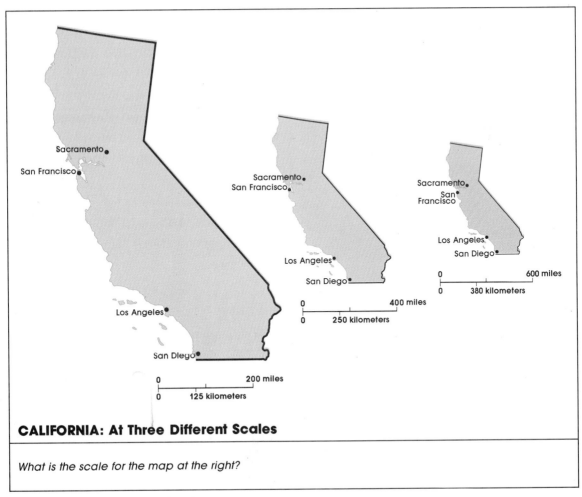

CALIFORNIA: At Three Different Scales

What is the scale for the map at the right?

A bird's-eye view Earlier you learned that a map is a special kind of drawing. Symbols, scale, directions, and a grid system are some of the things that make maps special. Another is that a map shows how the earth looks from straight overhead. A map is a bird's-eye view of a part of the earth. A map shows what a bird would see if it looked straight down on the earth from high in the sky. You would see what the bird sees if you were in an airplane looking down on the earth. The higher the airplane flies, the more of the earth you would see. If you went up high enough, you could see about one half of the earth.

The photograph on the next page was taken from an airplane. The map below it shows the same place as in the photograph. Find some shapes in the picture. Find those same shapes on the map. Find some water in the photograph. Now find the water on the map.

Find a symbol on the map. Look at the key to find out what the symbol means. Notice that the symbol is shown in the same place on the map as the real thing is in the photograph. Remember, the symbols stand for real things and places.

Looking ahead In the next chapter you will learn about the geography of California.

CHECKUP

1. Why do maps need symbols?
2. What is a map key?
3. Why are maps drawn to scale?

This photograph of an aircraft carrier was taken from an airplane directly overhead.

This photograph and map both show the coast near Monterey, California.

FROM PHOTOGRAPH TO MAP

KEY

Water		Roads	
Dock		Grass	
Beaches		Trees	
Sand traps		Other land	
Houses			

0		100		200 feet

| 0 | | 50 meters | |

KEY FACTS

1. Maps and globes are important tools used to represent the earth or parts of it.
2. Two thirds of the earth is covered with water.
3. A compass rose shows directions.
4. Lines of latitude and longitude form grids for locating places on the earth.
5. Symbols on maps stand for real things and places.
6. Scale helps us to draw maps showing places and distances many times smaller than their real size.

VOCABULARY QUIZ

Write the numbers 1 through 10 on a sheet of paper. Match these words with the definitions.

a. sphere   f. boundary
b. globe   g. Equator
c. continent   h. Prime Meridian
d. history   i. grid
e. geography   j. symbols

1. A line that separates one state or country from another
2. The longitude line numbered 0°
3. The latitude line numbered 0°
4. A round shape like a ball
5. The study of how people use the earth
6. A model of the earth
7. Shapes on a map that stand for real things
8. The study of the past
9. One of the seven large bodies of land on earth
10. A system of crossing lines or boxes

REVIEW QUESTIONS

1. What are the names of the seven continents of the world?
2. On what continent is our country found? What is our country's name? What country shares a boundary with California?
3. What is the most northern place on earth? The most southern place on earth?
4. Name the earth's four hemispheres.
5. What are the names of the lines drawn on maps that help us to find places?
6. How does a map show what the symbols mean?

ACTIVITIES

1. Use a world map to find each city at the latitudes and longitudes given below. On lined paper write the name of each city and the continent on which it is found.
a. 34°S and 58°W
b. 30°N and 31°E
c. 51°N and 0°W
d. 31°N and 122°E
2. Turn to the photograph on page 49. On a sheet of paper draw a map showing the places and things in the photograph. Remember to explain your symbols in a key box.
3. Use the map on page 43 to answer these questions:
a. Which state is on California's northern boundary?
b. How high is Mount Shasta? In which grid box is it found?
c. What symbol is used to show the state capital?

I/SKILLS DEVELOPMENT

USING A MAP GRID

WHAT IS A MAP GRID?

You have learned that some maps have a grid, or system of lines, that form boxes as they cross one another. The boxes are numbered across the top of the map. They are also lettered down the side of the map. You can use the letters and numbers to help find places on a map.

SKILLS PRACTICE

Use the map grid below. Name the city or town that is located within each of the boxes formed by the following letters and numbers.

1. A-2
2. D-1
3. B-4
4. A-6
5. C-4

For examples 6 through 10, decide which letter-number location matches the activity you could do there.

6. Camping
7. Mountain climbing
8. Watching airplanes take off and land
9. Gathering oranges off the trees
10. Watching cookies being made
a. D-2
b. A-6
c. A-1
d. C-3
e. A-2

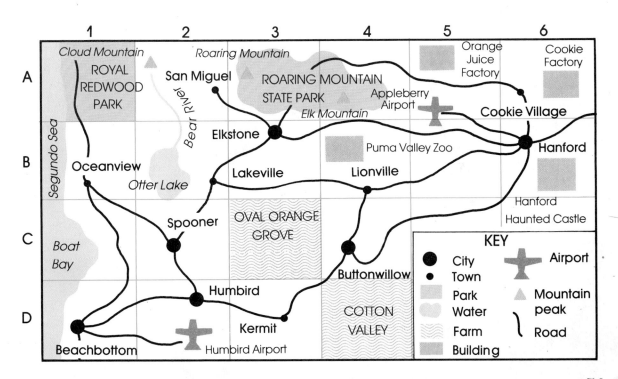

51

2 The Geography of California

Tools of Geography

```
┌─VOCABULARY──────────────────┐
│   mountains      counties    │
│   petroleum      population  │
│   plain          density     │
│   natural        graphs      │
│      resources               │
└──────────────────────────────┘
```

Learning from a song   In the Introduction of this book, you read the first verse of the song "I Love You, California." Turn back to page 10. Reread the verse. You will see that many of the words in the verse are geography words. Remember, geography is the study of the earth and how people use it. Below is the second verse from "I Love You, California." It also tells you something about the geography of our state.

I love your redwood forests,
love your fields of yellow grain.
I love your summer breezes,
and I love your winter rain.
I love you, land of flowers;
land of honey, fruit, and wine.
I love you, California,
you have won this heart of mine.

Questions to ask   All through this book you are going to be learning more about the geography of California. When you study geography, you must ask many *what*, *where*, and *how* questions. *What* are **mountains**? *What* is **petroleum**? *What* is a **plain**? *What* are **natural resources**? *What* are the names of our largest cities? *Where* are all of these things or places found in our state? And most important of all, *how* do people use them? These are but a few of the questions that will be answered in this book. You are sure to think of many other *what*, *where*, and *how* questions as you study about our state!

A large state   California is a large state. It is more than 800 miles (1,287 km) long and 250 miles (402 km) wide. Only Alaska and Texas are larger.

California is larger than 12 other states combined. Look at the map at the top of page 54. You will see that if California were placed over the lower part of Michigan, it would stretch from Michigan to Georgia.

California has many kinds of beautiful scenery, from ocean beaches and poppy-covered deserts to mighty waterfalls and rich farmlands.

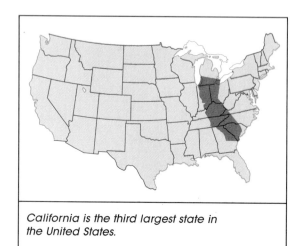

California is the third largest state in the United States.

Reading a table Look at the table on pages 308 and 309. It shows the names of all the counties. Look at the heads across the top of the table. What other facts are shown in this table?

The rows and columns of the table give you, in another form, some of the same facts shown on the map of California's counties. A table is a fast and handy way to organize facts. A table can

One state, 58 counties California is one of 50 states that make up the United States. California itself is divided into 58 parts called **counties**. The map on the right shows where the counties are located. What is the name of your county? Using the table below, find your county on the map.

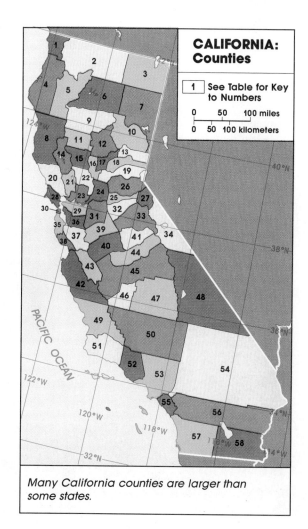

Many California counties are larger than some states.

1 .... Del Norte	30 .... San Francisco
2 .... Siskiyou	31 .... San Joaquin
3 .... Modoc	32 .... Calaveras
4 .... Humboldt	33 .... Tuolumne
5 .... Trinity	34 .... Mono
6 .... Shasta	35 .... San Mateo
7 .... Lassen	36 .... Alameda
8 .... Mendocino	37 .... Santa Clara
9 .... Tehama	38 .... Santa Cruz
10 .... Plumas	39 .... Stanislaus
11 .... Glenn	40 .... Merced
12 .... Butte	41 .... Mariposa
13 .... Sierra	42 .... Monterey
14 .... Lake	43 .... San Benito
15 .... Colusa	44 .... Madera
16 .... Sutter	45 .... Fresno
17 .... Yuba	46 .... Kings
18 .... Nevada	47 .... Tulare
19 .... Placer	48 .... Inyo
20 .... Sonoma	49 .... San Luis Obispo
21 .... Napa	50 .... Kern
22 .... Yolo	51 .... Santa Barbara
23 .... Solano	52 .... Ventura
24 .... Sacramento	53 .... Los Angeles
25 .... Amador	54 .... San Bernardino
26 .... El Dorado	55 .... Orange
27 .... Alpine	56 .... Riverside
28 .... Marin	57 .... San Diego
29 .... Contra Costa	58 .... Imperial

give you some specific facts that a map does not usually give. You can see from the map that San Bernardino is the largest county in the state. The map also shows you that San Francisco is the smallest county in the state. But the map does not show exactly how large San Bernardino County is. Nor does it show the exact size of San Francisco County. If you look at the table, you will see that San Bernardino County is 20,064 square miles (51,967 sq km). That is larger than the states of Rhode Island, Delaware, Connecticut, and Hawaii put together. What is the size of San Francisco County? How large is your county?

The county with the largest number of people is Los Angeles County. It has more people than any other county in the United States. In fact, only seven states have more people than Los Angeles County. Four other counties have more than 1 million people.

Geography, the study of people
The study of people is one of the most important parts of geography. There are more than 226 million people in the United States. About 24 million of these people live in California. This means that about one out of every ten persons in the United States lives in our state of California! More people live in California than in any other state in the United States.

Population density   The map on the next page shows the **population density** of California. Population density shows how crowded a place is. To find out the population density of a place, divide the number of people who live there by the size of the land. California has a population of 23,667,902. The size of California is 156,299 square miles (404,814 sq km). Divide 23,667,902 by 156,299. The answer is 151.4. So the population density of California is about 151 people per square mile. Many states have a higher population density. New Jersey has a population of only about 7 million, but its population density, 979, is much higher than that of California.

Which of these boxes is most crowded? Is that box larger than the other boxes?

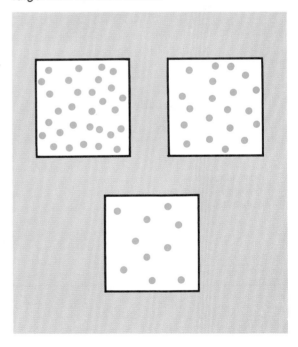

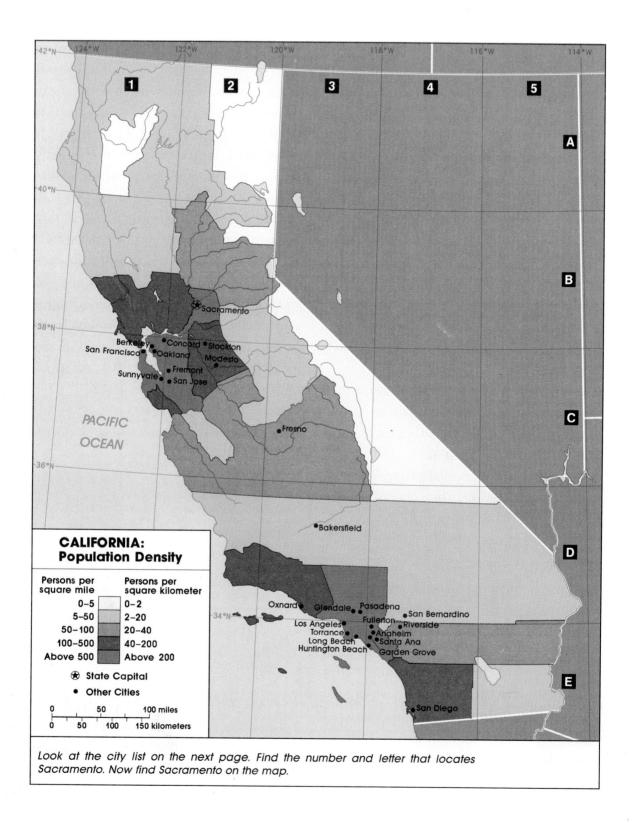

CALIFORNIA: Population Density

Persons per square mile	Persons per square kilometer
0–5	0–2
5–50	2–20
50–100	20–40
100–500	40–200
Above 500	Above 200

⊛ State Capital

● Other Cities

0   50   100 miles

0   50   100   150 kilometers

Look at the city list on the next page. Find the number and letter that locates Sacramento. Now find Sacramento on the map.

Cities with 1,000,000 or more		Fullerton	E-4
		Garden Grove	E-4
Los Angeles	E-3	Glendale	D-3
Cities with 500,000–999,999		Huntington Beach	E-4
		Long Beach	E-3
San Diego	E-4	Modesto	C-2
San Francisco	C-1	Oakland	C-1
San Jose	C-2	Oxnard	D-3
		Pasadena	D-3
Cities with 100,000–499,999		Riverside	E-4
Anaheim	E-4	Sacramento	B-2
Bakersfield	D-3	San Bernardino	D-4
Berkeley	C-1	Santa Ana	E-4
Concord	C-1	Stockton	C-2
Fremont	C-2	Sunnyvale	C-1
Fresno	C-3	Torrance	E-3

Cities   The map also shows all the cities in the state that have a population of 100,000 or more. Look at the city list above. The cities are grouped by population. How many cities have a population of 500,000 or more?

Drawings to compare things   You have been learning about our state through words, photographs, maps, and tables. Now let's learn by reading **graphs.** A graph, like a map, is a special kind of drawing. It uses pictures, circles, bars, and lines to compare things.

Pictographs   There are four different kinds of graphs. One of the simplest graphs is called a pictograph. It uses small symbols or pictures to stand for information. Look at the pictograph below. What is its title? Notice that each symbol stands for 1 million people. The numbers along the left side show years.

What was the population of California in 1900?

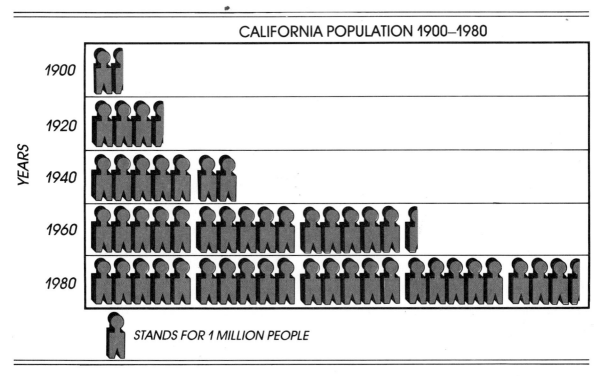

CALIFORNIA POPULATION 1900–1980

YEARS

1900
1920
1940
1960
1980

STANDS FOR 1 MILLION PEOPLE

Look at the row marked 1900. It shows 1½ symbols. Remember, each symbol stands for 1 million people. So 1½ symbols stand for 1½ million people. How many symbols are shown for 1960? How many people were living in California in 1960?

Pie graphs   The graph shown below is called a pie graph. If you have ever cut a piece of apple pie or another kind of pie, you know how a pie graph works. It is used to show the parts of a whole. In this pie graph the entire circle stands for all the cities and towns in our state. Each piece of the pie stands

Which size city or town is the most common?

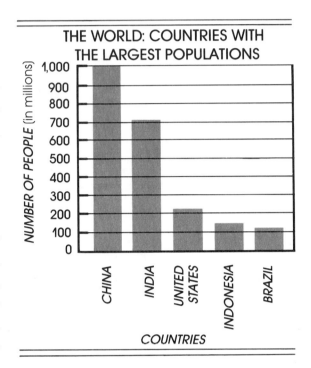

How many people live in India? In the United States?

for the number of places with a certain population. Which size city or town is the least common?

Bar graphs   One of the most useful kinds of graphs is a bar graph. Look at the one above. What is its title? Along the bottom are the names of countries. How many are there? Which country has the tallest bar? This means that it has the most people. Put your finger on the top of the bar for China. Now move your finger to the left. The numbers along the left show you how many people there are in each country. China has about 1 billion people.

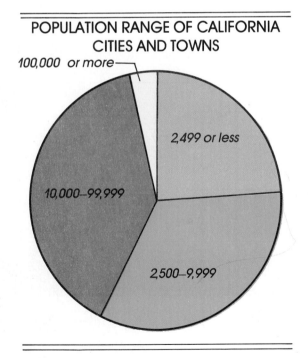

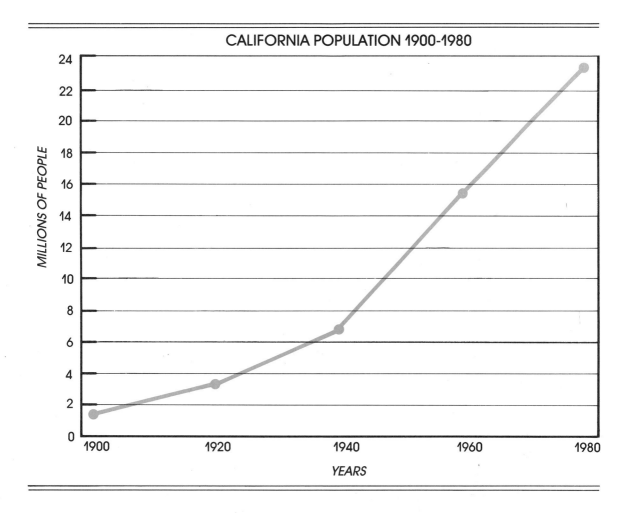

CALIFORNIA POPULATION 1900-1980

(y-axis: MILLIONS OF PEOPLE, 0 to 24; x-axis: YEARS, 1900 to 1980)

What do the numbers along the bottom of the graph show? What do the numbers along the left side show?

Line graphs   A line graph is another kind of graph. It is usually used to show how things change over a period of time. On page 57 you saw how a pictograph could be used to show the change in California's population over the years. Now let's look at that same information on a line graph. How many people were living in California in 1920?

About how many more people were living in California in 1980 than in 1920?

CHECKUP

1. How does California rank among the 50 states in size?
2. How many California counties have a population of 1,000,000 or more?
3. Name four kinds of graphs and explain how they are different.

California's Natural Resources

Nature and California California is rich in natural resources. A natural resource is something that is useful to people and supplied by nature. Land, water, forests, soil, and petroleum are all natural resources. Natural resources are not made by people. But people do use them to make other things. Forests might be used to make lumber. And oil, from petroleum, is used in our cars and to heat our homes.

Food for our nation Because of its rich soil, California has become our nation's leading farming state. Look at the table on the right. It shows where California ranks in growing certain crops and in raising farm animals.

The graphs on pages 304 and 305 show how some other states compare with our state of California in natural resources and farming wealth.

National parks Much of the natural beauty of California has been saved through state and **national parks.** These parks provide **recreation** for millions of people. Recreation is the activities people choose for fun and rest. People from

RANK OF CALIFORNIA FARM PRODUCTS IN THE UNITED STATES

Farm product	Rank	Farm product	Rank
Apples	5	Lettuce	1
Apricots	1	Lima beans	1
Cantaloupe	1	Rice	2
Cherries	2	Spinach	1
Grapefruit	2	Sugar beets	1
Grapes	1	Sweet potatoes	3
Lemons	1		
Oranges	2	Chickens	1
Peaches	1	Dairy cows	3
Pears	1	Sheep	2
Strawberries	1	Turkeys	2
Asparagus	1	Eggs	1
Barley	3	Almonds	1
Carrots	1	Cotton	2
Cauliflower	1	Honey	1
Celery	1		

all over the world come to visit the state and national parks in California.

A national park is a park that is cared for by the United States government. It belongs to all the people of our country. California has six of these parks. Find them on the map on page 43.

Three national parks are found in the Sierra Nevada. They are Yosemite, Sequoia, and Kings Canyon. Yosemite is on the western side of the Sierra Nevada. It is known for its beautiful waterfalls. Upper Yosemite Falls drops 1,430 feet (436 m). That is nine times higher than Niagara Falls in New York State.

Sequoia and Kings Canyon national parks are next to each other. A visit to either park is almost like going back 3,000 years. Giant **sequoia** trees grow in these two parks. They are among the oldest and largest living things on earth. In fact, sequoia forests grew on the earth before there were any people!

The trunk of the giant General Sherman sequoia is about 101 feet (30 m) around at the base.

Kings Canyon National Park has a giant sequoia named General Grant. It is 267 feet (81 m) tall. Sequoia National Park has another famous giant sequoia called General Sherman. It is about 275 feet (84 m) tall and about 3,500 years old. Mount Whitney, the second highest point in the United States, is in Sequoia National Park.

The newest national park in California is Redwood National Park. It is near Crescent City along the northern coast. Coastal redwoods grow there. They are the world's tallest trees. One of them grew to be 367 feet (112 m) high.

Lassen Volcanic National Park is in northeastern California. Lassen Peak is an old volcano. The volcano was active from 1915 to 1921. People have seen small amounts of steam coming from it since 1921. If you go through this interesting park, you will see other signs of volcanic activity. There are steep, rounded domes of lava. There is also Boiling Spring Lake. Its hot springs are heated by the hot lava inside the earth.

Channel Islands National Park is made up of eleven islands off the southern shore of California. The islands stretch 150 miles (241 km) from San Miguel Island to Santa Barbara Island. They lie between 10 and 70 miles (16 and 113 km) off the coast of California. These islands are home to many different kinds of plant and animal life. The brown

The pelican uses the big pouch under its bill to scoop fish up out of the water for food.

pelican lives on the islands of Anacapa and Santa Barbara. There are very few of these birds left in the world.

California also has more than 200 state parks, beaches, and historic places to visit. The state protects and cares for these places so that all Californians can enjoy them. The state park system was started in 1928 by a group of California citizens. Big Basin Redwoods, Jedediah Smith Redwoods, and Malibu Creek are just a few of California's state parks.

CHECKUP

1. Why are natural resources important?
2. Why are California's natural resources important to our nation?
3. Name the six national parks in California and tell something about each.

California's Climate

Weather and climate   Have you ever had to change your plans because it was colder than you had expected? Or maybe there was a time when it was too cloudy to go to the beach. Or maybe you have lived someplace where your school was closed because of a snowstorm. These are all things that happen because of nature. Rain, snow, wind, heat, and cold are all part of **weather.** Weather is the way the air is at a certain time. The weather may change from day to day, or even from hour to hour. It might be sunny this morning and cloudy this afternoon. Or it might be dry today and wet tomorrow.

The kind of weather a place has over a long period of time is called its **climate.** People outside of California speak of a "California" climate. Many people come to California because of its climate. However, there is no one type of California climate. Some parts of the state have a hot, dry climate, while others have a colder, wetter climate. Most Californians are within a 2-hour drive of another climate.

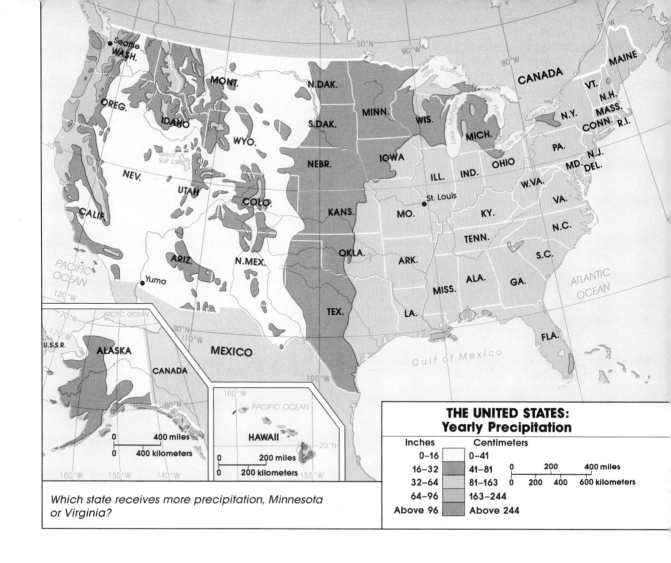

THE UNITED STATES: Yearly Precipitation		
Inches	**Centimeters**	
0–16	0–41	
16–32	41–81	
32–64	81–163	
64–96	163–244	
Above 96	Above 244	

Which state receives more precipitation, Minnesota or Virginia?

Precipitation   Rain, snow, and all the other forms of water that fall to the earth are called **precipitation**. Look at the precipitation graphs on page 306. Which are the driest months for Los Angeles? For Sacramento? Which are the wettest months?

Many parts of our state have a wet **season**, or time of year, and a dry season. Seasons are also part of climate.

During the dry summer season, many of the plants turn brown. But the winter rains make them green again. This is the opposite of what happens in many other states, where plants turn green in the summer and brown in the winter.

Look at the precipitation map of California on page 64. How much precipitation does your part of the state receive?

Temperature   The amount of precipitation is about one half of the picture of a place's climate. To understand

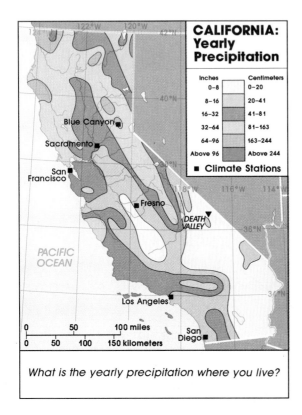

CALIFORNIA: Yearly Precipitation

Inches	Centimeters
0–8	0–20
8–16	20–41
16–32	41–81
32–64	81–163
64–96	163–244
Above 96	Above 244

■ Climate Stations

What is the yearly precipitation where you live?

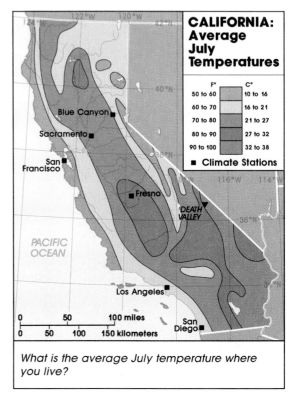

CALIFORNIA: Average July Temperatures

F°	C°
50 to 60	10 to 16
60 to 70	16 to 21
70 to 80	21 to 27
80 to 90	27 to 32
90 to 100	32 to 38

■ Climate Stations

What is the average July temperature where you live?

the entire picture we must learn about **temperature**. Temperature tells us how hot or cold something is. In order to find temperature we must have something to use as a measure. **Thermometers** are used to measure temperature.

Turn to the temperature graphs on page 307. The letters along the bottom of the graphs stand for months of the year. Which of the six places shown has the hottest July? Which has the coldest January?

Look at the map labeled Average July Temperatures above. Find Death Valley.

Death Valley has the hottest recorded temperature in the United States. On July 10, 1913, the thermometer reached 134° F (57° C). What is the average July temperature in Death Valley?

Other parts of the state are cold enough to have snow. Look at the map on page 65. It shows average annual snowfall for California.

Mediterranean climate   Most of California has a Mediterranean climate. In a Mediterranean climate, summers are dry and warm. Most of the precip-

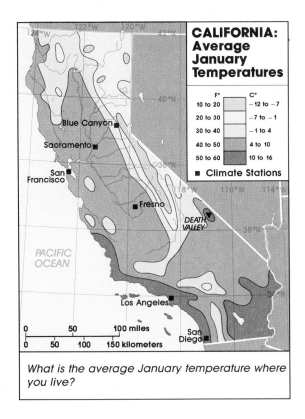

CALIFORNIA: Average January Temperatures

F°	C°
10 to 20	−12 to −7
20 to 30	−7 to −1
30 to 40	−1 to 4
40 to 50	4 to 10
50 to 60	10 to 16

■ Climate Stations

What is the average January temperature where you live?

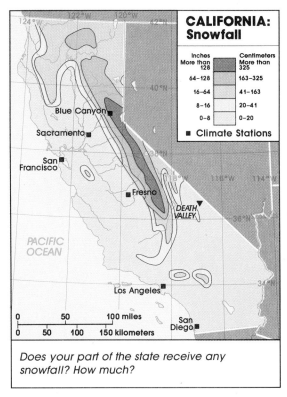

CALIFORNIA: Snowfall

Inches	Centimeters
More than 128	More than 325
64–128	163–325
16–64	41–163
8–16	20–41
0–8	0–20

■ Climate Stations

Does your part of the state receive any snowfall? How much?

itation comes in the winter when the temperatures are still mild. Many countries around the Mediterranean Sea have this type of climate. That is why it is called a Mediterranean climate. Find the Mediterranean Sea on the map on page 289.

Turn to the precipitation graphs on page 306. You will see that Los Angeles receives about two inches of precipitation in December. In December the average temperature for Los Angeles is about 55° F. Which are the driest months for Los Angeles? the wettest?

There is a lot of sunshine in a Mediterranean climate. That is why so many people talk about sunny California. Lots of sunshine allows California farmers to have a long season for growing crops. This is one of the main reasons why our state is the leading farming state in the United States. Later you will learn more about farming in California.

Ocean currents   Many factors affect climate. **Ocean currents** in the Pacific Ocean affect the climate of our state. A current is a steady flow of water

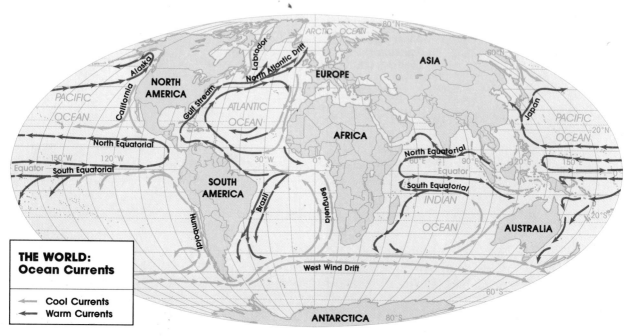

THE WORLD:
Ocean Currents

← Cool Currents
← Warm Currents

Find the California Current.

in one direction. There are cool currents and there are warm currents. Currents that move away from the Equator are warm. Those moving toward it are cool.

The California Current flows southward from Alaska toward the Equator. The water in this current is colder than the other water in the ocean. This current makes summers along the northern coast much cooler than they might otherwise be.

Look again at the temperature graphs on page 307. You will see that the average July temperature in San Francisco is about 16° F cooler than that in Sacramento. This difference is in part caused by the California Current.

The California Current also causes **fog** along the northern coast. Fog appears when clouds are formed near the ground. Most of the coastal fog appears during the late spring and early summer. At those times, warm air from the center of the state flows out over the water. When this warm air meets the cold water, it is cooled. This cooling causes water in the air to change into tiny droplets, or fog.

CHECKUP

1. What is weather?
2. What is climate?
3. Describe California's climate.
4. How do ocean currents affect California's climate?

Physical Regions of California

Four regions   California can be divided into four regions. They are the coastal region, the mountain regions, the Central Valley, and the **desert**.

The coastal region   The California **coastline**, or land along the edge of an ocean, or sea, is more than 1,200 miles (1,931 km) long. The coastline is made up of sea cliffs, beaches, and **bays**. A bay is a protected part of the ocean that reaches into land. Directly off the coast lie islands, such as Santa Catalina, San Miguel, and San Clemente.

The coastline provides Californians with recreation and beautiful views of nature. People travel from all parts of the world to drive along and look at the coastline. Many people also come to the coast to swim, surf, fish, or just rest. Malibu, Laguna, Carmel, and Santa Cruz are some of the coastal beaches that many people enjoy.

The coastline has been important to the growth of California. It has helped make California a world trade center. The Golden Gate Bridge stretches across the opening to San Francisco Bay. It is sometimes called the western gateway to the United States.

The Golden Gate Bridge is 8,940 feet (2,725 m) long. Its towers reach 746 feet (227 m) above the water.

San Francisco Bay, San Diego Bay, and Humboldt Bay are the three natural **harbors** along the California coast. A harbor is a bay that is deep enough for ships. San Francisco Bay is among the world's finest harbors. The ports of San Francisco, Oakland, Alameda, and Richmond are there. Ships from many other countries use the harbor at San Francisco.

San Diego Harbor is protected by the Point Loma and Coronado **peninsulas.** A peninsula is a piece of land that has water on three sides. The ideal location of San Diego Harbor makes it safe in all seasons. It is a base for the United States Navy. San Diego also has the largest fleet of tuna boats in the nation.

Humboldt Bay is the northernmost natural harbor in California. Eureka is its chief port. Eureka is known for fishing and lumber shipping.

The harbor at Los Angeles, Long Beach, was not formed naturally. It was improved by people. People made it safer for ships by dumping a long line of rocks in the water 3 miles (5 km) out from the coastline. The wall of rocks is high enough to break the strong waves from the Pacific. It is called a **breakwater**. An opening in this breakwater permits ships to sail in and out of the harbor. The port at Los Angeles, Long Beach, is one of the busiest in the world.

Most of the people of the coastal region live in the coastal **valleys**. A valley is a long, low place at the base of hills or mountains. The coastal valleys are known for their farming. The Napa, Sonoma, Santa Clara, and Salinas valleys are in the north. They are known throughout the world for their grapes and wine making.

The San Fernando, San Diego, San Juan Capistrano, and Santa Ana valleys are important southern coastal valleys. These once rich farmlands are now facing the problems of a rapidly growing population.

The land around Los Angeles is California's largest stretch of lowland along the ocean. The lowland covers 50 miles (80 km) of coastline between Santa Monica and Newport Beach. It is 1,750 square miles (4,533 sq km). This is less than 2 percent of California's land area. But about half of California's total population lives there.

Mountain regions   A mountain is land rising much higher than the land around it. Its tip may be peaked or round. The height of a mountain is measured in feet above sea level.

Look at the map on page 292. You will notice that over half of California is mountainous. You will see that many mountains form a long row. A long row of mountains is called a **range.**

The two major ranges in California are the Coast Ranges and the Sierra Nevada. The Coast Ranges run in a north-south direction. They follow the line of the coast. The mountains of the Coast Ranges are not very high. Mount Diablo, 3,849 feet (1,173 m) above sea level, is a landmark of the San Francisco Bay area. Clear Lake is found within the Coast Ranges. It is the largest natural lake totally within California.

Mount Shasta is no longer an active volcano. But if you could climb to the top, you would see a still active hot spring.

To the east across the Central Valley is the high Sierra Nevada. This mountain range forms a huge wall 400 miles (644 km) long and from 40 to 70 miles (64 to 113 km) wide. Some peaks are more than 14,000 feet (4,267 m) high.

The Sierra Nevada was named by the Spanish. *Sierra* means "mountain range." *Nevada* means "snow-covered." The higher parts of the Sierra Nevada are covered by snow most of the year. Many people like to ski in these mountains.

The 1960 Winter Olympic Games took place in Squaw Valley in the Sierra Nevada. The snow from this mountain range is also an important source of water for much of California.

The Klamath Mountains and the Cascade Range are in northern California. The Cascade is a volcanic range. Mount Shasta and Mount Lassen are inactive volcanoes. Mount Shasta, 14,161 feet (4,316 m) above sea level, is the highest peak in the Cascade Range.

An elevation map Distance above sea level is called **elevation**. The map below shows elevations in California. A map like this one is sometimes called a physical map. The lines that separate the colors used to show elevation of the land are called **contour lines**. All places along one contour line are exactly the same distance above sea level.

Find Sacramento on the map. What color is used to show the elevation of the land around it? Find this color in the map key. You will see that this color stands for 0 to 1,000 feet (0 to 300 m). What is the elevation of the land around Blue Canyon?

The Central Valley There are many valleys in California. The Central Valley is the largest. It also is the most important farming region in the whole state. Find the Central Valley on the map on this page.

The Central Valley is about 40 miles (64 km) wide and almost 500 miles (805 km) long. On a clear day a person standing in the valley can see the Coast Ranges to the west and the Sierra Nevada to the east. The Central Valley is really made up of two valleys. They are the Sacramento Valley in the north and the San Joaquin Valley in the south. The Sacramento River flows through the Sacramento Valley, and the San Joaquin River flows through the San Joaquin Valley. These two rivers are the longest rivers in California.

The Sacramento River flows south and the San Joaquin River flows north. They meet and empty into San Francisco Bay. A **delta** has formed where they meet. A delta is a piece of land made up of mud and sand. The rivers drop mud and sand as they flow into the bay. The delta forms over 1,000 miles (1,609 km) of inland waterways. These waterways are used

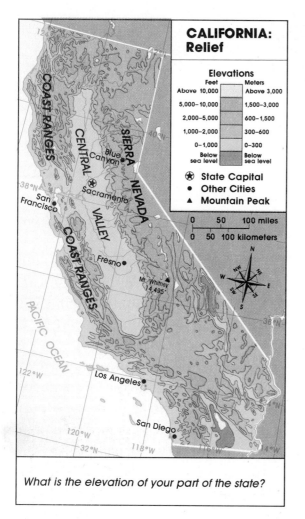

CALIFORNIA: Relief

Elevations

Feet	Meters
Above 10,000	Above 3,000
5,000–10,000	1,500–3,000
2,000–5,000	600–1,500
1,000–2,000	300–600
0–1,000	0–300
Below sea level	Below sea level

✪ State Capital
● Other Cities
▲ Mountain Peak

0   50   100 miles
0   50   100 kilometers

What is the elevation of your part of the state?

The Sacramento River winds through the rich farmland near Clarksburg.

for recreation and for supplying water to crops. Oceangoing ships can travel through the delta's waterways. They reach port at Sacramento and Stockton.

The Central Valley is one of the richest farmlands in the world. The soil is **fertile**, or rich, in what plants need to grow. The climate is sunny and mild. And there is plenty of water for the crops. Vegetables, fruits, nuts, and cotton are the major kinds of crops grown here. Some of the vegetables are tomatoes, carrots, and peppers. Some of the fruits are figs, grapes, oranges, peaches, and plums. Beef and dairy cattle, sheep, hogs, and poultry are also raised in this valley.

Much of the state's fertile valley farmland needs to be irrigated in order to grow many different crops.

The desert   To the east of the Sierra Nevada and the mountains in southern California is the desert region. A desert is a place that has very dry air, very little rainfall, and few plants. Desert days are very hot and desert nights can be very cool.

The deserts of California are caused by the mountains. Major winds travel from west to east across California. The moist winds from the ocean must rise over the mountains. As they rise they become cooler. Cool air cannot hold as much moisture as warm air can. The moisture changes into the form of rain or snow. By the time the winds drop to the eastern side of the mountains, they are drier. As they warm up, the winds absorb more moisture from the ground. The lands on the eastern side of the mountain are very dry.

The Mojave (mō hä'vē) Desert is the largest California desert. It stretches from the eastern side of the Sierra Nevada to the Colorado River. Most of the Mojave Desert is about 2,000 feet (609 m) above sea level. Small mountains with rounded sides cut across the Mojave. It rarely rains there. But when it does, many places fill in with water. The water is not very deep. The sun dries it up rapidly. These low places are called dry lakes.

Parts of the Mojave Desert also have forests. The forests are made up of Joshua trees. A Joshua tree is evergreen

Most trees cannot grow in deserts because they need more water than a desert provides. But the rare Joshua tree is well suited to the Mojave Desert.

and grows no higher than 30 feet (9 m). Look at the picture of the Joshua trees on page 72.

A small river, the Mojave, flows down from the San Bernardino Mountains. When it reaches the Mojave Desert, there is plenty of water. But before long it sinks into the sand. The water is still there, under the ground! Farmers have dug wells to get the water for their crops. Farmers grow crops such as onions, melons, and alfalfa. Alfalfa has very deep roots. It makes good cattle feed.

At the northern edge of the Mojave Desert is Death Valley. It is the lowest, hottest, and driest place in the United States. At one point it is 282 feet (86 m) below sea level. The summer temperature rises to over 115°F (46°C) almost every day. It has only about 2 inches (5 cm) of rain each year.

Today you can drive through Death Valley. The floor of the valley is flat. Some parts are covered with dried, cracked mud. Other parts are covered with rocky mountains, sand dunes, or deep canyons. There is some life in Death Valley. Small bushes and shrubs come up after a rain. But they soon dry up. Bristlecone pines grow in the mountains at the edge of Death Valley. They are the oldest living things in the world. One bristlecone pine is known to be about 4,600 years old. A few animals such as lizards, kangaroo rats, ground squirrels, and snakes

This lizard perches on a rock in Death Valley. Why, do you think, is it called a collared lizard?

also can live in Death Valley. Death Valley has been made a **national monument**. Like a national park, special care is taken to keep the land the way it is.

Looking ahead   In Unit 2 you will begin learning about the early history of California.

CHECKUP

1. What are the four physical regions of California?
2. Why has the coastline been important for California's growth?
3. What are the names of the two major mountain ranges in California?
4. What is a desert?

73

KEY FACTS

1. California is the state with the largest population and the third largest land area in the United States.

2. The study of people and how they use the earth is one of the most important parts of geography.

3. Tables and graphs are important tools for studying geography.

4. California is our nation's leading farming state.

5. Most of California has a Mediterranean climate.

6. The four most important physical regions of California are the coast, the mountains, the Central Valley, and the desert.

VOCABULARY QUIZ

Beside the number of each sentence, write the word or phrase that best completes the sentence. Use a sheet of paper.

1. You can tell how crowded a place is by finding the _____.

2. Four kinds of graphs are _____, _____, _____, and _____.

3. _____ is the way the air is at a certain time.

4. Rain and snow are forms of _____.

5. A steady flow of water in one direction is a _____.

6. When clouds are formed near the ground we call it __.

7. Land along the edge of the ocean is a _____.

8. On maps elevation is shown by drawing _____.

9. A piece of land formed by mud and sand from a river is called a ____.

10. A _____ is a protected body of water deep enough for ships.

REVIEW QUESTIONS

1. What two numbers must you have to find population density?

2. Why is it important to save land for national and state parks?

3. What is the difference between weather and climate?

4. How does a mapmaker show elevation on a map?

5. Why are the Sacramento and San Joaquin rivers important to the Central Valley?

6. Compare the Mojave Desert and the Central Valley. How are they different? Are they alike in any way?

ACTIVITIES

1. List at least five things in your home or in school that come from natural resources. Next to each item write at least one natural resource used to make it, for example: paper, tree.

2. Keep a record of the weather in your area for 2 weeks. Record the temperature at the same time of day each morning and afternoon. Note whether it is rainy, cloudy, partly cloudy, foggy, or sunny. Also note changes from morning to afternoon.

2/SKILLS DEVELOPMENT

USING THE PARTS OF THIS BOOK

CONTENTS

This book has many special parts to help you learn about California. The first of these parts is the Contents. This tells you how the book is divided into units and chapters. Turn to the Contents pages at the front of the book. Answer these questions:

1. What is the name of Unit 3?
2. Name the Chapters in Unit 3.
3. On what page does Chapter 6 begin?

INDEX

Another helpful part of the book is the Index. It tells you the numbers of the pages on which various topics are discussed. Turn to the Index, starting on page 313. Answer these questions:

1. Which pages would you turn to if you wanted to read about California missions?
2. On what pages would you find information about Cabrillo?
3. On what pages would you find information about deserts? About mountains?

GLOSSARY

The Glossary is another important part of this book. The Glossary, arranged alphabetically like the Index, defines all the key social studies words. These are the words found in the boxes at the beginning of each lesson. Turn to the Glossary on page 298. Answer these questions:

1. What is a peninsula?
2. What is a delta?

3. What is the difference between fog and smog?
4. What is a tailrace?

GAZETTEER

Another part of the book arranged alphabetically is the Gazetteer. It gives information about many places—cities, mountains, rivers, and other geographic features. For many of these places the Gazetteer also gives latitude and longitude. The page number at the end of each definition directs you to a map that shows where the place is. Turn to the Gazetteer, starting on page 293. Answer these questions:

1. What is the latitude and longitude of San Diego?
2. Where does the Sacramento River start?
3. What is the highest peak in the Sierra Nevada?

GRAPH APPENDIX AND ATLAS

The Graph Appendix and Atlas are two other parts of this book that will help you. The Graph Appendix provides you with more information in the form of graphs. Turn to the Graph Appendix, starting on page 304. Answer the following questions:

1. What state leads in cotton production?
2. What is the average January temperature of Blue Canyon?

The Atlas is a special collection of maps. Turn to the Atlas, starting on page 288. Name the maps that you find there.

I/UNIT REVIEW

1. Maps and globes are important tools that are used to represent the earth or parts of it. — *Name the four oceans and the seven continents and locate them on a globe or world map.*

2. Lines of latitude and longitude are used to locate places on a map. — *On a map of California find the latitude and longitude of Oakland, Anaheim, Eureka, Lake Tahoe, and Death Valley. What is the latitude and longitude of your community?*

3. Symbols on maps stand for real things and places. — *If you were to make a map of your community, what are some of the things and places that you would show with symbols?*

4. Maps are drawn to scale. A certain number of inches on a map stand for a certain number of feet or miles on the earth. — *What are the scales on the three maps of California on page 47?*

5. Tables are fast and easy ways to organize facts. A table gives you some specific facts that a map does not usually give. — *Using the table of counties on pages 308 and 309, rank the five largest California counties according to their population. Rank the five largest counties according to area.*

6. Graphs are special drawings that use pictures, circles, bars, and lines to compare things. — *If you had $50 and you spent $10 to repair your bicycle, $15 to go to the ball game with your friend, and you put the rest in the bank, what kind of graph would best show what you did with your money? Why would you use this kind of graph?*

7. Most of the things that people need and use depend on natural resources. — *List some of California's most important natural resources. Name some of the ways people make use of these resources.*

8. Photographs are important sources of information and are good learning tools. — *If you wanted to tell a friend in another state about California's four major physical regions, what kinds of photographs would you send him or her?*

Early California History

3 The First Californians

Living with the Land

VOCABULARY

native	craft
Californian	pitch
tribe	tar
nature	tule balsa
sweathouse	dugout canoes
sauna	

California Indians Were you born in California? If so, you are a **native Californian.** However, the term *native Californian* can be used in another way. It also means the first people who lived on the land that today we call California. People have been living here for thousands of years. These first people are often called Native Californians. They are also called California Indians. They were living here long before the Spanish, Mexicans, and others came to settle in California.

There were many different **tribes** of California Indians. A tribe was made up of groups of people who were related. Each group lived in its own village. There were many villages along the coast and in the river valleys. Each tribe spoke a different language.

Living with nature The California Indians were very smart in living with **nature**. Nature includes all the living and nonliving things that make up the world. Soil, rocks, minerals, deserts, rivers, plants, animals, and mountains are all parts of nature. The California Indians used wood from the trees to build their homes. Soil was also used as a building material. They fished in the rivers and in the ocean, and they hunted deer and other animals. They gathered nuts and seeds and berries for food. They learned how to live in California's deserts and mountains.

Each tribe learned to live with nature in a different way. For example, the Yurok (yü´räk) Indian group lived in a cold, rainy part of northern California. They used trees for making their homes. They used animal skins as their clothing. In the desert area of southern California lived another Indian group known as the Mojaves (mō hä´vēs). These people learned to live in the heat of the desert. They kept cool by wearing little or no clothing. In similar ways other tribes learned to live with the natural things they found around them.

In early times, more than 40 Indian tribes lived in what is today California.

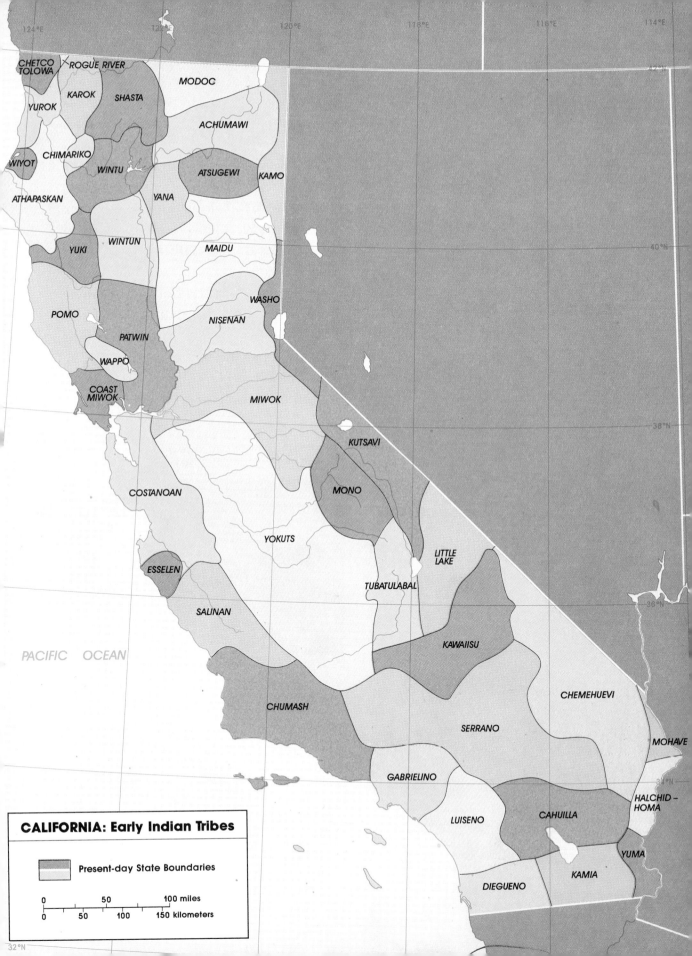

CALIFORNIA: Early Indian Tribes

Present-day State Boundaries

| 0 | 50 | 100 miles |
| 0 | 50 | 100 | 150 kilometers |

CHETCO
TOLOWA
ROGUE RIVER
MODOC
KAROK
SHASTA
YUROK
ACHUMAWI
CHIMARIKO
WIYOT
WINTU
ATSUGEWI
KAMO
ATHAPASKAN
YANA
YUKI
WINTUN
MAIDU
POMO
WASHO
NISENAN
PATWIN
WAPPO
COAST
MIWOK
MIWOK
COSTANOAN
KUTSAVI
MONO
YOKUTS
ESSELEN
LITTLE
LAKE
TUBATULABAL
SALINAN
PACIFIC OCEAN
KAWAIISU
CHEMEHUEVI
CHUMASH
SERRANO
MOHAVE
GABRIELINO
HALCHID –
HOMA
LUISENO
CAHUILLA
YUMA
KAMIA
DIEGUENO

Indian dwellings The California Indians built their houses of materials found near their villages. The tribes that lived near the redwood forests made thick boards from the trees. They used these thick boards, called planks, for building their houses. These planks were split from logs with wedges made of animal bones or antlers. Other tribes used willow trees and sometimes smaller plants as building materials. The Indians could build their houses quickly with such materials. They could easily move their villages and then they could build new houses.

Some Indian homes, like the one below, were built of slabs. The basket is made from twigs or roots.

Sweathouses Many villages had a special house called a **sweathouse**. A fire was used to heat the house. Stones and rocks were heated in the fire. These hot stones and rocks kept the sweathouse warm for a long time. Many times the houses were covered with earth to keep the heat in. Usually the men of the village would come to the sweathouse. They would sit in the house until their bodies were covered with sweat. Then they would run outside and jump into some nearby cold water, such as a river. This helped to clean their bodies. Also it seemed to help keep them healthy.

The sweathouse was a favorite gathering place. The men sat by the fire until they were covered with sweat.

Some people today do much the same thing. The room they use is called a **sauna** (sou′nä). After heating themselves in the sauna, they take a cold shower. Like the California Indians, they believe this keeps them healthy.

After sitting in the sweathouse, the men ran outside and leaped into a stream.

Baskets Basketmaking was the major **craft** of some of the Indians. A craft is a trade or work that requires special skill. The beautiful baskets were used to hold many different things. They were used as traps for fish. They were even used like pots to cook food! How could the Indians cook their food in baskets? Of course they did not put the baskets over the fire. The baskets would have burned. Some of the baskets were made so tightly that they could hold water. So the Indians put water in the baskets along with the food. Then they added rocks that had been heated in the fire. They moved the rocks around inside the basket to keep the sides and bottom from burning. The Indians sometimes covered the sides of baskets with **pitch** or **tar**. The pitch or tar made the baskets waterproof. Pitch is a sticky sap from some evergreen trees. Tar is sticky and black. It is often used as blacktop to pave streets.

A woman of the Pomo tribe makes a tightly woven bowl that will probably be used to hold food.

Types of boats The California Indians also used the materials supplied by nature to make their boats. A simple boat called a **tule balsa** (tü′lē bôl′sə) was made by tying together plants called tules. These plants, also called river rushes, grew along the edge of the water. This kind of boat was used for crossing rivers and streams.

Tule balsa boats were made from bundles of tule tied with vines. Such boats were light but did not last long.

Other kinds of boats were made to last much longer. Some of the northern tribes made boats from redwood logs. These were called **dugout canoes**. The Indians used tools made of stone to hollow out the logs. Some of the other tribes used stone tools to shape planks. They tied the planks together and made very strong boats. With these boats, they could fish in the ocean waters along the coast.

CHECKUP

1. Tell how different tribes learned to live with nature in different ways.
2. Name some of the ways Indians used baskets.
3. Describe the boats used by the California Indians.

Making a dugout canoe from a log took great skill. The sides and the bottom of the canoe could be neither too thick nor too thin. It took many months to make a canoe.

Food from Nature

Fish   The Indians who lived near the ocean or the rivers ate many different kinds of fish. One of their favorites was salmon. In the spring the salmon came up the rivers from the ocean. Many of the Indian tribes had special places on the rivers where they fished. These places were called **fishing grounds**. The Indians often used basket traps for catching fish. They also used spears, harpoons, and nets weighed down with stones. The California Indians were peaceful most of the time, but they would fight to defend their fishing grounds.

Along the coast the Indians gathered **shellfish**. Shellfish are animals, such as clams or abalone, that have shells on their body. Of course, the shells could not be eaten. They were piled up outside the villages. Some of these mounds of old shells can still be seen.

Hunting   Many California Indians hunted for deer and other animals. They used bows and arrows to shoot deer and smaller animals. They caught wild rabbits and birds in nets and traps. The hunters watched for signs of animals, such as tracks or broken tree limbs.

These women belong to a group studying early Indian life. They have dug into a mound of old shells near the site of an Indian village along the coast.

Seeds, corn, beans, and pumpkins   The California Indians also gathered seeds from grass and other wild plants for food. The seeds were gathered in baskets and later were ground into meal. Most groups were hunters and food-gatherers but not farmers. However, the Yuma (yü′mə) and Mojave Indians did some farming. These people lived in the area that is now southern California near the Colorado River. In the spring the river was full of water from melting snows in the mountains. Often the river would overflow. This made wet places along the river. The Yuma and Mojave Indians scattered seeds in the wet places. They grew such foods as corn, beans, and pumpkins.

Notice how the acorn grows on the oak tree such as these California oaks.

Acorns The most important food for many California Indians was the **acorn**. It was used for food the year round. The acorn is the nut that grows on oak trees. The nut is inside a shell that must be broken. Acorns are a good food, and they can be stored for a long time. The Indians gathered acorns in the fall. There was only one problem with eating them. Acorns have **tannic acid** that makes people sick when they eat it. So the California Indians discovered a way to take the acid out of the acorns. First, they took the nuts out of the shells and dried the acorns. With stone tools they ground the nuts into tiny pieces, or meal. They dug a hole in the earth shaped like a bowl. The hole was then lined with pine needles, sand, and small pebbles. Then they put the acorn meal in the hole. Next, they poured hot water over the meal. This was done eight or ten times, and the hot water washed out the tannic acid. The acorn meal was then safe to eat. The acorn meal was as important to the California Indians as cornmeal was to other North American Indians. They cooked the meal in many different ways. Breads, puddings, and hot cereals were some of the foods made from acorn meal. Berries and nuts were often used to flavor the foods.

CHECKUP

1. What is a fishing ground?
2. What important item was used for food the year round?
3. On what kind of tree does the acorn grow?
4. How was acorn meal used?

Making Acorn Meal

1. Gathering acorns

2. Shelling the acorns

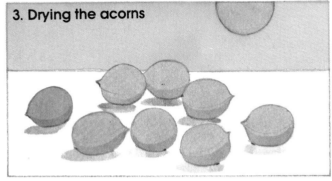

3. Drying the acorns

4. Removing the brown layer

5. Grinding the nuts

6. Removing the tannic acid

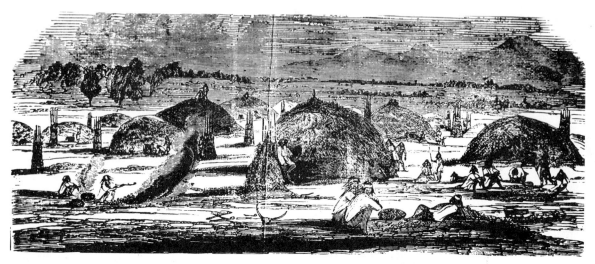

This indian village of reed houses was in California's Central Valley.

Life in the Villages

The village   Almost all villages of the California Indians were small. A village had about 130 people. These Indians spent most of their time with the people of their village. But sometimes the people of nearby villages would get together. Often, this was for special celebrations, such as a first-acorn feast. A first-acorn feast was much like the Thanksgiving feast of the Puritans of New England.

The chiefs   Each village had a leader called a **chief**. The chief had several jobs. One job was to make sure that people obeyed the rules of the village. These rules were made by the people of the

An Atsugewi Indian woman displays a model of a baby carrier, which could be stuck into the ground.

village. It was the chief's job to decide when celebrations would be held. The chief decided when the village would move to a new place. Also, it was the chief's job to settle arguments and to solve other problems in the village.

Usually the title of chief was passed from father to son. If the son was not thought to be acceptable for the job, then another chief was chosen by the people of the village.

The people in neighboring villages were often friendly with each other. Wars and fighting were not common. Generally they were peaceful people. If a need for warfare arose, a war chief was chosen to lead the fighters of the village.

Music, dance, games   In an Indian village the people were helpful and fun-loving. They often shared their food and were helpful in other ways. They loved music, dancing, games, and storytelling. In some villages, singing and dancing lasted all day and all night. Dancing was carried on in the villages both for fun and for **ceremony** (ser′ə mō nē). A ceremony is an event that honors something important that has happened. The Indians honored many important events. Instruments that made music were often part of the fun. The flute, made of wood, was one of their favorite musical instruments. Flutes were often used in ceremonies.

The village people enjoyed many different games. They needed to be strong and skillful to compete in some of the games. Ball games and jumping matches were just some of the things they did. There were also games of chance. Luck, not skill, decided the winner.

Carefully carved Indian flutes such as these were often used in ceremonies.

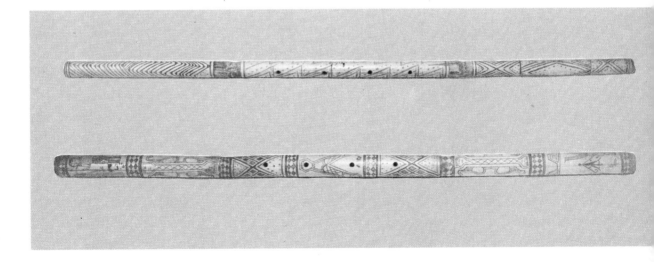

Ishi

Ishi is one of the most well-known California Indians. Ishi was the last California Indian to live the same way his ancestors had lived for several thousand years before him.

Ishi was a member of the Yahi tribe. The Yahi lived in the foothills of Mount Lassen in northern California. He was born around 1862. By the time Ishi was 10 years old, only a few Yahi were still alive. When his mother died in November 1908, Ishi was the last member of the Yahi tribe left. For several years Ishi lived by himself in the mountains.

In August 1911, Ishi was found by a rancher near the town of Oroville. He was starving, exhausted, and very lonely. The people of Oroville fed Ishi and gave him clothes. Then some people took him to San Francisco. There he lived in the University Museum.

Ishi was the last member of the Yahi tribe. He died in 1916.

Ishi was surprised at the way other people lived. For the first time Ishi saw running water, beds and chairs, and electric lights.

While living at the museum, Ishi taught the people many things about the Yahi way of life. Thousands of museum visitors watched Ishi as he showed how to shape and string a bow or how to make fire using a fire drill. The visitors especially enjoyed watching Ishi chip arrowheads from rock.

In 1914 Ishi and some of his new friends from the museum made a trip back to Yahi country. It was a sad trip for Ishi but also an exciting one. The trip made Ishi think of his old friends and his family. However, it gave Ishi a chance to show his new friends how the Yahi had lived. He hunted for food by setting traps and using his bow and arrows. He also showed them how to catch salmon, using nets or harpoons. Ishi lived in the museum until he died in 1916.

Californian Jim Plunkett, a star football player in college, is now a well-known professional player.

Californian Navarre Scott Momaday, author and educator, received the Pulitzer prize for fiction in 1969.

Indians today   There are still many Indians living in California. Some live together in tribes. Others choose to live in towns and cities with other people. Many California Indians want to keep the ways of their parents and grandparents. The Indian traditions and customs are shared and taught to family members. All California Indians are very proud of their history.

Looking ahead   In the next chapter you will learn how new people came to California. Their arrival affected the lives of the Indians in many ways.

CHECKUP

1. What were some of the jobs of the village chief?
2. Describe the types of games enjoyed by the village people.

KEY FACTS

1. People have been living in what is now California for thousands of years.
2. The California Indians were known for their skill in living with nature.
3. California Indian dwellings were built quickly with materials from nature.
4. Basketmaking was a major craft of some of the California Indians.
5. The California Indians caught fish, gathered seeds, and hunted for animals.

VOCABULARY QUIZ

Fill in each blank with the word or phrase that best completes the sentence.

1. The _____ was a boat made by tying together plants called tules.
2. _____ is found in acorns.
3. A special place where an Indian group fished was called _____ .
4. _____ are animals that have shells on their body.
5. A sticky black substance that is often used as blacktop to pave streets is called _____ .
6. The _____ is the nut that grows on oak trees.
7. The village leader was called a _____ .
8. The California Indians hollowed out logs to make _____ .

REVIEW QUESTIONS

1. Who were the first people to live in what is now California?
2. What kind of materials did the California Indians use for building their houses?
3. Describe some of the ways the Indians caught fish.
4. Name some of the important foods of the California Indians.
5. Describe a California Indian village.
6. What was life like in a California Indian village?

ACTIVITIES

1. Imagine that you are a member of a tribe of California Indians. Think about the jobs of the village chief. Would you like to be a village chief? Write a paragraph explaining why or why not.
2. The California counties listed below have Indian place-names. On an outline map of the state, mark the county lines. Then label each of the following counties: Colusa, Modoc, Mono, Napa, Shasta, Tehama, Tuolumne, Yolo, and Yuba. Make a title for your map.

3/SKILLS DEVELOPMENT

USING A DICTIONARY

WHAT IS A DICTIONARY

A dictionary is a book that contains the words of a language. A dictionary tells several things about these words. The pronunciation and the meaning of each word is given. The pronunciation shows you how to say a word. It divides the word into parts and identifies the sounds of the letters.

The words are listed in alphabetical order. This helps you find the words easily. It also makes it possible for you to easily check the spelling of a word.

When you see a word that you do not know, you can find the meaning of the word in a dictionary. If you do not know how to use a word, a dictionary can help.

Look up the word *Indian* in a dictionary. Why is it easy to find? (Words are in alphabetical order.) Notice that the word is divided into parts. Look at the pronunciation. Say the word using the pronunciation. How many definitions are given for the word *Indian?*

SKILLS PRACTICE

Look up the following words in a dictionary. Write a sentence using each word.

1. settle
2. village
3. language
4. desert
5. redwood
6. skill
7. trap
8. planks
9. salmon
10. peaceful
11. clams
12. meal
13. feast
14. rule
15. flute

Some students say, "If I can't spell a word, how can I look it up in the dictionary?" Usually, you can spell a word close enough to search and find it in the dictionary. Use a dictionary to correct these misspelled words. The misspelled part is underlined.

1. saw̲na
2. cano̲c
3. miner̲els
4. har̲boons
5. cel̲abration
6. bask̲it
7. pro̲wd
8. argumen̲d
9. instrum̲ant
10. willo̲u trees

4 The Explorers and Early Settlers

Spain in the New World

VOCABULARY

explorer	voyages

Two explorers Do you know what an **explorer** is? If you said a person who travels in search of something new, you would be correct. Neil Armstrong is a well-known American explorer. He was the first person to set foot on the moon. Another well-known explorer was Christopher Columbus. In 1492 he sailed to America from Spain. It took him over 2 months to make the trip. In July 1969 Neil Armstrong flew from the United States. He landed on the moon in 4 days.

Interest in the New World After Columbus returned to Spain, other explorers from that country sailed to America. They called it the New World. These explorers were looking for two things. One was a way to sail to what they called the Orient. Today we know it as Asia. Asia had spices, silks, and other treasures. The explorers wanted to bring these items back to Spain.

The Spanish were also looking for gold in the New World. They had heard many stories from the natives about "cities of gold." Some of these stories were true. Spanish soldiers marched into Mexico and South America. They found great cities with much gold. They sailed back to Spain in ships loaded with this wealth.

The gold from the New World created excitement in Spain. More people became interested in exploring. They thought other great cities and more gold might be found in the New World. In the early 1500s many Spanish explorers set out in all directions. Some explorers in Mexico headed north. They did not find gold. But they did find California.

California gets its name In the 1500s there was a popular Spanish book. It was a make-believe story about an island named California. The island was ruled by a queen named Calafía. There were no men on the island. The women were strong and had various weapons. There were also creatures called griffins on the island. A griffin had a head and wings like an eagle and a body like a lion. The griffins protected the island.

Many people believe California was named after the island in this old Span-

Christopher Columbus and Neil Armstrong both went on long, dangerous trips. Columbus sailed to America, and Armstrong flew to the moon.

ish story. The first Spanish explorers thought they had found an island when they sailed from Mexico and found the tip of Lower California. In Spanish, the lower part of California is called Baja (bä′ hä) California. Not until some years later did they find that Lower California was not an island. Instead, it is a long piece of land called a peninsula.

Hernando Cortés   One of the first explorers to reach Lower California was Hernando Cortés (hėr nan′ dō kôr′ tez). About 1520 Cortés took Mexico for Spain. Then he explored some more. From 1527 to 1539 many **voyages** were made into the Pacific. A voyage is a trip by water. In 1535 one of Cortés's ships reached the peninsula of Lower California. At this time the Spanish still thought Lower

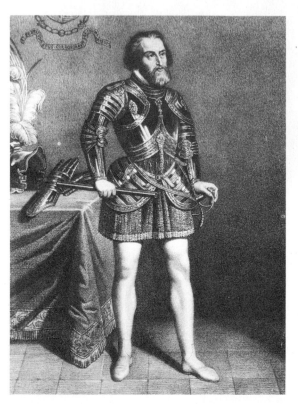

Hernando Cortés was one of the first Spanish explorers to see what is now California.

Did the Spanish set up missions in California soon after it was discovered, or did they wait more than 100 years?

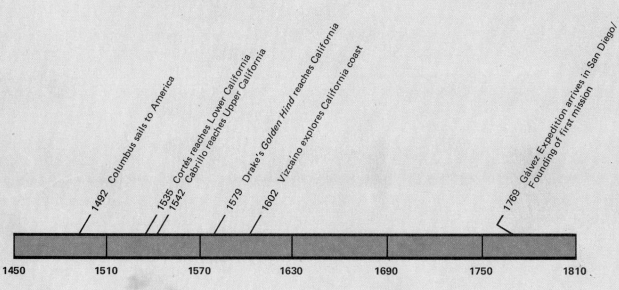

1492 Columbus sails to America
1535 Cortés reaches Lower California
1542 Cabrillo reaches Upper California
1579 Drake's *Golden Hind* reaches California
1602 Vizcaíno explores California coast
1769 Gálvez Expedition arrives in San Diego/ Founding of first mission

1450   1510   1570   1630   1690   1750   1810

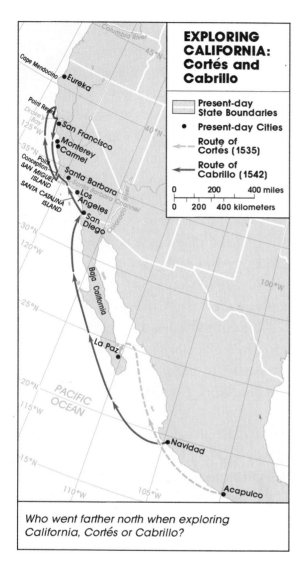

EXPLORING CALIFORNIA: Cortés and Cabrillo

- Present-day State Boundaries
- Present-day Cities
- Route of Cortés (1535)
- Route of Cabrillo (1542)

0   200   400 miles
0 200 400 kilometers

Who went farther north when exploring California, Cortés or Cabrillo?

California was an island. Cortés later returned to Spain. But Spanish exploration of the New World continued.

Juan Rodríguez Cabrillo   The first known explorer to see the land that is today the state of California was Juan Rodríguez Cabrillo (hwän rō ŦHrē′ gäth kä brē′yō). This land was called Upper California. In Spanish it was called Alta California. In 1542 the Spanish govern-

ment in Mexico ordered Cabrillo to find a shorter water route to Asia by way of North America. Cabrillo had two small ships called the *San Salvador* and the *Victoria*. On September 28, 1542, Cabrillo's two ships sailed into what is now San Diego Bay. Their entrance into this bay marked the Spanish discovery of what today makes up the state of California.

Cabrillo's ships then sailed north to the Santa Barbara Channel. They stopped at what is now known as San Miguel (san′ mə gil′) Island, then continued north. They failed to see either Monterey Bay or San Francisco Bay. Near Fort Ross they started south again and discovered a body of water now called Drake's Bay.

Cabrillo died on January 3, 1543. Before Cabrillo died, he asked his men to explore once more the coast to the north. It is believed they sailed as far north as present-day Oregon. By this time, however, most of the men were sick. They returned to Mexico. Cabrillo and his sailors found no gold and no route to Asia. But they did explore the coast of Upper California. Soon the whole world would know of this new land.

CHECKUP

1. What two things were the early Spanish explorers looking for in the New World?
2. Describe the make-believe island that California was probably named after.
3. Why did Cabrillo explore Upper California?

95

An Englishman Finds California

The Manila galleons After Cabrillo's exploration, the Spanish lost interest in California. They were more interested in the Philippine Islands in the Pacific Ocean. There, in the city of Manila, they used gold and silver to buy spices and silks from the Orient. In sailing ships called **galleons** (gal′ ē əns), they took the spices and silks back to Mexico. There they sold these goods for large amounts of money.

The Spanish used large sailing ships called galleons to carry treasures from Mexico to the Philippines.

Within a few years many galleons were sailing between Mexico and Manila. They were called the Manila galleons. But there were many problems for the sailors on the ships. The winds were against them when they sailed from Manila. The trip back to Mexico took from 5 to 8 months. On the way they often ran out of food and water. On each trip many men died from **scurvy** (skėr′ vē). This is a disease of the gums caused by not eating fresh vegetables or fruit.

A pirate for the queen The world soon learned about the Manila galleons and their treasures. One person much interested in them was Queen Elizabeth I of England. England and Spain were old enemies. The Manila galleons carried wealth that England wanted. Queen Elizabeth decided to send out men and warships to steal the wealth.

Queen Elizabeth selected Francis Drake for this job. He sailed from England on the warship *Golden Hind*. The voyage led him south around the tip of South America.

Drake sailed along the west coast of South America. As he found towns, he stopped and attacked them. He took much of their gold and silver. To the people in England, Drake was a hero. But the Spanish called him a **pirate** (pī′rit). A pirate is a person who steals treasures from ships.

The Mystery of the Brass Plate

In the 1930s a brass plate was said to have been found near Drake's Bay. It was lettered with the words that Drake used to claim the new land for England. Was the brass plate really the same one that Drake had left? Or was it a fake made to look like that plate? For many years, people had been trying to find out the truth. Several people believed that it was real. But in 1977 a team of scientists studied the brass in the plate. They compared it to brass that was made

The brass plate shown above was found in the 1930s near Drake's Bay.

in the 1500s. They found that the brass in the plate was different from the old brass. So they said that it was a fake. What is the truth? We cannot be sure. The brass plate may be real or it may be a fake. But we can be sure of one thing. Where the brass plate came from is still a mystery.

Farther north, Drake attacked some Manila galleons and took their treasures. Finally, he sailed north past Mexico to the Upper California coast. With his ship leaking, he entered a bay somewhere near the present-day Point Reyes. Years later the bay he most likely entered was named Drake's Bay.

Drake and his men traded gifts with the friendly Indians. And Drake had a brass plate made that claimed the new land for Queen Elizabeth. The brass plate was nailed to a post near the bay. The leaks in the boat were also fixed. Then Drake sailed from the California shores. He sailed around the world to get back to England.

CHECKUP

1. Why did the Spanish become interested in the Philippine Islands?
2. What kinds of problems did the men on the galleon ships have?
3. Who sent Francis Drake on his journey?
4. What did Francis Drake do to show his claim of the land for the Queen?

More Spanish Voyages

> **VOCABULARY**
>
> anchor   settlement

Problems for the galleons Francis Drake was not the only one who attacked the Manila galleons. Others also raided the ships for treasures. As you learned earlier, another problem was that the sailors often ran short of food and water. The Manila galleons could not sail straight back to Mexico. The winds were against them. To get the best winds, they had to sail north from the Philippines. Then they sailed east to California. Then they turned south, and good winds took them to Mexico. By the time they reached California, they were often out of food and water.

The Spanish in Mexico thought California would be a good place to keep ships to protect the galleons. They also thought it would be good to have Spanish settlers in California. Settlers could provide food and water for returning galleons.

So once again the Spanish started exploring the California coast. They looked for good places to **anchor** ships. To anchor means to "hold in place." A ship's anchor is a heavy metal object hooked on to the ship. It is thrown overboard to hold the ship in place. The best place to anchor a ship is in a bay. Remember, a bay is an inlet from the sea. A good bay is protected from the wind. This helps keep big waves from driving ships into the shore.

Sebastián Rodríguez Cermenho The captain of one of the Manila galleons was Sebastián Rodríguez Cermenho (sē bas′chan rô Ŧhrē′ gäth sėr men′ ō). His ship was the *San Agustin*.

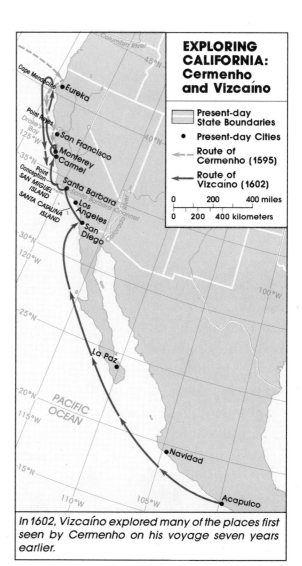

EXPLORING CALIFORNIA: Cermenho and Vizcaíno

- Present-day State Boundaries
- • Present-day Cities
- Route of Cermenho (1595)
- Route of Vizcaíno (1602)

0   200   400 miles
0   200   400 kilometers

In 1602, Vizcaíno explored many of the places first seen by Cermenho on his voyage seven years earlier.

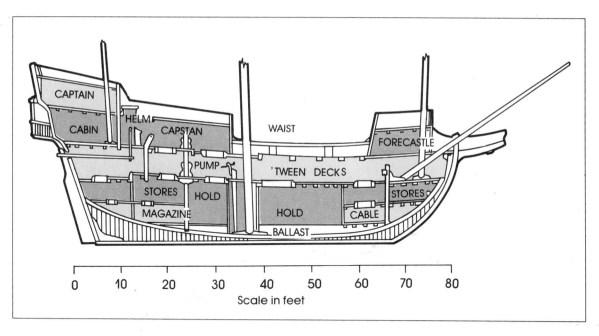

This cutaway drawing shows how the San Agustin *would have looked if you could see inside it. Galleons were built to carry big loads of supplies or treasure.*

Cermenho was asked to explore the California coast on his way home from Manila.

In July 1595 the *San Agustin* sailed from the Philippines. Cermenho and his men reached the coast of California in November. It is believed they first landed near the present-day city of Eureka (yů rē′ kə). Then they sailed south and stopped in another bay. This may have been the same bay that Francis Drake had entered some years before. While they were there, a sudden storm wrecked the ship. Only a small boat that the men had put together earlier was saved. The men crowded aboard the small boat and slowly sailed southward. As they sailed they saw the entrance to Monterey Bay.

Cermenho wrote about what he saw.

Cermenho and his men arrived home on January 7, 1596. The men were close to death from starvation and illness. Cermenho was blamed for losing the *San Agustin* and its valuable load. After this, the Spanish did not risk losing another rich Manila galleon. They began using smaller ships to explore the California coast.

Sebastián Vizcaíno In 1602 the Spanish sent Sebastián Vizcaíno (sē bas′ chan vēth′ kä ē′ nō) on a California voyage. With three small ships, Vizcaíno explored the California coast. He gave many places the names we know them by today. He named San Diego, Santa Catal-

Sebastián Vizcaíno probably sailed past Drake's Bay on his voyage along the California coast in 1602. Today, Drake's Bay is part of the National Seashore at Point Reyes.

ina Island, Santa Barbara, Monterey, and Carmel. Seven years after Cermenho's discovery of Monterey Bay, Vizcaíno wrote that Monterey Bay would be an outstanding place for a **settlement**. A settlement is a new place where people build homes. A settlement is like a small village.

Vizcaíno's men suffered from much sickness on their 11-month voyage. Forty-five of his men died. That was half his sailors. Only five men were healthy when they finally returned to Mexico.

CHECKUP

1. Why did the Spanish in Mexico begin to show new interest in California?
2. What happened to the *San Agustin?*
3. Describe the condition of Cermenho's men when they arrived home.

The Gálvez Expedition

VOCABULARY

sea otter	mission
expedition	presidio

New interest in California   After Vizcaíno's voyage, over 150 years passed without further important Spanish exploration in California.

Around 1770 the Spanish in Mexico again became interested in California. This was the result of a leader named José de Gálvez (hō sā′ ₸Hā gäl′ vāth). Gálvez worried that California might be lost to another country. He knew that the Russians had ships close by. They were supposed to be hunting the **sea otter**. This is an animal that lives along

Sea otters are furry animals that like to eat and sleep while floating on their backs.

the Pacific coast. It is hunted for its fur. Gálvez was afraid the Russians wanted to claim the land of California. He also worried about the English and the Dutch. Their warships had been seen off the coast of Lower California.

Gálvez had the support of the Spanish king. He planned an **expedition** to California. An expedition is a trip that is made for a special purpose. Gálvez hoped that Spain would be able to settle the land.

The expedition plan   Gálvez wanted to settle two places in California. Both had been well described by earlier explorers. One settlement would be at San Diego and the other would be at Monterey.

Gálvez planned that settlers in each place would do two things. One thing was to build a **mission** (mish′ən). A mission is a church with other buildings and enough land to support a settlement. The purpose of a mission was to turn the natives into Christians. The natives believed in their own gods. The Spanish were Roman Catholics. They wanted the natives to believe in the Christian God.

The second job for the settlers was to build a **presidio** (pri sid′ ē ō). A presidio is a fort from which soldiers can defend a settlement.

Gálvez had four groups of settlers. They were to leave from the southern tip of Baja California. Two groups would travel in ships. The other two would travel on land. All four groups were supposed to meet in San Diego.

The ships reach San Diego   Two ships were made ready. One was the *San Carlos*, which sailed in January 1769. The other ship, the *San Antonio*, left a month later. It was the first to reach San Diego. It arrived on April 11. For a while it was feared that the *San Carlos* was lost. Then, on April 29 the *San Carlos* sailed into San Diego Bay. But no one could be seen on the ship. No landing boats were lowered. That was strange! When the crew of the *San Antonio* took boats out to the *San Carlos*,

101

Flags were flying and cannon boomed when the San Carlos *left for California. When the ship reached San Diego 110 days later, 24 sailors had died and many more were ill with scurvy.*

they learned the reason. The men were too weak and sick to lower the boats. They were suffering from scurvy. During the 110-day trip, 24 of the 62 men had died. Most of the others died later.

The land expeditions get ready
The two groups going by land were also getting ready for their journey. They were going to take 200 cattle on the journey. These would be raised at the missions. The land groups were also planning to take along horses, mules, and food for the settlements. The first group finally left on March 22, 1769.

This group was led by Captain Fernando Rivera y Moncada (fer nän' dō rē vä' rä ē mông kä' ₣Hä) and Father Juan Crespi (hwän krās'pē), a church leader. In the group were 25 soldier-cowboys called "leather-jackets." They wore sleeveless leather jackets made of seven layers of deer skin. This protected them from most Indian arrows. Many also carried bull-hide shields, swords, lances, and short guns called muskets.

The second land group left on May 15, 1769, with two leaders. One was a church leader. He was Father Junípero Serra (hü nē' pā rō ser' rä). The second leader was a military leader. He was Captain Gaspar de Portolá (gäs pär′ ΤHā pôr′ tō lá′), who was known as a brave soldier.

The land groups arrive   The first land group, led by Rivera and Crespi, arrived in San Diego on May 14. Their trip across the dry land of Baja California had been hard. But they were in better shape than the men who had come by sea.

Captain Portolá and Father Serra arrived with the second land group on July 1. Father Serra had been in poor health when they left. In fact, two men had to lift him onto his mule. But he was eager to go to work after the long journey. Father Serra was a very strong-minded person.

Portolá goes north   Many of the men who arrived in San Diego were sick or weak. Many had died on the trip. Portolá decided to send a few of the men back to Mexico on the *San Antonio*. They were to get food and supplies. Portolá then picked about 60 of the healthiest men. They would go north with him. Their plan was to travel by land and try to find Monterey Bay.

Portolá's group started north on July 14, 1769. Portolá wrote that his men were as thin as skeletons. But they traveled slowly and rested often. They gave names to many places. Names like Santa Margarita (sant′ ə mär′ gə rēt′ ə), Santa Ana, Carpintería (kär′ pən tə rē′ ə), and San Lorenzo (san′ lə ren′ zō) are well-known today.

Portolá and his men did reach Monterey Bay. But they did not know it. The bay they found was not mostly surrounded by land. It was not protected from north winds. So they thought that Monterey Bay must be farther north.

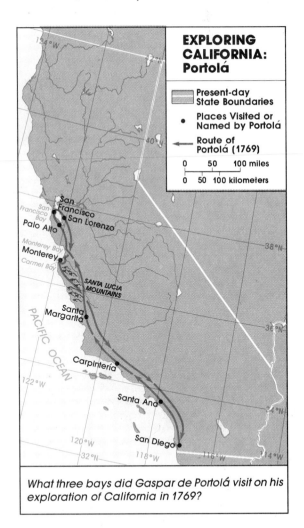

EXPLORING CALIFORNIA: Portolá

Present-day State Boundaries
• Places Visited or Named by Portolá
← Route of Portolá (1769)

0   50   100 miles
0   50   100 kilometers

What three bays did Gaspar de Portolá visit on his exploration of California in 1769?

Portolá's search for Monterey Bay was long and hard. He went as far north as San Francisco Bay before returning to San Diego.

back to camp very excited. They had seen a large bay. All the men went to look. They had found San Francisco Bay. It was November when they saw the bay for the first time. Portolá now knew they had passed Monterey Bay. Vizcaíno had not been correct when he described Monterey Bay. Portolá and his men decided to go back southward. Near the shore of Carmel Bay, they set up a cross. A letter was buried at the base of the

This statue honors Father Junípero Serra who founded the first mission in California.

San Francisco Bay Portolá and his men left Monterey Bay and headed north. Eleven of the men were very sick. They were carried in blankets between mules. Farther north, Portolá was surprised at the big trees with red wood. They named the trees *palo colorado* (pa′ lō kol′ ə rad′ ō). In Spanish this means "redwood." Later they saw a giant redwood. They called it *palo alto*, which means "high tree" in Spanish. This is how the city of Palo Alto got its name.

One day in November 1769, some of the men were hunting deer. They came cross. This would tell people who might come later that Portolá's group had been there. They also set up another cross near Monterey Bay. But they still did not recognize the bay as Monterey Bay. Then they started back toward San Diego.

Portolá returns to San Diego   It was December and winter was coming. Portolá's group was crossing the Santa Lucia Range. The mountains already had snow. The group had run out of food. Portolá urged his men to go on. They had to eat 12 of the mules. They found some friendly Indians who gave them dried fish. They finally made it back to San Diego on January 24, 1770.

Portolá found hungry, sad people when he returned to San Diego. The ship *San Antonio*, which he had sent for supplies, had not returned. On February 10, 1770, Portolá sent Captain Rivera and a few other men to Baja California. They were to find supplies. Portolá said the rest would have to leave also if the *San Antonio* did not arrive by March 20.

Father Serra and the other priests did not want to leave San Diego. The past July they had started the first mission in California. It was named *San Diego de Alcala* (san' dē ā'gō ŦHā al'kə lä'). The priests prayed that the supply ship would come so they could stay. On the last day before they were to leave, someone saw the sails of a ship. The ship passed San Diego. No one knows why the ship passed, but it came back 4 days later. It was the *San Antonio*. It carried food and other things they needed.

The mission of San Diego de Alcalá is the oldest mission in California.

Back to Monterey   Within a few days, Portolá was preparing for a new expedition to find Monterey Bay. Portolá ordered the *San Antonio* to sail to Monterey Bay with supplies. Then he and Father Serra started out with a group on horses and mules. They took the same trail he had taken before. On May 24 they reached the place near Monterey Bay where they had set up the second cross. Portolá knew this time that it was Monterey Bay.

The land party arrived a week before the *San Antonio* sailed into Monterey Bay. Then Father Serra held a religious ceremony above the bay. The ceremony

This painting shows the religious ceremony that was held when the second mission in California was founded at Monterey in 1770.

The presidio at Monterey was a building much like a fort. It protected the people of the mission in times of danger.

was held under a large oak tree. Vizcaíno had held a service under the same tree in 1602. This ceremony began the second mission in Upper California. It was named San Carlos Borroméo (san' kär' ləs bōr' rō mā' ō).

Miguel Costansó, who was aboard the *San Antonio*, recorded the events in his journal:

> In this place, according to order, a fort was built, and a Mission established; which was named the Mission of San Carlos; every one cooperating with equal diligence and solicitude, soldiers and sailors, with their respective officers, in the humble beginning of that important settlement; in which were included the particular conveniencies allotted for the Missions, and garrison of the Fort; and the other parts were then marked out, which were to be erected in the future.

Later, Father Serra moved the San Carlos mission to Carmel. It was only 4 miles from Monterey. The mission at San Carlos then became Father Serra's headquarters.

Portolá and his men also built a small presidio above Monterey Bay. This was called the Presidio of Monterey. On July 9, 1770, Portolá sailed away on the *San Antonio*. No one knows if he ever returned to California.

Looking ahead In the next chapter you will learn how 19 more missions were started and how they grew.

CHECKUP

1. Name the places Gálvez wanted to settle.
2. How many groups did Gálvez send to San Diego? How did they travel?
3. Why were the men who sailed on the *San Antonio* worried about the *San Carlos*?
4. Why did Portolá send the *San Antonio* back to Mexico?

KEY FACTS

1. Explorers looking for a route to Asia and treasures in the New World found California.
2. Cortés was one of the first Spanish explorers to reach Lower California.
3. Juan Cabrillo was the first known explorer to see Upper California.
4. Francis Drake claimed California for Queen Elizabeth of England.
5. Gálvez planned an expedition to California to settle San Diego and Monterey.
6. Under Gálvez's plan, two groups traveled in ships and two groups traveled on land from Baja to San Diego.
7. Father Junípero Serra founded the first mission in California at San Diego in 1769.

VOCABULARY QUIZ

Write the numbers 1 to 10 on a sheet of paper. Match these words with the definitions.

a. anchor   f. mission
b. expedition   g. voyage
c. explorer   h. sea otter
d. presidio   i. pirate
e. galleon   j. scurvy

1. An animal that lives along the Pacific coast and is hunted for its fur
2. A sailing ship
3. A disease of the gums caused by not eating fresh vegetables or fruit
4. A trip that is made for a special purpose
5. A person who travels in search of something new
6. A church with other buildings and enough land to support a settlement
7. To hold in place in the water
8. A trip by water
9. A fort from which soldiers can defend a settlement
10. A person who steals treasures from ships

REVIEW QUESTIONS

1. How was California probably named?
2. What goods did the Spanish buy in the Philippine Islands?
3. Why was Queen Elizabeth interested in the Manila galleons?
4. What are some of the places named by Vizcaíno?
5. Why did Gálvez think that another country might claim California?
6. What two things were the settlers in San Diego and Monterey supposed to do?
7. How did Palo Alto get its name?
8. Describe Portolá's return trip to San Diego.

ACTIVITIES

1. Make a chart of California explorers. Tell what was important about the exploration made by each.
2. Using a state map to help you, list ten places in California that have Spanish names. Then use an encyclopedia to find out what each of the names means in Spanish.

UNDERSTANDING A LEGEND

WHAT IS A LEGEND?

Have you ever heard the word *legend*? Do you know what it means? A *legend* is "a story handed down through the years." It may or may not be true. Sometimes these old stories tried to explain things that people did not understand.

In this chapter you learned about a Spanish book that was popular in the 1500s. The book was written by a man from Spain named Garcí Ordónez de Montalvo. You read that it told a story about an island named California. The story became a legend. This is what the legend said about California.

LEGEND OF CALIFORNIA'S NAME

California was an island. People were not certain just where it was located. Some people said it was in the Caribbean Sea. It was quite an unusual place. Griffins flew in the sky. Griffins were half eagle and half lion. They could lift a man and carry him straight up. Then they would drop him to his death!

California was a land of many delights. There were beautiful trees, sparkling rivers, gems and gold. A group of black women lived on this island. They were soldiers. They fought with bows, arrows, and spears. The women were called Amazons.

The island was ruled by Queen Calafía. She was more beautiful than all the other women. She wanted to do great things. She was brave and strong. That was why she was queen.

No men lived on this island. If a ship was tossed by a storm onto the island, the men were taken as prisoners. Then they were killed.

(Taken from Garcí Ordónez de Montalvo's *Las Sergas de Esplandían*. Retold in George William Sanderlin's *The Settlement of California*, New York: Coward, McCann and Geoghegan, 1972, pp. 19–20.)

SKILLS PRACTICE

Answer these questions about the legend on a sheet of writing paper. Number your answers.

1. What would be a good title for this legend?
2. Draw a picture that shows what you think the griffins looked like.
3. Why was the island called a land of many delights?
4. Tell about the people who lived on the island.
5. What happened to men if they came to the island?
6. We said earlier that a legend may not be true. Do you think this legend is true? Why or why not? (Before you write your answer, think about what you read about the explorers of California.)

The Twenty-one Missions

---VOCABULARY---
| padre | transportation |
| livestock | |

Father Serra takes the lead   When Captain Portolá left California, there were two missions. One was at San Diego, and the other was at Monterey. Father Serra wanted to start more missions, but there were not enough soldiers to guard more missions.

Father Serra returned to Mexico and asked the Spanish leaders there to help him. They agreed that he should go ahead with his plans. During the next 2 years, Father Serra set up 3 new missions. They were called San Antonio, San Gabriel (san gā′brē el), and San Luis Obispo (san lü′ə sə bis′pō). Before Father Serra died in 1784, he and his helpers had started 9 missions in all.

These missions were on the coast of California or in valleys nearby. They were connected by a dusty trail. The trail became known as El Camino Real (el kə mē′nō rā′ əl), or the King's Highway. (See the map on page 113.)

More missions   A few years later, Father Fermin de Lasuén (fär mēn ŦHā lä sü ən′) took over Father Serra's work. Father Lasuén was another strong leader in the church. He set up 9 more missions. After his death, 3 others were started. This made 21 missions in California. They lay along the King's Highway like beads on a string.

Placing a mission   The religious leaders, or **padres** (pä′drāz), looked for certain things when deciding where to set up a mission.

First, they wanted land with good soil. They needed to grow food. They had to have grass for their **livestock**, or farm animals.

Second, they needed water. California does not get much rain in the summer when most crops are growing. So they had to bring water to the fields.

Third, missions had to be near the California Indian settlements. The main purpose of a mission was to bring the California Indians the Christian religion. Also the padres wanted the Indians to learn to live like the Spanish and other Europeans. It would be the

San Carlos Borromeo was one of the earliest missions set up by Father Serra.

Indians who would do most of the work in building a mission and in carrying on the daily jobs.

The padres also thought about **transportation**, or the moving of people and goods from one place to another. The Spanish in California often rode on horses or mules. The padres tried to place new missions within one day's ride of each other. Neighboring missions were not much more than 30 miles (48 km) apart. You can see on the map how they were spaced.

CHECKUP

1. Where were the first two California missions located?
2. Why was El Camino Real important to the missions?
3. What did the religious leaders look for when choosing a place for a mission?
4. About how far apart did the padres try to space the missions?

The Growth of the Missions

┌─VOCABULARY─────────────────────┐
adobe	tallow
irrigation	hemp
vaquero	
└────────────────────────────────┘

Building the missions The first buildings at a mission were often little more than huts. They were made of sticks held together with mud or clay. The roofs were made of bundles of tules. You learned in Chapter 3 that tules, also called river rushes, were plants that grew along the edge of the water. The floors were of dirt, and there was no glass for the windows. These huts served as shelter until better buildings were made.

Work was soon under way on buildings that would last for a long time. **Adobe** (ə dō′bē) was most often used for

How long was it between the founding of the first mission and the last one?

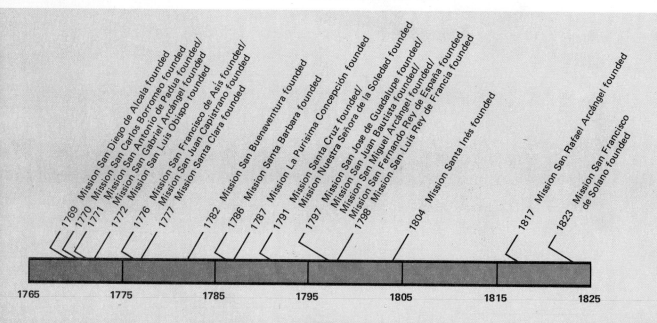

1769 Mission San Diego de Alcala founded
1770 Mission San Carlos Borromeo founded
1771 Mission San Antonio de Padua founded/
    Mission San Gabriel Arcángel founded
1772 Mission San Luis Obispo founded
1776 Mission San Francisco de Asís founded/
    Mission San Juan Capistrano founded
1777 Mission Santa Clara founded
1782 Mission San Buenaventura founded
1786 Mission Santa Barbara founded
1787 Mission La Purísima Concepción founded
1791 Mission Santa Cruz founded/
    Mission Nuestra Señora de la Soledad founded
1797 Mission San Jose de Guadalupe founded/
    Mission San Juan Bautista founded/
    Mission San Miguel Arcángel founded/
    Mission San Fernando Rey de España founded
1798 Mission San Luis Rey de Francia founded
1804 Mission Santa Inés founded
1817 Mission San Rafael Arcángel founded
1823 Mission San Francisco de Solano founded

1765   1775   1785   1795   1805   1815   1825

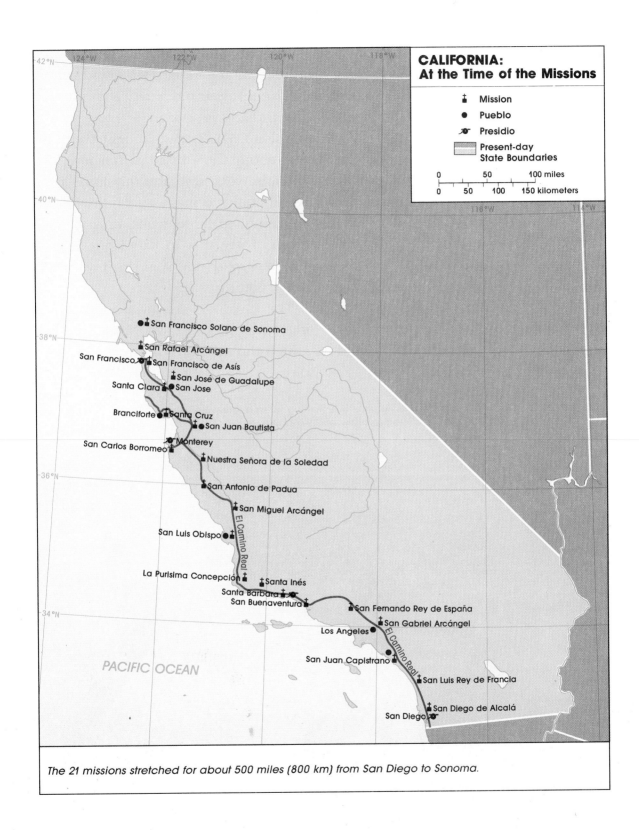

CALIFORNIA: At the Time of the Missions

- ✝ Mission
- ● Pueblo
- ⊙ Presidio
- ▭ Present-day State Boundaries

| 0 | | 50 | | 100 miles |
| 0 | 50 | 100 | | 150 kilometers |

San Francisco Solano de Sonoma

San Rafael Arcángel

San Francisco · San Francisco de Asís

San José de Guadalupe

Santa Clara · San Jose

Branciforte · Santa Cruz

San Juan Bautista

San Carlos Borromeo · Monterey

Nuestra Señora de la Soledad

San Antonio de Padua

San Miguel Arcángel

San Luis Obispo

El Camino Real

La Purísima Concepción · Santa Inés

Santa Barbara · San Buenaventura

San Fernando Rey de España

San Gabriel Arcángel

Los Angeles

San Juan Capistrano · El Camino Real

San Luis Rey de Francia

San Diego · San Diego de Alcalá

PACIFIC OCEAN

The 21 missions stretched for about 500 miles (800 km) from San Diego to Sonoma.

these buildings. It was a mixture of wet clay and straw. The mixture was made into bricks and dried in the sun. Red tiles made of clay were used to cover the roofs.

A mission was a little community. The church and the padres' living quarters were built first. Then storerooms and workshops were added. The main buildings were often connected and built around an open square. Along the inner part of the square were shady hallways open to the outdoors. The largest building was the church at one corner of the square. As time went on, other buildings were often added.

The missions grow   The padres tried to get the Indians who lived nearby to give up their old ways. They wanted the Indians to live in or close to the missions. The padres taught the Indians about the Christian religion. The Indians worked at the missions. They were taught to make adobe bricks and roof tiles, to build walls, and to raise crops. Later this Indian labor helped provide goods for Spain to trade with other countries.

The Indians were given food, clothing, and a place to live. Not all Indians joined the missions, but many of them did.

Missions were usually built around an open square. This drawing shows a typical mission plan. The buildings included a church, living quarters, and workshops.

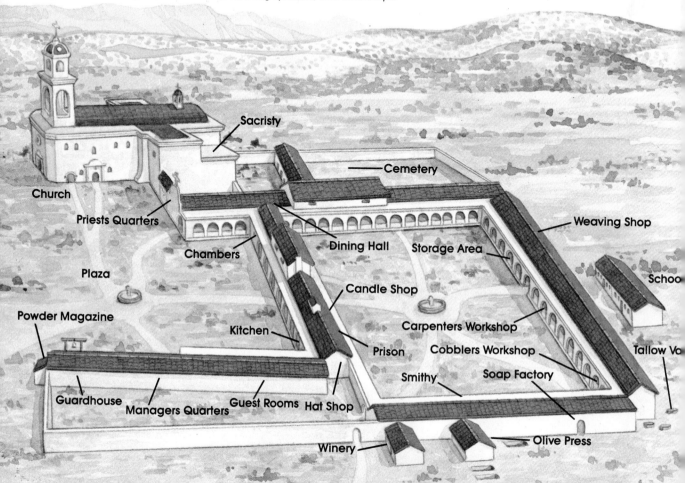

Sacristy
Cemetery
Church
Priests Quarters
Weaving Shop
Chambers
Dining Hall
Storage Area
Plaza
Schoo
Candle Shop
Powder Magazine
Carpenters Workshop
Kitchen
Cobblers Workshop
Tallow Vo
Prison
Guardhouse
Smithy
Soap Factory
Managers Quarters
Guest Rooms
Hat Shop
Winery
Olive Press

California vaqueros were skilled horsemen. Here one prepares to rope a steer.

The padres and Indians worked very hard. They grew many kinds of food crops. They started orchards of oranges, lemons, figs, dates, and olives. They built canals and dug ditches to bring water to the crops. This is called **irrigation** (ir′ə gā′ shən). You will learn more about irrigation in Chapter 10. The cattle herds grew large. Some of the California Indians who took care of the cattle became **vaqueros** (vä ke′ rōz). *Vaquero* is the Spanish word for "cowboy."

After a few years, some of the missions grew or made more things than they needed for their own use. They sent their extra goods to Mexico. They also traded with the sailing ships that stopped at California. They traded **tallow**, or beef fat, and leather made from the hides, or skins, of cattle. Tallow was used to make candles that were needed for lighting in those days. They also traded **hemp**, a tall plant grown in the fields. The strong threads of the plant were made into rope.

In return for these things, the missions received other things that they could not make for themselves. They received things like tools, glass, cloth, nails, pots, and pans.

CHECKUP

1. How did the first buildings at a mission differ from those that were put up later?
2. In what ways were the mission buildings used?
3. What part did the Indians play in the life of the mission?
4. What were some of the goods that the missions used for trade? What did they receive in return?

The End of the Missions

California becomes part of Mexico
In 1821 Mexico won its **independence** from Spain. *Independence* means "freedom from the control of another country." So Mexico, not Spain, now ruled California.

The Mexican leaders did not like the way the missions were run. They said that the Indians were treated almost as slaves. The Indians worked in the fields and shops. If they ran away, they were brought back and punished.

By this time, more and more people were coming to California. They wanted to settle there, and they expected there would be land for them. But they soon found that the missions owned much of the good land. So these people, too, were against the missions.

Finally, the Mexican leaders decided that the missions would have to give up most of their land. The churches were all that they could keep. Half the land was supposed to be given to the Indians who had worked on it. But that did not happen. Many Indians did not know about their rights to the land. Many others who did receive some land were cheated out of it. Most of the mission lands ended up in the hands of the settlers and the big landowners.

Mission San Gabriel Arcángel was the fourth mission founded by Father Serra.

Mission San Antonio de Padua near Jolon was founded on July 14, 1771.

Leaving the missions   Thousands of California Indians had lived and worked in the missions. Now they had to leave. But many of them did not want to go. They did not know where to go or what to do. The mission was the only home they had known. They felt lost.

Few were able to return to the old way of life, the way the Indians had lived before the Spanish came. With more people moving in, that way of life was gone.

A few of the Indians were able to make a living using the skills they had learned. Some of the vaqueros got jobs on the **ranchos** (ran′chōz). *Rancho* is the Spanish word for "ranch." Some went to the **pueblos** (pweb′lōz). *Pueblo* is the Spanish word for "town." But not many could find jobs in the towns. Those who

The Rise of the Ranchos

During the mission days, Spain gave California land to Spanish soldiers. These soldiers wanted to stay in California after their time of service was over. This gift of land was called a **land grant.** The land grants became the ranchos, where great herds of cattle were raised. The owners of the ranchos were called **rancheros.**

After Mexico took over California, the ranchos grew. Land that belonged to the missions was given to people who wanted to become rancheros. Over 800 land grants were made.

A big rancho might have 15,000 to 20,000 cattle. Sheep and horses were also raised. Many miles of pastureland were needed for grazing.

The cattle hides and tallow were often traded to American and British traders for goods, such as cloth, dishes, and furniture.

Vaqueros looked after the cattle. Each spring they would round up the cattle so that the calves could be branded. This roundup was called a **rodeo.**

Usually the rodeo lasted a week. Everyone enjoyed good food, games, and dancing. There were also **fiestas.** These events were held for religious holidays, weddings, and just for fun.

The rancheros were friendly to anyone who traveled by the rancho. Visitors received meals, lodging, and even new riding animals. The rancheros refused payment for their hospitality.

Houses on the rancho were made of adobe brick. The thick walls kept the houses cool in summer and warm in winter. The house shown below at Petuluma Adobe State Historical Park is an example of a rancho adobe house.

Notice how the adobe brick was used to build this rancho house.

Mission San Carlos Borroméo was founded in 1770. It was moved in 1771 to the Carmel River valley. It is also called Mission San Carlos del Rio Carmelo.

did were often treated badly and were paid almost nothing. Many Indians caught diseases that had been brought in by the new people. A great many died because their bodies were not used to fighting such diseases.

For most of the Indians, life was much harder after they left the missions. They had not been free to do as they wanted at the missions. And they had not been trained for life away from the missions. But they had been safe from outsiders.

Now they found they had no one to stand between them and the settlers. Those who were moving into California were often cruel. They destroyed the Indian settlements and took their lands. The Indians were sometimes killed or were left to die of hunger and disease. For those who lived, there were years of hardship ahead.

Looking ahead   In the next chapter you will learn how other countries besides Mexico became interested in California. You will find out who some of the first people were to come to California from the United States. And you will learn how California came under American rule.

CHECKUP

1. What country got control of California in 1821?
2. What changes did this bring about in the missions?
3. What happened to the mission lands?
4. What did the California Indians do after they left the missions?

5/CHAPTER REVIEW

KEY FACTS

1. Father Serra and other Spanish religious leaders set up 21 missions in California.

2. The first purpose of the missions was to bring the California Indians to accept the Christian religion.

3. Each mission was a community in which fields of crops and herds of cattle were tended by the Indians. They were also taught crafts and skills.

4. After Mexico became independent from Spain, the mission system was ended.

VOCABULARY QUIZ

Write the numbers 1 to 10 on a sheet of paper. Match these words with the definitions below.

a. livestock   f. transportation

b. vaquero   g. pueblo

c. rancho   h. hemp

d. irrigation   i. padre

e. adobe   j. independence

1. Moving people and goods
2. A cowboy
3. A ranch
4. A plant from which rope is made
5. A town
6. A religious leader
7. Farm animals
8. Bringing water to crops
9. Building material made of sun-dried clay and straw
10. Freedom from the control of others

REVIEW QUESTIONS

1. Why did the Spanish set up missions in California?

2. What things did the padres look for when choosing a place for a mission?

3. What were the different parts of a Spanish mission?

4. What things were grown or made in the missions? What things did the missions have to trade for?

5. Why did the Mexican leaders break up the missions?

6. What effect did the breakup have on the California Indians who had lived and worked there?

ACTIVITIES

1. On an outline map of California, locate the missions that were set up by Father Serra and other religious leaders. Place a dot at the location of each mission. Beside each of the dots, write the name by which the mission was known.

2. Pretend that you are a California Indian who has grown up in a mission. Now the mission system is ending, and you must leave. Write a paragraph telling how you feel about leaving the mission. Also tell how you intend to get along after you have left the mission.

3. Make a list of the Spanish words in this chapter. Beside each Spanish word, write the English meaning.

5/SKILLS DEVELOPMENT

USING A TIME LINE

WHAT IS A TIME LINE?

We can better understand events in history if we know the order in which the events happened.

Below is a list of events from this chapter and earlier chapters. However, the events are not in the order in which they took place. On a separate sheet of paper list the events in the proper order.

a. Spanish exploration of California
b. Ending of mission system
c. Only Indians in California
d. Building of the missions
e. Mexico's independence from Spain

You have listed these events in the order in which they happened. This means according to time. You listed from the earliest happening to the latest happening. Another way to show the order of events is by a time line. A time line shows events and dates. A time line, like a map, is drawn to scale. On a time line each inch stands for a certain amount of time.

READING A TIME LINE

Look at the time line below. It is 5 inches long. It begins in 1940 and ends in 1990. Each inch on the line stands for 10 years. The time line shows when each of the following became governor of California.

Earl Warren	1943
Goodwin Knight	1953
Edmund Brown	1959
Ronald Reagan	1967
Edmund (Jerry) Brown, Jr.	1975
George Deukmejian	1983

The first inch of the time line runs from 1940 to 1950. Earl Warren became governor in 1943. So we place a dot on the line where we think the date 1943 should be. Then we write above the dot Warren's name. The same method is used to place the other names on the time line.

SKILLS PRACTICE

Now you can make your own time line. You may wish to make a time line of important events in your family. To help you get started, answer the following questions:
1. What events will be included? (List only important events.)
2. In what years did the events happen?
3. In what year will your time line begin? End?
4. Each inch in your time line will stand for how many years?

You are now ready to draw your line and add the dates in the proper places. Use a dot to place and then label each event from your list. You have now created a time line.

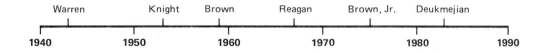

The Russians in California

The Russians sail southward In the early 1800s other countries besides Spain became interested in California. One was Russia. The Russians were already in Alaska. They had come to Alaska in search of furs. They set up a **trading post** in Sitka (sit′kə), about 1,200 miles (1,920 km) north of California. A trading post is a store where goods are exchanged, bought, and sold.

At times the Russians came south hunting sea otters and seals. The furs of these animals were very valuable. The Russians liked what they saw in California. They were pleased to see how easy it was to grow food crops there. Alaska was too cold for many crops.

A Russian and a California lady In 1806 an important Russian official from Alaska sailed into San Francisco Bay. His name was Nicolai Rezanov (nē′ko lä ē re zä′nof). He had been sent to Alaska to look at the Russian settlements. Rezanov found that many of the people there were almost without food. So he came south to California to buy food for them.

When Rezanov arrived in San Francisco, the Spanish **governor**—the top official—would not sell him food. The governor was afraid that Spain would not like his giving food to foreigners. But Rezanov fell in love with the 16-year-old daughter of the military leader. Her name was Concepcion Arguello (kən sep sē ōn′ är′gwel ō). Rezanov asked her to marry him, and she said yes.

Now Concepcion wanted to help Rezanov. She asked the governor to help the Russians. Rezanov was allowed to buy a shipload of food.

Rezanov sailed back to Alaska with the food. He then had to return to Russia to report to his **government**—his country's ruling group. Concepcion waited almost 40 years for Rezanov to return and marry her. Only then did she learn that on his way home to Russia, Rezanov had been killed in an accident. Concepcion refused to marry. She joined

Fort Ross has been restored to look much as it did when the Russians held it.

a religious group and spent the rest of her life helping the poor.

Fort Ross   Six years after Rezanov left, another Russian ship came from Alaska to California. The Russians were looking for a good place to set up another trading post. They also wanted a place where crops could be grown for food for the Alaska settlements. The place they chose was near Bodega (bə dā′gə) Bay. It was about 45 miles (72 km) north of San Francisco.

The Russians built a fort to protect their settlement. They named it Fort Ross. The name came from *Rossiya*, the word the Russians used for the name of their country.

The Spanish were not happy about the Fort Ross settlement. But they did not try to stop the Russians from building it. Yet the Spanish worried about losing part of California to the Russians.

So did the Mexican government after it took over California.

The Russians' attempts to raise crops were not very successful. During their stay at Fort Ross, they had to buy grain from the Californians.

Finally, in 1842, the Russians left California. But it was not because the Mexicans made them leave. It was because so many of the sea otters had been killed by hunters. Unless the Russians could get furs, they could not afford to stay in Fort Ross. They did not come back, but such place-names as Fort Ross and the Russian River are reminders of the Russians' stay in California.

CHECKUP

1. Why did the Russians come to Alaska?
2. Why did Nicolai Rezanov sail to California? What happened to him?
3. Why did the Russians build Fort Ross?
4. Why did the Russians leave California?

Which group reached California first—the Jedediah Smith party or the Bidwell party?

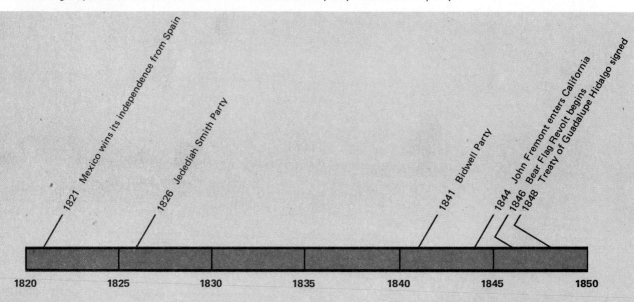

The Americans Start Coming

To California by sea   In 1796 the *Otter*, a sailing ship from Boston, came to Monterey. It was the first ship from the United States to come into a California port.

From that time on, ships from the United States came to California more and more often. Even though the Spanish had a law against trading with foreigners, trading went on just the same. Sometimes American traders were caught and put in jail. Whaling ships also stopped along the California coast to make repairs. The sailors on these ships traded with the Californians. The sailors brought back to the United States stories of California's good soil and pleasant weather.

After California came under Mexican rule, trade became easier. The Mexicans allowed much more trade with ships from other countries than the Spanish had allowed. For cattle hides from the ranchos, Americans exchanged everything from plows to needles. Now, foreigners who agreed to obey California's laws were also allowed to settle there. Some of the American traders did settle there, and some married the daughters of Spanish families.

The oxcart is loaded with cattle hides that have been brought to the coast for trading.

To California by land   The first Americans to reach California by land were led by Jedediah (jed'ə dī ə) Smith, a young fur trapper. In 1826 he and 15 or 20 others set out from what is today northern Utah. They crossed the dry lands that are in southern Nevada. Then they went across the Mojave Desert in southern California. They were weak with hunger when they walked into the San Gabriel mission.

The padres were surprised to see the Americans. The Americans were fed and cared for by the padres for 2 months. The Mexican governor was not so friendly. When he found out about the Americans arriving in California, he had Smith thrown in jail. The governor said that Smith and his men had not had permission to come into California. He feared, too, that the Americans would try to overthrow Mexican rule.

The Americans were finally allowed to leave California. However, Smith had to promise never to return. On the way back to Utah, these men became the first whites ever to cross the high lands of the Sierra Nevada.

Smith soon broke his promise. After a short stay in Utah, he went back to California. Again he was jailed, and once more he was set free and told to get out. When he was 32 years old, he was killed by Comanches at a desert watering hole in what is now New Mexico.

John Sutter came to America from Switzerland. He wanted to settle in the Sacramento Valley.

Soon other Americans began to cross the deserts and go through the mountains to California. They were fur trappers, hunters, and traders. When they returned to the United States, they spread the word that California was a great place in which to live.

Sutter's Fort   John Sutter had come to America from Switzerland. After spending some time in the United States and Mexico, he went to the Hawaiian (hə wī'yən) Islands. Then he decided to settle in California. Sutter hired some

Soon after John Sutter's fort was built, a busy town grew up around it. Today this community, shown above, is the city of Sacramento, California's capital.

workers in Hawaii and brought them with him to California. He wanted to settle in the Sacramento (sak rə men′tō) Valley. Sutter offered to help the Mexican governor in ruling that inland region. The governor liked the idea and gave Sutter a large piece of land. It was near the spot where the Sacramento and American rivers come together. This is where Sacramento, the capital of California, is now located.

Sutter's workers built a large fort. Sutter hired people to grow crops, raise cattle, and cut timber. He kept a store with trading goods. He got along well

Pío Pico was the last Mexican governor of California.

with the Indians, and he saw that Mexican laws were obeyed.

Sutter's Fort was on the trail used by Americans coming into California. It passed through the Sierra Nevada. Sutter liked Americans. The more Americans that came, the better he liked it. They were good customers for his store. Most Americans who came to California through the Sierra Nevada stopped at Sutter's Fort.

John Frémont   Another American who stopped at Sutter's Fort was Captain John Frémont. He had been sent by the United States government to explore the West and make maps of it. In 1844 one of his trips brought him to California.

Frémont liked California very much. When he returned to the United States, he wrote a report about what he had seen. People all over America read the report. They learned about California's beautiful weather. They read about its uncrowded land. And they started thinking about going to California.

The Bidwell party   Even before Frémont excited people with his report about California, Americans were starting to settle there. The first group of settlers to go by land was the Bidwell **party**. *Party* means a "group of people taking part together in some action."

John Bidwell was a 20-year-old school teacher. He was one of the leaders of a party that left Missouri in 1841. More than 60 people started out on the trail to California. They had 18 carts and wagons pulled by horses, mules, and oxen. After 7 weeks, they reached a fork in the trail. Some of the group went north to Oregon. Bidwell led his group of 32 people south.

Near the Great Salt Lake the animals tired. The people threw away the furniture stored in their wagons. They got rid of almost everything that was heavy.

By the time they reached the High Sierra, the party was almost out of food. To get meat, they had to kill many of their animals. As they climbed the mountain trails, they had to go through deep snow. But Bidwell kept them moving forward. Finally the day came when they looked down into a wide valley. Soon they reached a California rancho. It had been 6 months since they started. But they had come through safely. All the people that Bidwell led to California praised him for being such a strong leader.

The Donner party   Many more groups followed the Bidwell party to California. It was a long, hard trip, and none of the groups had an easy time. A party led by George Donner had a very bad time.

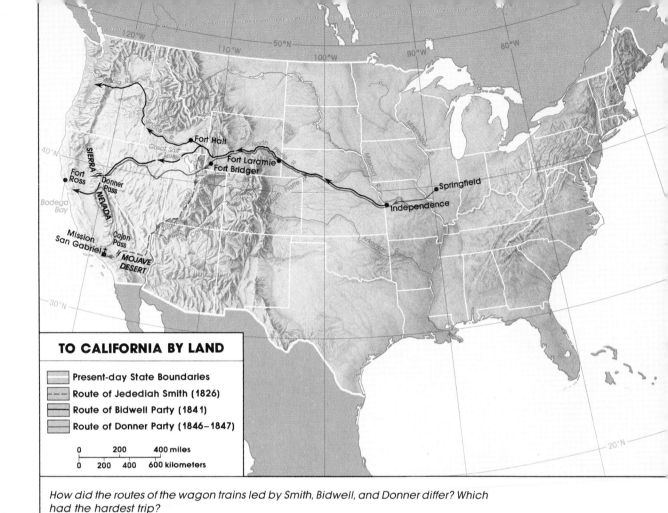

TO CALIFORNIA BY LAND

☐ Present-day State Boundaries
--- Route of Jedediah Smith (1826)
☐ Route of Bidwell Party (1841)
☐ Route of Donner Party (1846–1847)

0   200   400 miles
0   200   400   600 kilometers

How did the routes of the wagon trains led by Smith, Bidwell, and Donner differ? Which had the hardest trip?

The Donner party set out in the spring of 1846 from Springfield, Illinois. They planned to get through the Sierras before snow fell. After about 2 months on the trail, they tried what they thought was a shorter way. But soon they were lost. When they reached the Sierras, it was much nearer winter than they had planned.

In early November they started through the mountains. An early snowstorm struck. Soon they were trapped in 10 feet (3 m) of snow. For 4 months they tried to keep alive in a cold, windy mountain pass. In December, 15 men set out on foot to get help. Weeks later, 7 of them reached a California rancho. The other 8 died on the way.

Several groups now tried to save those who were trapped in the deep snows. Some people were brought out, but many others had to stay in the mountains for 4 months. The snow was 22 feet (7 m) deep. By spring, 34 people had died. Only 45 of 79 people came out of the mountains alive.

During the winter of 1846–1847, the Donner party underwent great suffering in the snows of the Sierras.

CHECKUP

1. How did the first people from the United States get to California?
2. Why is each of the following remembered: the *Otter*, Jedediah Smith, John Frémont, John Bidwell?
3. What was Sutter's Fort, and where was it located?
4. What hardships did people have when going by land to California?

Americans Take California

Interest in California Once the United States had been a small country along the Atlantic coast. But it had become bigger. Now, in the 1840s, many people wanted the United States to take over more lands in the West.

One place these people were interested in was California. Some American leaders hoped to push the borders of the United States to the Pacific Ocean. San Francisco Bay, it was thought, would make a fine base for American ships.

The United States was not the only country interested in California. France and England were also interested. American leaders did not want those countries to get control of California.

Several American Presidents had wanted to buy all or part of California from Mexico. But Mexico would not sell it. By 1845 there was bad feeling between Mexico and the United States. The two countries did not agree on where the boundary was between Mexico and Texas.

At the same time, Americans in California were becoming unhappy with Mexican rule. They did not like having Mexico tell them with whom they could trade. They were afraid that Mexico might decide to keep Americans from coming into California. Some Americans already in California were afraid they might be made to leave.

The bear flag is raised   In June 1846 a group of Americans who had settled in California learned that some Mexican officers were driving a large number of horses south. The horses were for the use of Mexican soldiers. The Americans thought that the soldiers, mounted on horses, might turn on them and drive them out. So the Americans stole the horses.

Then they went to the home of General Vallejo (və lā′hō), the Mexican Army leader. They told him he was under arrest. The Americans made a red and white flag. On it they sewed a red star and the picture of a grizzly bear. They raised this flag over the **plaza** in Sonoma. A plaza is a public square in a town or city.

What these Americans did is called the Bear Flag **Revolt**. A revolt takes place when people rise up against their own leaders.

The Americans said that Mexico no longer ruled California. They said that California would be a free country called a **republic**. This is a kind of government that is run by the people.

Frémont's return   Those who raised the bear flag were not the only group of Americans in California. John Frémont had made another overland journey there. With him were some 60 soldiers. Frémont was supposed to be doing more exploring.

But he had received word that war with Mexico was likely. Now he was ready to help bring California under American rule.

The Mexican War   In 1846 there were no telephones, radios, or television sets. It took a long time for news to get to California from the United States. So no one in California knew that the United States had been at war with Mexico for a whole month before the Bear Flag Revolt took place.

For a few weeks in 1846, the bear flag flew over what those who raised it called "the republic of California." Today the bear flag serves as California's state flag.

The war had started in Texas in May 1846. Word reached California early in July when ships of the United States Navy sailed into Monterey Bay. The navy leader was John Sloat. He had the American flag raised at Monterey and at Sutter's Fort. At Sonoma the bear flag was hauled down, and the American flag went up. From that time on, California was claimed as American territory.

While Sloat was in charge, everything was peaceful. The Americans promised the Californians that they would be treated well. The Californians seemed ready to accept American rule. However, Robert Stockton soon became the new navy leader to take Sloat's place. Stockton was much harder on the Californians than Sloat had been. Stockton made harder rules. With Stockton's support, Frémont added some Americans who had settled in California to his group of soldiers. He called his new, larger group the California **Battalion** (bə tal'yən). A battalion is a large group of soldiers. Frémont's men then marched

The American flag flies at Monterey in 1846 after the arrival of the American navy.

The California Battalion, led by John Frémont, rides on its flag-raising trip.

through many towns and raised the American flag.

Trouble in Los Angeles   In northern California the takeover by the Americans went smoothly. But southern California was a different story.

In August the American flag was raised in Los Angeles, and a small group of American soldiers was stationed there. But the American leader was harsh and rude to the Californians. They revolted against American rule. The Americans might have been badly defeated if they had not received some help.

This help came from General Stephen Kearny (kär′nē) of the United States Army. When war broke out, he was ordered to march west with his soldiers to California. On the way he had claimed New Mexico for the United States. From there

Kearny and his men kept on into the dry lands of the Colorado Desert in southern California.

The Californians had good leaders in Jose Maria Flores (hō sä′ mə rē′ə flōr′əs) and Jose Antonio Carillo (hō sä′ ən tō′nē ō kär rē′yo). Their soldiers were very good horsemen. The soldiers carried long poles called lances, which they used as spears. The first time Kearny's soldiers met the Californians was near the Indian village of San Pasqual (sän pas′ kyủ əl). The Americans were badly beaten. But with help sent by Stockton, they finally reached San Diego.

Now the Americans were ready to move on Los Angeles. The soldiers of Kearny and Stockton marched on Los Angeles from the south. Frémont and his men moved down from the north. This time the Californians could not stop the Americans. In January 1847 Los Angeles again came under American rule. A few days later the Californians gave up, and the war in California was over.

The war ends   Fighting went on for 8 months more in Mexico. It ended there in September 1847 when the American soldiers took Mexico City. A peace treaty was signed in 1848. It was signed in the Mexican village of Guadalupe Hidalgo (gwä dǝ lüp hid al′gō).

By the terms of the Treaty of Guadalupe Hidalgo, California belonged to the United States. The United States also got from Mexico the land between Texas and California. Later the United States paid Mexico 15 million dollars.

In 1853 the United States added new land from Mexico. It paid 10 million dollars for the Gadsden Purchase. Find it on the map. The land shown on the map as Texas Annexation had already become part of the United States. This land, like the Mexican Cession, had also once belonged to Mexico.

From Atlantic to Pacific   For the United States, the end of the war meant that its lands now stretched from the Atlantic to the Pacific. But for Spanish-speaking Californians, the end of the war had other meanings.

The Spanish language would now in most places give way to the English language. Customs and ways of life that were once Spanish would become American.

Under a law passed a few years later, Californians had to prove their right to the lands they lived on. Many had owned these lands for years but had no papers

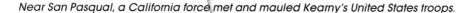

Near San Pasqual, a California force met and mauled Kearny's United States troops.

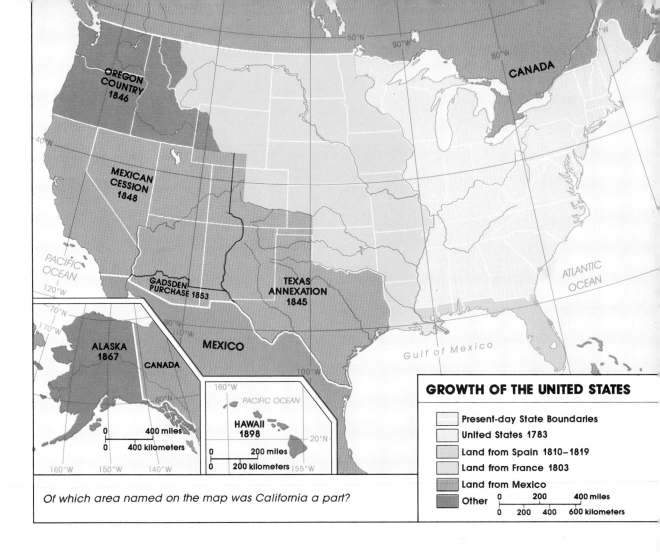

OREGON COUNTRY 1846

MEXICAN CESSION 1848

CANADA

PACIFIC OCEAN

120°W

GADSDEN PURCHASE 1853

TEXAS ANNEXATION 1845

ATLANTIC OCEAN

ALASKA 1867

CANADA

MEXICO

Gulf of Mexico

0 400 miles
0 400 kilometers

160°W   150°W   140°W

160°W

PACIFIC OCEAN

HAWAII 1898

20°N

0 200 miles
0 200 kilometers

155°W

Of which area named on the map was California a part?

GROWTH OF THE UNITED STATES

- Present-day State Boundaries
- United States 1783
- Land from Spain 1810–1819
- Land from France 1803
- Land from Mexico
- Other

0   200   400 miles
0 200 400 600 kilometers

to prove it. So some of those living on the old ranchos for years now had to give up their lands.

The Spanish past   But though the old Spanish way of life became weaker, it would never die. Today it is a part of the state's past that Californians are proud of. Many towns and cities still have Spanish names. Many Californians can trace their families back to Spain or Mexico. In art, music, food and other ways, the Spanish past lives on.

Looking ahead   In the next chapter you will learn how the discovery of gold brought many people to California. You will find out how people came and about their search for gold.

CHECKUP

1. What was the Bear Flag Revolt?
2. How did the Californians react to the American takeover?
3. What part did each of the following play in the Mexican War in California: John Sloat, General Vallejo, John Frémont, Jose Maria Flores, General Kearny?

KEY FACTS

1. In the early 1800s the Russians had a trading post in northern California, but they left when they could no longer get many furs.

2. In about the same period, Americans came to California in larger numbers, both by sea and by land.

3. The United States government wanted to buy California, but Mexico would not sell it.

4. The Mexican War between the United States and Mexico was fought mostly outside of California. It resulted in Mexico's giving up California to the United States.

5. California's Spanish past is seen today in the state's place-names, architecture, music, food, and in other ways.

VOCABULARY QUIZ

On a separate sheet of paper, write the word that completes each sentence.

1. The public square in the early towns of California was called the (a) pueblo, (b) presidio, (c) rancho, (d) plaza.

2. When people rise up against their leaders, this action is called a (a) return, (b) revolt, (c) resort, (d) resource.

3. A kind of government in which the people rule is called a (a) kingdom, (b) capital, (c) republic, (d) mission.

4. The people who make up a battalion are (a) soldiers, (b) padres, (c) fur traders, (d) sailors.

REVIEW QUESTIONS

1. Why did the Russians come to California? Why did they finally leave?

2. For what purposes did American ships stop at California?

3. Why is Jedediah Smith remembered in the history of California?

4. What did John Frémont do to make Americans more interested in California?

5. Why did some American Presidents try to buy California? What did Mexico say?

6. Where did the Mexican War start? Why were Californians late to learn about the outbreak of war?

7. What actions took place in California during the Mexican War?

8. What did the Treaty of Guadalupe Hidalgo say about California?

9. What parts of the United States in addition to California once belonged to Mexico?

ACTIVITIES

1. On an outline map of the western United States, draw the overland route used by many Americans who went to California. On the map write the names of the present-day states through which the trail led. Label the Sierra Nevada and Sutter's Fort.

2. Pretend that you are a member of either the Bidwell party or the Donner party. You have finally arrived in California. Write a letter to a friend back home, telling what happened on your journey.

6/SKILLS DEVELOPMENT

UNDERSTANDING CAUSE AND EFFECT

WHAT IS CAUSE AND EFFECT?

One thing sometimes causes something else to happen. For example, a child climbed a tree and sat on a dead limb. The limb broke and the child fell. We call this **cause and effect**. The **cause** of what happened was the child sitting on a dead limb. The **effect** was the child falling.

It is important to learn how to tell when one event causes another. Picking out cause and effect is a part of the skill of thinking clearly.

MATCH THE PICTURES

Look at the pictures below. See if you can match an **EFFECT** picture with each **CAUSE** picture.

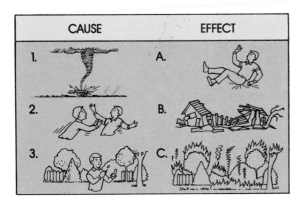

Now let's see how well you matched the cause and effect pictures.

1 matches B
The effect of the tornado was the collapsed house.

2 matches A
The effect of the children pushing was that one child fell to the ground.

3 matches C
The effect of the child lighting the match was that the grass and trees caught on fire.

SKILLS PRACTICE

Write the numbers 1 to 5 on a sheet of paper. Match each **CAUSE** to the correct **EFFECT**.

CAUSE

1. Lyn lives in a forested state.
2. Juan lives in a state that gets a small amount of rain.
3. Phil's state has large areas of rich and fertile soil.
4. Hal lives in a state with large amounts of coal.
5. Marilyn's state has a rainy season.

EFFECT

A. This state is a leading producer of food crops.
B. This state is often troubled with floods.
C. This state has many people who work as miners.
D. This state has a large lumbering industry.
E. This state uses irrigation to help grow crops.

2/UNIT REVIEW

1. There were many different tribes of California Indians. — *Can you name one tribe that lived or still lives in your area?*

2. The California Indians were known for their skill in living with nature. — *Why can we say that this statement is true?*

3. The California Indians caught fish, gathered nuts and seeds, and hunted animals for food. — *What are the important foods for you today? Are they the same foods that were important to the Indians? Why or why not? Do you get your food the same way as did the Indians? Why or why not?*

4. Explorers have to be brave. — *Why do explorers have to be brave? Compare an early explorer of the California coast, such as Cabrillo, with the well-known explorer Neil Armstrong, the first astronaut to walk on the moon.*

5. The explorers who went to the New World were looking for two things. They were looking for gold and for another way to sail to the Orient. — *Why were the Spanish in Mexico interested in exploring the California coast?*

6. After Mexico became independent from Spain the mission system ended. — *Why did the Mexican leaders end the mission system? Was ending the mission system a good or bad thing for the California Indians?*

7. In the early 1800s other countries besides Mexico became interested in California. — *List two other countries that were interested in California. Tell why each country was interested in California.*

8. The Mexican War, fought between Mexico and the United States, ended in 1847. — *What did the end of the Mexican War mean to the Mexicans, the Americans, and the Californians?*

Becoming a State

The Discovery of Gold

VOCABULARY

waterwheel	pyrite
tailrace	prospector

Sutter builds a sawmill James Marshall was one of the men who worked for Captain Sutter. Captain Sutter wanted to build a sawmill because more lumber would be needed by new settlers.

Captain Sutter sent James Marshall to look for a place to build the sawmill. He looked for a place with a river and trees. The mill was to be powered by a **waterwheel.** The running water of the river would turn the waterwheel. The waterwheel would then turn the saws that cut the logs into lumber.

Marshall found a good location for the sawmill on the south fork of the American River, about 45 miles (72 km) from Sutter's Fort.

Marshall finds gold January 24, 1848, was a cold, clear day in the hills of central California. The sawmill was almost completed. Marshall walked along a sandy trail by the American River.

A **tailrace,** or ditch, had been dug to move water from the sawmill pond back to the river. Marshall wanted to see if the newly dug ditch was deep enough.

He pushed aside the branches of the trees. As he stood staring at the clear water, a bright yellow gleam caught his eye. He stooped down to scoop a gold flake from the icy water. Then he saw another flake and took it.

He asked himself, Is it real gold? Or is it only **pyrite** (pī′ rīt), or fool's gold?

There was an easy way to find out. Marshall walked up the riverbank, looking for two smooth rocks. He placed the gold flake on one rock and then pounded the flake with the second rock. The flake was soft and flattened easily like gold. If it had been fool's gold, it would have been brittle, breaking into bits.

"Gold! I've found gold!"

It is gold Marshall ran to the sawmill and shouted to the workmen, "Boys, I believe I have found a gold mine!" He showed them the gleaming flake of gold in his hand.

The workmen stared in disbelief. They were doubtful. The next day the work-

Collection of the National Cowboy Hall of Fame, Oklahoma City

A gold prospector travels alone carrying his shovel, pan, and other needed tools.

men were amazed to find pieces of the shining metal in the ditch.

Four days after his discovery, Marshall burst into John Sutter's office. Sutter wrote in his diary about what happened next: "He told me he had something of the utmost importance to tell me, that he wanted to speak to me in private, and begged me to take him to some isolated place where no one could possibly overhear us."

They moved to a private place. Then Marshall showed Sutter what he had discovered. Sutter thought it was gold, but he was not sure. They decided to test the gold. They pounded the flakes. They weighed them in water. They tested them with an acid. The shiny flakes were gold!

The news spreads Sutter went back to the sawmill with Marshall. He saw how much gold there was. He asked the workmen to keep the gold a secret until the sawmill was built. That would be about two more months. Few travelers came to the mill. So Sutter and Marshall hoped that word of the gold discovery would not spread.

Marshall told the millworkers that they could look for gold. Only one, Henry Bigler, did. He wrote in his diary, "I took the gun and went along down the creek to hunt for ducks, but in reality to look for gold." He was the first **prospector** (pros' pek tər). Prospectors were people who looked for gold.

Keeping the gold discovery a secret was hard. Word spread rapidly in many ways. A week after the discovery, Sutter wrote to tell a friend about it. Local children told about the gold. Many people wrote letters to their friends. And travelers spread the news.

In what year was gold discovered by James Marshall?

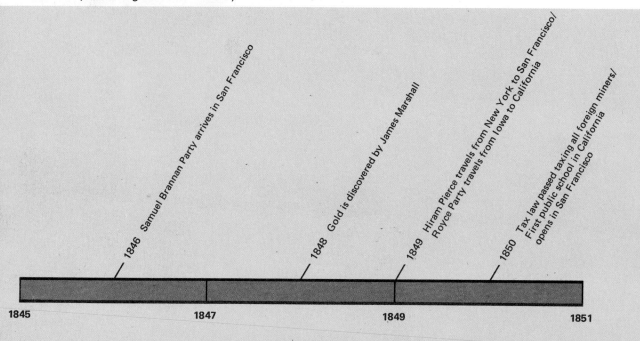

1846 Samuel Brannan Party arrives in San Francisco

1848 Gold is discovered by James Marshall

1849 Hiram Pierce travels from New York to San Francisco/ Royce Party travels from Iowa to California

1850 Tax law passed taxing all foreign miners/ First public school in California opens in San Francisco

1845   1847   1849   1851

Visiting Sutter's Mill Today

You can see the replica (rep' lə kə) of Sutter's sawmill when you visit Coloma (kə lō' mə), California. It sits just west of the Sutter's mill site on the American River. Floodwaters destroyed the mill in 1862.

Coloma was the first mining town in California. It had the first mountain sawmill, the first cradle for collecting gold, and the first mining ditch. It was also the first county seat of El Dorado (el' də räd' ō) County.

Today Coloma is smaller than it was in the 1850s. Wood and brick buildings are along the streets and the dirt paths. But only a few of the early buildings remain.

A replica of Sutter's sawmill was built in 1968. You can see how the mill works on weekends. Logs are moved up to the saws and split into lumber.

The sawmill is no longer directly on the American River. But you can stand on the original site. A cement marker is located about 50 feet (15 m) into the river. You have to hop across the rocks to get there. About 200 feet (61 m) downstream from the mill site is the gold-discovery site. When you look into the clear water, you might see some gleaming flecks on the dark sand. Some of the precious metal is still in the river.

In Coloma you can also visit a Chinese store made of stones. Another store has a replica of a mine tunnel. You can see a jail cell that was used until 1912. Behind the cell there is a jail building that was built in 1865. You can visit the gunsmith shop and see the original Colt and Allen revolvers.

To the west you can see a statue of a man looking down on the Coloma Valley. This statue is a monument to James Marshall. A foot trail leads to the monument from the mill. At the monument you will learn that Marshall's gold discovery changed California history. Near the monument you can see the cabin where Marshall lived until 1868. When you visit Sutter's mill, you can also visit the museum.

When this replica of Sutter's sawmill was built, oak pins were used to join the boards. Metal nails were used only on the roof.

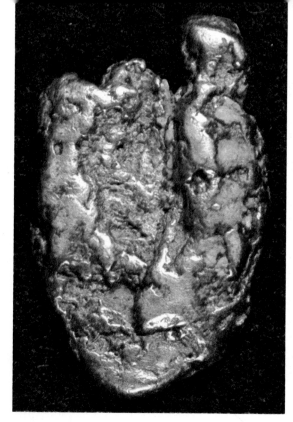

This gold nugget, shown above in an enlarged photograph, was among the first pieces of gold found by Marshall.

Gold! Gold from the American River!" he shouted. Brannan wanted many miners to come to California. He sent to Mississippi and Missouri thousands of copies of a newspaper telling about the gold. He also sent newspapers to the East Coast.

CHECKUP

1. What did James Marshall find in the American River?
2. What is the difference between real gold and pyrite, or fool's gold?
3. Why did Sutter and Marshall want to keep the gold discovery a secret?
4. Why did Sam Brannan want the gold discovery news to spread?

Gold was melted, refined, and finally formed into gold coins like these shown below. Can you find the date on any of the coins?

Gold seekers arrive   Soon many people came looking for gold. They were so excited they just left whatever they were doing. Sutter lost many of his workers. People came from all over California, Oregon, and Mexico. Some people came across the Pacific Ocean from Hawaii and even Australia (ô strāl′ yə).

A man named Sam Brannan (bran′ an) owned a store near Sutter's Fort. He saw some of the gold from the American River and got very excited. He wanted to sell supplies to the miners. He went through the streets of San Francisco. He waved his hat and a medicine bottle filled with small pieces of gold. "Gold!

Traveling to California

VOCABULARY

forty-niners	**bargain**
isthmus	**wagon train**

The rush begins   Word of the gold discovery began to spread over the world. Some of the California gold was put on display in Washington, D.C. The President spoke of the gold discovery in a speech. Many people came to California to search for gold during 1849. They were called the **forty-niners.**

The gold hunters were interested in the fastest way to California. Men and women discussed routes. They read newspapers and books. They talked to people who had been to California.

The shortest way to the goldfields in the West was to drive wagons there. The trails were covered with snow when people in the East first heard about the gold. So there would be no grass for the animals to eat. Wagons from the East could not leave until spring.

Many gold hunters did not want to wait for spring. Most of the people who traveled to California from December of 1848 through March of 1849 went by sea.

There were two sea routes. One was around South America past Cape Horn. The second was across the Isthmus of Panama in Central America. An **isthmus** (is′ məs) is a narrow strip of land

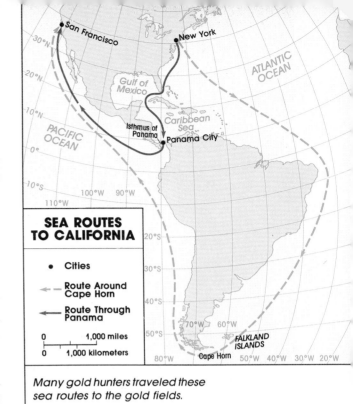

SEA ROUTES TO CALIFORNIA

- Cities
- Route Around Cape Horn
- Route Through Panama

0   1,000 miles
0   1,000 kilometers

Many gold hunters traveled these sea routes to the gold fields.

connecting two larger pieces of land. It has water on both sides. The safest route by sea was around South America. But it was a 6- to 9-month voyage. The route through Panama was faster but more dangerous. This route was a 3- to 5-month trip.

Going by sea   One of the people who traveled the Panama route was Hiram Pierce of Troy, New York. He left his wife and children to join gold hunters sailing from New York City. On March 8, 1849, the trip began. They traveled down the Atlantic coast and landed in Panama.

Their trip to the Chagres (chäg′ rəs) River on the Isthmus of Panama went

The Chagres River on the Isthmus of Panama was part of the route across Panama.

smoothly. Then the trip became difficult. The travelers had to **bargain** (bär′ gən) with the natives for a way to get across the isthmus to Panama City. A bargain is an agreement to make a trade or an exchange.

The group used a small boat for the trip up the river. Their boat could travel only 17 miles (27 km) on the shallow river. Then they had to bargain again with other natives.

This time they got on flat-bottomed boats. Natives using poles pushed the boats upstream to a small village. From there the group would travel to the Pacific by land.

They walked most of the 24 miles (39 km) through the jungle. Insects bit them.

The sun was hot. And they were tired when they arrived in Panama City.

Hiram joined nearly 2,000 other gold hunters who had been waiting weeks for a ship to San Francisco. They got on a ship 35 days later. The trip to California took them 2 months. The ship was overcrowded, and the food was bad. Many of the people got sick. At times, storms tossed the ship about. On July 26, Hiram and the others arrived in San Francisco Bay. It had taken them almost 5 months to travel to California.

Going overland   Although they had to wait until spring, most gold seekers came by land. Twice as many came by land as by sea.

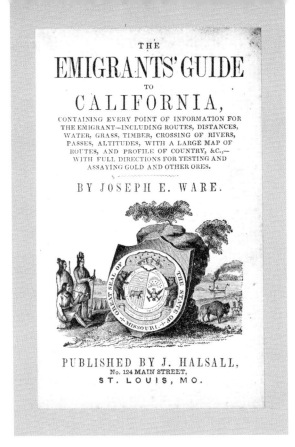

THE
EMIGRANTS' GUIDE
TO
CALIFORNIA,
CONTAINING EVERY POINT OF INFORMATION FOR
THE EMIGRANT—INCLUDING ROUTES, DISTANCES,
WATER, GRASS, TIMBER, CROSSING OF RIVERS,
PASSES, ALTITUDES, WITH A LARGE MAP OF
ROUTES, AND PROFILE OF COUNTRY, &C.,—
WITH FULL DIRECTIONS FOR TESTING AND
ASSAYING GOLD AND OTHER ORES.

BY JOSEPH E. WARE.

PUBLISHED BY J. HALSALL,
No. 124 MAIN STREET,
ST. LOUIS, MO.

This guide provided the traveler with routes, distances, maps, and even directions for testing gold.

Sarah Eleanor Royce (sãr′ a el′ a nėr rois) and her family were among those who traveled by land. They were from Iowa. In the spring of 1849, they started for Council Bluffs, Iowa. There they joined other gold hunters for the trip to California.

Sarah's husband hitched some oxen to their wagon. They had cows to give them milk. They did not know much about where they were going or about the dangers. But they wanted to find gold.

At Council Bluffs they crossed the wide Missouri River on a ferryboat. Then they joined other forty-niners in a **wagon train.** A wagon train is a group of wagons traveling together.

This ferryboat carrying gold miners and their wagons was made by joining canoes.

Many people—ministers, doctors, lawyers, blacksmiths, shoemakers, and printers—traveled to California. In 1849 over 80,000 people went to California to hunt for gold.

Like many of the forty-niners, Sarah kept a diary of their trip. On June 10, 1849, she wrote, "The Captain gave the word of command, 'Roll out!' and wagon after wagon fell into line."

The trail was hard   At first, Sarah and her family enjoyed the excitement of the journey. But as they traveled on, many in the wagon train got sick. Some of the wagons were too heavy. They had to be unloaded along the way. Thunderstorms beat down on the travelers. The journey to California was long and hard.

These California-bound travelers have stopped along the way. What do you think they are doing?

Finally Sarah and her family arrived at Salt Lake City. It was the only town between Council Bluffs and the mining towns of California. Travelers were able to buy supplies and rest there.

The journey became even harder and more dangerous as they crossed the desert and the mountains. The travelers often lost their way. They had trouble finding water. It was hard to find grass for the animals to eat. Some of the animals died. Along the way many wagons were left by their owners.

Government sends help   The government sent out groups of guides to help the people traveling over the Sierras (sē er' əs). Sarah and her family were met by two of these guides. With the help of these men, they arrived at Pleasant Valley, a small mining settlement. Further on was a mining camp that Sarah called Weaverville. The family set up camp there and stayed for the winter. It had taken them almost 6 months to make the journey from their Iowa home to the goldfields of California.

CHECKUP

1. Why were the people who went to California to hunt for gold called forty-niners?
2. What was the shortest route to California?
3. What was the safest sea route to California?
4. How did Hiram Pierce travel to California?
5. What were the dangers of traveling overland to California?

Hunting for Gold

Source of the gold   For thousands of years, rivers had been **eroding** (i rōd′ ing), or wearing away, the mountains. Some of the rocks that washed down contained gold. As rocks hit against each other, they broke up into smaller and smaller pieces. Gold is heavier than most other rocks and settles in the bottom of rivers. Have you ever looked into the clear waters of a river or lake and seen the rocks at the bottom? Imagine if one of them shone with a golden glow!

Most gold was in fine pieces in the sand and gravel of the streams and rivers. The gold found on the bottom of rivers was called **placer** (plas′ ər) **gold.** Later, gold was also found in solid rock.

Panning for gold   To gather placer gold, the gold hunters used a process called **panning.** They used a round pan with a flat bottom and slanted sides. They often had to wade into the icy water. Then they put sand, gravel, and water into the pan and swirled it around. They tilted the pan so the water and the lighter things would fall out. Since the gold was heavy, it was among the last things left in the pan.

To pan for gold the prospector squatted on the banks of a stream and filled his pan with sand, gravel, and water hoping to find gold.

Panning for gold was hard, back-breaking work. It took a lot of time. The water was cold, and the prospectors' knees and muscles ached. Many of them said panning was the hardest work they had ever done in their lives.

Improvements in mining   Panning for gold was a slow process. People soon invented ways to collect gold faster. The **cradle** was one new way. It looked like a baby's cradle and usually needed two people to use it. The bottom of the cradle was sloped and had strips of wood nailed crosswise. One person put sand, gravel, and water into the cradle. Then another person rocked it. The water ran over the sand and gravel. The lightest material was washed off. The gold settled at the bottom of the cradle and was caught on the crosspieces. At the end of the day, the gold was divided between the two people.

Soon the cradle was replaced with the **sluice** (slüs) **box.** The sluice box was a long, narrow, sloping box with no top. Sand and gravel were shoveled into the box. Then water was carried to or piped into the box from a stream or river. There were boards crosswise in the bottom. After lots of washing with water, the gold was trapped behind the strips of wood.

Gold mines   There was more gold inside the rocks of the hills. Have you ever had vanilla ice cream with chocolate ripples in it? Gold ran through the rocks in the same way the chocolate ripples run through the vanilla ice cream. The miners dug into the ground to remove the rocks. They crushed the rocks and then used a sluice box. If there was no gold, they would dig in another place.

The work was so difficult and dangerous that miners had to work together. They invented machines to make the work easier. Power-driven drills were used to dig out the rocks. Then later, dynamite was made in California. Miners used it to dig tunnels into the hills and to break up rocks. Some tunnels went far into the ground. The Empire (em' pīr) Mine in Grass Valley was begun in 1850. Before it was closed about a hundred years later, miners had dug its tunnels 7,000 feet (2,134 m) into the ground!

The cradle used for separating gold was made of wood and was about three feet long. The sluice box was also made of wood but was longer and more narrow.

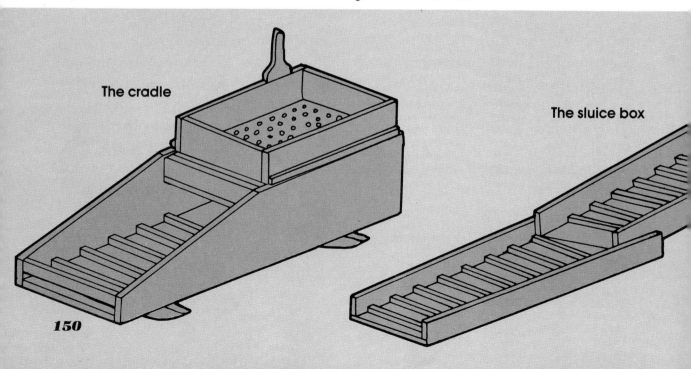

The cradle

The sluice box

Stores like these welcomed the business that came during the gold rush.

Making a fortune   Some prospectors found lots of gold. Many others did not. They moved from place to place, always hoping to find gold. Hiram Pierce was one of those who never struck it rich. After 3 years of prospecting, he went home to his family. He had spent more money than he had made. But he could tell his friends about his adventures in California.

The real winners in the gold rush were the **merchants** (mėr′ chənts). They were the storekeepers, hotelkeepers, bankers, and transporters. The merchants charged high prices. Part of the reason was that it cost a lot of money to deliver supplies to the miners.

Life in the gold camps   Life was hard in the gold camps. At first, law and order was no major problem. Each camp had its own rules. The miners met to discuss and solve problems.

In some camps, miners set up their own courts. They punished people who broke the rules. Whipping was a common punishment. Those who were accused of stealing usually were hanged. Many people were hanged in the town of Placerville. It was called Hangtown.

Living in the gold camps was costly. Eggs often cost $50 a dozen. An apple might cost $1. Bread that cost 5¢ a loaf in New York cost 75¢ or more in the gold camps.

151

The 1850 tax law   Some American miners did not like prospectors from other countries searching for gold. People from Australia, China, Chile, Mexico, France, and many other countries all came to look for gold. But some Americans thought the gold should be hunted by Americans only.

In 1850 the California government passed a tax law. This law placed a tax of $20 per month on all foreign miners. Many of them could not pay the tax. So they were not allowed to look for gold.

A miner's life   Most forty-niners had long hair and beards. They often wore a red or gray flannel shirt, pants, and an old crushed hat. Their high boots were pulled up over the pant legs. Many bought the heavy pants of Levi Strauss (lē' vī strous). These pants were first made from old canvas ship sails. Later,

A flannel shirt, heavy pants, boots, and an old hat were the usual clothing of the gold miner.

Cooking dinner over an open fire was part of the life of a prospector.

This well-known author, Mark Twain, wrote humorous gold-mining stories.

The typical forty-niner had to do his own cooking, laundering, and house-keeping. The forty-niners' cooking utensils were only a frying pan and a pot. They ate a lot of pork and beans. The pork and beans were boiled in the pot. Often, they left the pot uncovered. They would eat from the pot until it was empty. Then a fresh supply was made.

Sunday was the day they rested from mining. The men did their housekeeping. They visited the general store. They also spent time reading and writing. And many enjoyed singing and dancing.

Miners told each other stories to pass the time. Many of these stories were later written by such authors as Bret Harte (bret härt) and Mark Twain (twān). People all over the world have enjoyed the stories.

Miners adopt a newborn baby, as pictured in one of Bret Harte's gold-rush stories.

Strauss used a material called denim (den′ əm). This was the start of jeans.

The miner's home usually was a crude structure. Nearly all miners camped out. Often they used homemade tents. Later some miners built log cabins.

Most of the miners were men. There were few women and few families. Many of the men had wives and children thousands of miles away. These men were lonely and homesick. The men looked forward to letters from home and often wrote long replies.

These pictures show the changes that took place in San Francisco between 1848 (top) and 1851 (bottom). The changes were caused by the gold rush.

Placerville started as a mining camp. It was named Dry Diggings, then Hangtown, then Placerville.

San Francisco in search of gold. The town grew rapidly. By 1850 over 30,000 people lived there.

Families in San Francisco built homes and businesses. Public schools were started in the mid-1850s. Restaurants, hotels, and shops were opened. San Francisco soon became the leading seaport and an important city in the West.

As the gold rush ended, life became more settled in San Francisco and in the gold country. People who had come to California to "get rich quick" now turned to other ways to make a living. More women came and people began to settle into family life.

The gold rush had changed California. Its population had grown. It had become important to the United States.

Growth of San Francisco   The gold rush changed California. Many people came to California. Small cities became larger. The cities of San Francisco, Sacramento, and Stockton grew. Miners could buy needed supplies and spend their gold in these places. New towns were started. Auburn, Placerville, Grass Valley, Columbia, Jackson, and Sonora (sə nōr′ ə) began during the gold rush.

The little village of San Francisco had 2 hotels, 2 wharves, and 812 people when gold was discovered. In 1848 it became the gateway to the goldfields. In that year over 40,000 people passed through

Looking ahead   The gold rush brought hundreds of people to California. Soon after the gold rush, California became a state. In the next chapter you will learn about how California became a state.

CHECKUP

1. What were three ways used by the first prospectors to find gold?
2. How did the miners get the gold from the rocks?
3. How did the government of California try to keep out foreign miners?
4. What was a miner's life like?

7/CHAPTER REVIEW

KEY FACTS

1. Marshall's discovery of gold in January 1848 changed the history of California.
2. The forty-niners traveled to California by land and by sea.
3. Placer gold was obtained by panning, cradling, or using a sluice box.
4. The real winners during the gold rush were the merchants.
5. Life in the gold camps was hard.
6. During the gold rush, San Francisco became the most important city in the West.

VOCABULARY QUIZ

Write the numbers 1 to 10 on a separate sheet of paper. Match these words with the definitions.

a. pyrite
b. sluice box
c. isthmus
d. bargain
e. prospector
f. wagon train
g. tailrace
h. forty-niners
i. panning
j. placer gold

1. Gold found on the bottom of rivers
2. A gold-collecting process using a round pan with a flat bottom and slanted sides
3. Also called fool's gold
4. An agreement to make a trade
5. A ditch to move water from the millpond to the river
6. The people who came to California in 1849 to search for gold
7. A narrow strip of land connecting two larger pieces of land
8. A person who looked for gold
9. A long, narrow, sloping box used to wash gold from sand and gravel
10. A group of wagons traveling together

REVIEW QUESTIONS

1. How did Marshall decide the flakes were real gold?
2. What were some of the ways the news of the gold discovery spread?
3. Why did it take so long to travel to California?
4. Why was life in the mining camps hard?
5. How did San Francisco change during the gold rush?

ACTIVITIES

1. Draw a picture of the way you would have tried to collect gold in California. You may show a way of collecting placer gold. Or you may show a mining method. You may want to think of your own way of collecting gold.
2. Imagine that you are a business person in San Francisco during the gold rush. You want to make money selling supplies to the miners. And you want many miners to come to California. Write a newspaper advertisement or article to attract people to the gold country.

WRITING DESCRIPTION

WHAT IS DESCRIPTIVE WRITING?

A description paints a picture of something with words. When you write a description, you want the reader to see the picture.

How do you paint a picture with words? Read the example of descriptive writing below and look for words that help you make a picture. This example describing the California gold rush is from *California Gold Days* by Helen Bauer.

For two weeks out of New York the trip was pleasant. Then the ship unloaded on the Isthmus at the mouth of the Chagres River. Here there were only a few bamboo huts with palm-leaf roofs. To the travelers it was a beautiful place. But it was here that their troubles began.

The gold hunters had to hire natives to take them up the Chagres River. No price was too high for them to ask. Sometimes money was taken and the guides ran away. Sometimes they disappeared with the baggage. Many had to wait here because there were no boats. They had a terrible time.

The lucky men were taken up the river in little boats. Their long, polelike paddles sent the boats gliding up the stream. The trip up the jungle river was one the men never forgot! Tree branches dipped down into the muddy river. Bright flowers, yellow and purple, hung from the trees. Monkeys chattered and swung from the long, thick vines. Parrots and other birds screeched in the treetops. Once in a while there were wild cries from the jungle. Sometimes alligators pushed their noses against the sides of the little boats. It was enough to frighten anyone! The jungle seemed thicker as they went along. Very little sun came through. "We'll never forget the trip up the Chagres!" the men said. They would never forget the hot, steamy days, either. Nor the swarms of biting mosquitoes and insects! Nor the miserable nights spent in the native villages. But they were on their way to Panama!

At last they came to the end of the river trip. But this was not the end of their travels. They had to travel twenty more miles overland to the coast to get a ship.

SKILLS PRACTICE

Complete the following. Use a separate sheet of paper.

1. What words did you find that helped you see what the author was describing? "Bright flowers, yellow and purple" and "long, thick vines" are examples that help you "see" the jungle. List at least six other words that helped you see the scene the author was describing.

2. Imagine you were one of the forty-niners traveling to the goldfields. Perhaps you traveled by sea around Cape Horn. Maybe you went by wagon. Use your imagination and write a letter home. Describe what you saw along the way. Describe your feelings as you made the long trip. Paint a picture with your words. Your letter should be one page in length.

8 Making a State

California Becomes a State

---VOCABULARY---

military governor	slaves
alcaldes	free state
constitution	Congress
delegates	capital
natural boundary	capitol

Military government You learned in Chapter 6 that California broke away from Mexico. You read about the Bear Flag Revolt and the raising of the American flag a few weeks later. California then needed a new government. This means California needed leaders to make the laws and to see that the laws were carried out. The United States Army controlled the state until a new government was formed. The person in charge for the army was known as the **military governor** (mil' ə ter ē). This person made government decisions for the whole state of California. The army helped make sure that people obeyed his orders.

There were also local officials. They were called **alcaldes** (al kal' dēz). California had alcaldes before the Americans took over the area. They carried out the laws and judged people who did not obey the laws.

The Americans in California wanted a government more like what they were used to. They wanted to elect officials. They did not want the military governor controlling them. They did not want one person carrying out the laws and judging the people. They wanted these things done by different people. That is what they had been used to in other states.

In 1849 the military governor, General Bennett Riley, called for a convention. The reason for the convention was to write a state **constitution** (kon stə tü' shən). A constitution is a set of laws by which a state or country is governed.

Constitutional convention The people of California voted for **delegates** (del' ə gits) to the constitutional convention. A delegate is a person who has the right to act or speak for others. The convention met at Monterey in September 1849. The 48 delegates were to write

The design for our state seal was formally accepted at the 1849 constitutional convention.

the laws for governing the state. They looked at other state constitutions to get ideas. After six weeks they had finished writing the constitution. The people voted in favor of the constitution on November 13, 1849.

Two major decisions   The delegates at the constitutional convention made two major decisions. One decision was the location of the eastern boundary of California. Some people wanted California to be a very large state. They wanted to include the land that is today Nevada. Other people thought that would make the state too large and hard to govern. Some delegates did not want the boundary to be farther east than the Sierra Nevada. They said the mountains were a **natural boundary**. A natural boundary is a boundary that exists in nature. Finally, the delegates decided on a boundary just to the east of the Sierra Nevada. So California became a long, narrow state. Find the boundaries of California on the map on page 292.

The delegates also talked about slavery. In some parts of the United States, black people were kept as **slaves**. Slaves were people who were owned by other people. They were bought and sold. They had to do as they were told. Many Americans in California came from states that had slaves. But the California delegates decided that California should not have slaves. California would be a **free state**, or a state in which owning slaves was not allowed.

Leaders elected   The new constitution stated that the people of California would elect their leaders. So Californians voted for a governor and other

In what year did California become a state? Who was governor at that time?

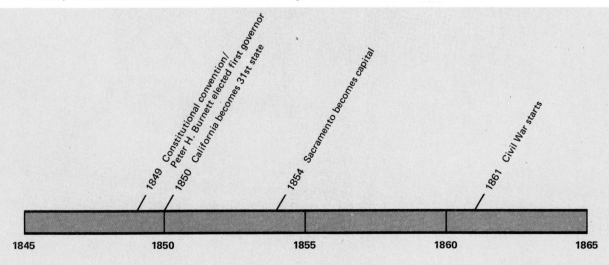

1845   1850   1855   1860   1865

1849 Constitutional convention/Peter H. Burnett elected first governor
1850 California becomes 31st state
1854 Sacramento becomes capital
1861 Civil War starts

leaders. The governor is the top leader of the state. The governor is responsible for running the state government. Peter H. Burnett was elected as the first governor under the new constitution.

All this was done without the approval of the United States government. California was not yet officially a state. So some of the new California officials went to Washington, D.C. They wanted the new California constitution to be approved.

The thirty-first state   The constitution had to be approved by the United States **Congress** (kong′ gris). Congress is a group of men and women who make the laws for the United States. Members of Congress are elected by the people.

Peter H. Burnett served as governor of the new state of California until January 1851.

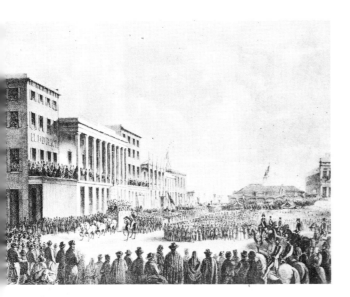

This old picture shows a grand parade celebrating California's admission into the United States.

Some members of Congress were upset because the Californians had written a constitution and elected leaders before getting permission. And California wanted to join the United States as a free state. At that time the slave states and free states were equal in number. But if California joined the United States, there would be one more free state than slave state.

Congress did approve the California constitution on September 9, 1850. California became the thirty-first state in the United States. September 9 is celebrated as Admission Day in California.

161

Find Sacramento on the map.

CALIFORNIA: State Capitals

Locating the capital   The new constitutional government of California now needed a location. The place where the government leaders work is called the **capital**.

You know that the capital of our whole country is Washington, D.C. But every state in the United States also has its own capital city. Many cities in California wanted to be the capital city of their state. San Jose (san ə zā´) became the capital of California, and the new leaders first met there in 1850.

In 1851 the capital was moved to a new city called Vallejo (və lā ō). General Mariano Guadalupe Vallejo had given money and land to start the new city as the capital of the state. Vallejo is between San Francisco and Sacramento.

This picture shows the state capitol in Sacramento not long after it was completed.

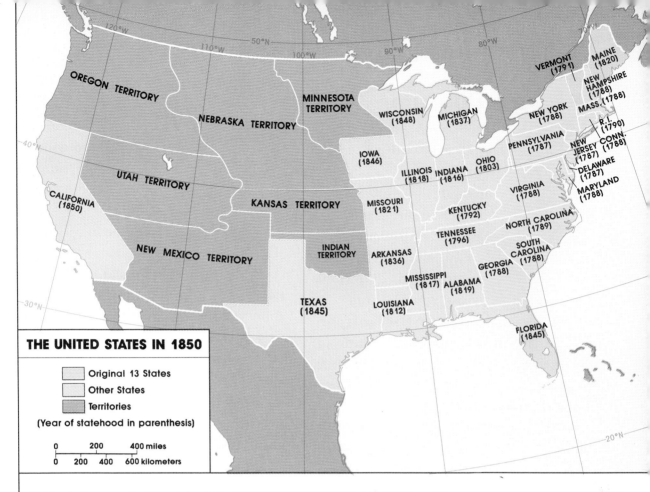

California became the thirty-first state in 1850. When did Wisconsin become a state?

It was hard to run the new government in a city that was still being built. In 1853 the capital was moved to a small town called Benicia (bə nē′ shə). But there were very few places for the government workers to live in Benicia. Some of the workers lived in Sacramento. Most of the government leaders wanted to be in Sacramento. So in 1854 the capital was moved to Sacramento, where it is today.

In 1860 the government leaders voted for a special building. It was the state **capitol**. In that building the business of the state government would be handled. The capitol was first used in 1869 but was not completed until 1874.

CHECKUP

1. What did the military governor do? What did the alcaldes do?
2. What two big decisions did the constitutional convention make?
3. Why were some members of Congress upset when California wanted to join the United States?
4. Where is the capital of California today?

163

Ruling California

VOCABULARY

bribes   vigilantes

Creating order   It took time for the new constitution to help bring order to the new state. The elected leaders, along with the people of the state, had to make the constitution work. It was important for people to choose good leaders.

Each county and city in California also formed its own government. Many of these governments were weak when they first started. The elected officials were not always good leaders. Sometimes they were in office because people did not vote carefully. Some people did not vote at all. Some people voted more than once. This is against the law. The leaders could not control the people who did not obey the laws. There were government leaders as well who did not obey them.

Not all the elected leaders were honest, either. Some took **bribes,** or money given for special favors. Some leaders did not even punish the criminals.

Crime increased, and many citizens did not feel safe. On their own, some citizens began to capture and punish the criminals. These citizens were called **vigilantes** (vij ə lan′ tēz). They did not receive any help from the sheriffs or other government leaders.

Some vigilante groups were careful to punish only lawbreakers. Others were not so careful. Innocent people were sometimes punished. The job of enforcing the laws belongs to government leaders. But the vigilantes felt the government leaders were not doing their job.

Many people had not been very careful about voting for government leaders. When people do not take voting seriously, poor leaders often are elected. When people began voting more seriously, better leaders were elected. Then the governments began to have better rule in the state. The vigilantes were no longer needed. The Californians learned that voting is a responsibility and must be done with great care.

Mining-camp law   The discovery of gold brought many people to California. The number of mining camps grew quickly. Many of these camps were separated from others. There was no outside government that could help the miners. As you learned earlier, the miners made their own rules. Mostly they did as they pleased so long as no one was hurt.

One of the first things the miners had to do was record their land claims. Each miner could claim a piece of land on which to look for gold. The miners needed a system of recording who had what piece of land. They generally found one person to be a recorder. This

Punishment of those captured by the vigilantes followed swiftly after trial.

recorder wrote down the details of each person's claim in a book. A claim had to be of a reasonable size. The group of miners decided how big their claims could be. In places with much gold, the claims were small. Some of them were as small as 10 feet by 10 feet (3 m by 3 m). How many claims of that size would fit into your classroom?

The miners had a simple system for punishing those who broke the rules. After catching a wrongdoer, they held a trial. In a small camp, all the miners decided on the guilt of the accused. In a larger camp a small group decided.

The miners had no jails. So usually a murderer was hanged. A thief was often whipped. Some thieves were sent away from the camp. Sometimes the miners cut off part of a thief's ear. It was a well-known sign of the crime.

CHECKUP

1. Why is it important to vote carefully?
2. Who were the vigilantes? Why were they needed?
3. Why did the people in the mining camps make their own rules?
4. What did the miners do to people who broke the rules?

Problems of the New State

Ownership of land   Much of California was owned by Spanish and Mexican settlers. Some of them had very large amounts of land. Because so much land was available, the landowners did not worry about the exact borders of their land. Few fences were built. And records of who owned the land were not kept carefully.

However, these things changed because of the California gold rush. Thousands of people came to California. The new people wanted some land for themselves. Some of them just stopped at places they wanted and settled down. They were called **squatters.** They did not care who owned the land.

In some other parts of the United States, people were allowed to settle on unused land. If they built a house and used the land, it became theirs. The people who came to California wanted that same right.

Land Commission   The United States government helped to settle the many arguments about landownership. It set up the Land Commission. The Land Commission tried to find out who owned the land in question. Landowners had to present proof of their ownership. Not all people were able to do this. In many cases a family had held the land for years. However, the legal papers had been lost, or perhaps they had never been in order. For such reasons, many people lost their land. Other people had to hire lawyers to prove what land they owned. It took many years to settle the disputes. Sometimes the squatters were so settled on the land that they could not be moved. Then some landowners just gave up and let the squatters stay.

Arguments over who owned land slowed down the development of the state. Many people wanted to come to

Fertile California land, such as this land in the Sacramento Valley, attracted thousands of new people.

California. But first they wanted to be sure of their right to own land.

California and the Indians   The new state of California also had to settle some problems with Indians. The Indians you read about earlier had not left California.

The people who came to look for gold and to settle in California did not understand the Indians. They made fun of the way the Indians dressed and acted.

Many new people were settling on land where the Indians lived. In the Central Valley the Indians were pushed out by the gold miners.

The Indians were upset when they saw oak trees being chopped down for firewood. As you know, the Indians used the acorns from the oak trees as food. In some parts of the state, the Indians had to steal cattle to survive.

From 1850 to 1863, there were many battles about ownership of the land. The new settlers often killed the Indians to take their land. Other Indians fought back and attacked a number of settlements. Then the new people attacked the Indians. Many Indians died in battles.

A new plan   Some treaties were made with the Indians to give them land. But settlers sometimes thought they could make better use of the land. So they took land away from the Indians.

These portable houses were built for some California Indians who were forced to move from their village.

Edward Beale was in charge of Indian affairs in California. Beale wanted to help the Indians. In 1852 he made a plan for land to be set aside for the Indians. There would be soldiers on the land to protect the Indians' land. The soldiers would also help control the Indians. There would be a person to help them learn the ways of white Americans. The Indians would learn how to farm. They would also be taught trades, including jewelry making. This land would be called a **reservation** (rez ər vā′ shən). Many reservations were started in California as well as in other parts of the country.

CHECKUP

1. What did the Spanish and Mexican settlers argue about with the squatters?
2. What did the Land Commission do?
3. What is an Indian reservation?

167

The Civil War

North against South   For many years the Northern and Southern states had argued over slavery. The Northern states did not allow slavery. The Southern states did. But the North did not want slavery to spread. In 1860 and 1861 some Southern states broke their ties with the United States. They formed a separate country, the Confederate States of America. Now the argument became a war. It is known as the **Civil War**. A civil war is a war between people of the same country. The North hoped that the United States would be reunited. The Civil War, which began in 1861, went on until 1865.

While California helped the North in many ways during the Civil War, it was spared actual warfare.

What should California do?   When the Civil War began, Californians talked about what they should do. Should they join the North, since theirs was a free state? Or should they join the South? Both the North and the South wanted California's gold and soldiers. Some Californians joined the Southern army. Some joined the Northern army. Other Californians felt that their state, too, should break with the United States. They wanted to start a separate country, the Pacific Republic.

The Californians finally decided to remain loyal to the North and to the United States. The California government declared, "The people of California are devoted to the Constitution and Union."

California was not affected very much by the war. Some states were almost ruined by the battles, but California was far away from the fighting.

California helps win the war   The North won the war at last, and the South rejoined the United States. California helped to save the country. Fifteen thousand Californians joined the Union army. Only a few hundred of them were sent to fight. The others guarded California. They kept the Southern forces from attacking California's harbors and ports.

Also important to the Northern victory were the supplies from California.

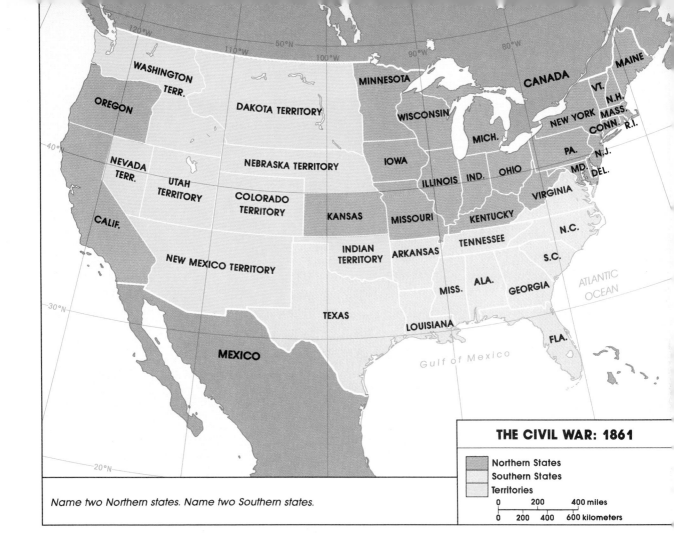

WASHINGTON TERR.
OREGON
MINNESOTA
CANADA
MAINE
VT.
N.H.
WISCONSIN
NEW YORK
MASS.
CONN. R.I.
MICH.
DAKOTA TERRITORY
NEVADA TERR.
UTAH TERRITORY
NEBRASKA TERRITORY
IOWA
PA.
N.J.
MD. DEL.
ILLINOIS IND. OHIO
COLORADO TERRITORY
CALIF.
KANSAS
MISSOURI
KENTUCKY
VIRGINIA
N.C.
TENNESSEE
S.C.
NEW MEXICO TERRITORY
INDIAN TERRITORY
ARKANSAS
MISS. ALA. GEORGIA
ATLANTIC OCEAN
TEXAS
LOUISIANA
FLA.
MEXICO
Gulf of Mexico

THE CIVIL WAR: 1861

Northern States
Southern States
Territories

0   200   400 miles
0   200   400   600 kilometers

Name two Northern states. Name two Southern states.

Gold from California helped to pay the costs of the war. California wool was used to make uniforms. Wheat grown in California helped to feed the Union forces.

California gave more money than any other state to an organization that helped the sick and wounded. It was called the Sanitary Commission.

After the Civil War, many soldiers looked for a new place to live. People from the Northern and Southern states came to California to start anew.

Looking ahead In the next chapter you will read how railroads connected California with the eastern part of the United States. And you will learn how farming, livestock raising, and other businesses grew in California.

CHECKUP

1. What is a civil war?
2. Why did the North and South fight each other in the Civil War?
3. How did California help the North win the war?

KEY FACTS

1. The constitutional convention of 48 delegates met in Monterey in September 1849.

2. California began using its new constitution and elected its leaders before becoming a state.

3. California became the thirty-first state in the United States on September 9, 1850.

4. Sacramento became the capital in 1854.

5. Many of the county and city governments were weak when they first started.

6. The Land Commission was formed to help settle problems about landownership.

7. In 1852 a plan was made to set aside land for the Indians. These land areas became known as reservations.

8. During the war between the North and the South, California remained loyal to the North.

VOCABULARY QUIZ

Write the word or words that best complete each sentence below. Use a separate sheet of paper.

1. A _____ is a set of laws by which a state is governed.

2. A person who has the right to act or speak for others is called a _____.

3. Some constitutional convention delegates said the Sierra Nevada were a _____ _____.

4. A state that did not allow slavery was known as a _____.

5. The city where the government leaders work is called the _____.

6. Citizens who caught and punished criminals on their own were called _____.

7. People who claimed and settled on land they wanted were called _____.

8. A _____ is a war between people of the same country.

REVIEW QUESTIONS

1. Why were the Americans unhappy with the military governor's control?

2. After the constitution was written and approved, what city became the capital?

3. Why did some citizens become vigilantes?

4. Who were the squatters?

5. What kind of land plan did Edward Beale make in 1852?

6. How did California help the North win the Civil War?

ACTIVITIES

1. If you had been a delegate to the constitutional convention, what five laws would you have suggested for governing the state? Write the laws as you would have presented them to the convention.

2. Find out about an Indian reservation located in your part of the state. You may look for such information as when the reservation was formed and how many people are living on the reservation today. Write a paragraph or two about the reservation.

UNDERSTANDING PLURALS

RULES FOR PLURALS

Some nouns name *one* person, place, or thing. They are in the singular form. Other nouns name *more than one* person, place, or thing. They are in the plural form.

These four main rules will help you change many nouns from singular to plural.

1. Add *-s* to form most plurals.

law   laws

2. Add *-es* to a word that ends in *s, ss, sh, ch, x,* or *zz.*

box   boxes
church   churches

3. If a word ends in a vowel and *y,* add *-s.*

boy   boys

4. If a word ends in a consonant and *y,* change the *y* to *i* and add *-es.*

army   armies

5. A few words change their spellings to form the plurals.

person   people
woman   women

A DICTIONARY CAN HELP

Sometimes you may need to use a dictionary for the words that are respelled to form the plurals. Look up the singular form of the word *ox.* The dictionary will show you the plural form of *ox* next to the singular form. What is the plural form of *ox?*

Sometimes words do not change their spelling from singular to plural. *Deer* is an example.

The deer is drinking water.

Several deer ran across the field.

When you are not sure whether a noun needs a plural form, check the word in a dictionary.

SKILLS PRACTICE

The words in this list are nouns from Chapter 8. Each noun on the list is singular. Copy the list on a piece of lined paper. Then write the plural form next to each word.

1. Californian
2. delegate
3. boundary
4. bribe
5. squatter
6. gold
7. country
8. Indian
9. victory
10. wheat

After you have written the plural forms, use each one in a sentence. Write sentences that tell things you have learned about California.

Before the Railroad

VOCABULARY

clipper ships   telegraph lines

Distance problems   California had problems after it became a state. One of the biggest problems was its distance from the eastern part of the country. There were no roads or telephone service between the east and west coasts. It often took several months for people in California to get mail from their families in the East. So they asked the government leaders to solve this problem.

The clipper ships   In the 1850s the trip around South America to California became easier. Shipyards in the East were building fast sailing ships called **clipper ships**. Many of these ships traveled around South America to California. They were called California clippers. These ships were much faster than the ships that had been used before.

The most famous of the California clippers was the *Flying Cloud*. In 1851 it sailed from New York to San Francisco in 89 days. That was the fastest that any sailing ship had ever made the trip. The California clippers carried mostly mail and goods. Most people thought the clippers were too uncomfortable for their own travel.

The Panama Railroad   In 1855 a railroad was completed across Panama. It connected the Atlantic Ocean with the Pacific Ocean. With the new railroad the trip across Panama took only about 4 hours. It used to take 3 or 4 days by boat and mule. The new railroad allowed people to go from New York to San Francisco in about a month.

The stagecoaches   There was another way of going to and from California. In the early 1860s, stagecoach routes were started between Missouri and California.

A stagecoach could carry 9 or 10 people inside. And as many as 12 others could ride on the top. The stagecoaches also carried luggage and mail.

Stagecoach drivers were the heroes of their time. They had to guide six horses. There were no roads, only trails.

The coming of the railroad to California brought new settlers and opened eastern markets for California's farm products.

The mountain trails were narrow and rocky and often steep. The drivers had to worry about bad weather and robbers. They also had to keep a speed of about 10 miles (16 km) an hour. The stagecoach drivers had a hard job. It took about 25 days for the mail to go from Missouri to California by stagecoach. But even that was too slow for some people.

The Pony Express   In 1860 the Pony Express was started. The Pony Express carried the mail the same distance as the stagecoach in just 10 days. Riders on horseback carried the mail between St. Joseph, Missouri, and Sacramento. No letter could weigh more than one-half ounce. Only one thin sheet of paper in an envelope weighed that amount.

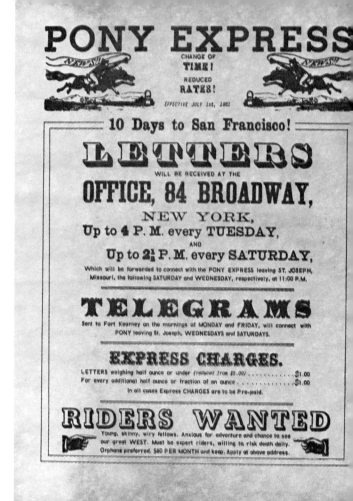

The fastest way to get a letter from New York to San Francisco in 1860 was by Pony Express.

How many years passed from the time of the Flying Cloud's trip to San Francisco and the completion of the transcontinental railroad?

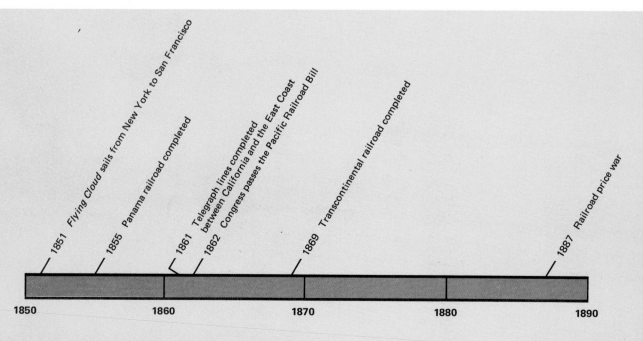

The postage for carrying such a letter was $5.00. That was a lot of money in those days.

There were stations with fresh horses every 10 miles (16 km) on the Pony Express route. Each rider rode as fast as possible and changed to a new horse at each station. A rider would ride 30 miles and use three horses, then a new rider would take over. The new rider would take the mail for another 30 miles (48 km). About 80 riders were used to carry the mail the whole distance.

The telegraph   In October 1861, **telegraph lines** were completed between California and the East Coast. Telegraph lines are a system of electrical wires used to send messages. By using a telegraph, messages could be sent through the wires at very fast speeds. It took less than a minute to send a message. As a result the Pony Express was out of business in less than 2 years.

CHECKUP

1. How were the clipper ships built in the 1850s different from some of the other ships used earlier?
2. What happened in 1855 in Panama that made the trip from New York to San Francisco shorter?
3. What kind of difficulties did the stagecoach drivers have?
4. What was the major reason why the Pony Express was started?

Starting the Railroad

A railroad is needed   People were not happy having to ride stagecoaches to and from California. The trip between Missouri and California took 25 days, and that was too long. Trains were used in the eastern part of the United States. The trains were easier, safer, and much faster.

Theodore Judah   Theodore Judah (thē′ ō dōr jü′ dä) was an expert on building railroads. He was from the East. In 1854 he came to California to help build the state's first railroad. That was a 23-mile (37 km) line between Sacramento and Folsom.

Judah was not satisfied building only one railroad. He talked about railroads to anyone who would listen to him. Some people thought Judah was railroad crazy. They even called him Crazy Judah. But Judah's dream was to build a railroad eastward through the Sierra Nevada. That railroad would meet another one that was being built westward toward California. The two railroads would become one and would link California and the East. It would be a **transcontinental** railroad, which means that it would cross the continent.

Judah went to Washington, D.C., to tell the government about his idea. He wanted the government to supply the money to build the railroad. He talked to people in California about forming a new company to build the railroad.

The Big Four   Judah found four store owners in Sacramento who were interested. They were Leland Stanford, Collis P. Huntington, Mark Hopkins, and Charles Crocker. They were known later as the Big Four. The Big Four formed a new company with Judah. They called it the Central Pacific Railroad Company.

The government acts   In 1862, Congress passed the Pacific railroad bill. This bill made possible the building of the railroad. The Central Pacific Railroad Company was to start building a railroad going east from Sacramento. And the Union Pacific Railroad Company was to start building one going west from Omaha, Nebraska. Congress gave both companies money for each mile of railroad they built. Each company wanted to build as fast as possible. The more track they laid, the more money they could make.

Judah got the Central Pacific Railroad started in Sacramento. But he argued with his partners, so he went back East to find some new partners. He died after he got to New York. But the Big Four went on building the railroad.

CHECKUP

1. What did Theodore Judah do to get a railroad to California built?
2. What is a transcontinental railroad?
3. Who were the Big Four?
4. Why did the workers of both railroad companies work as fast as possible?

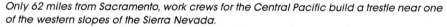

Only 62 miles from Sacramento, work crews for the Central Pacific build a trestle near one of the western slopes of the Sierra Nevada.

The Big Race

Charles Crocker   After Judah died, Charles Crocker took over the job of building the Central Pacific Railroad. But he had many problems. His first job was to lay track through the steep, rocky Sierra Nevada. Crocker had trouble finding workers for this job. He tried to hire workers from Mexico. He even asked to use prisoners who had been captured during the Civil War. Finally he found some Chinese workers.

A large number of Chinese people had come to California to work during the gold rush. Many railroad builders thought the Chinese could not do the heavy work on a railroad. But Crocker found that the Chinese were strong and hard-working.

Most of the Chinese were not treated fairly. Many were robbed and beaten and even murdered. In 1871 some white people from the city of Los Angeles shot or hanged 20 Chinese. The people who harmed the Chinese were not often punished. This was partly because in the mid-1800s the Chinese were not allowed to speak in court against white persons.

The race   Laying track through the mountains was hard. Crocker's workers had to dig a **tunnel**, an underground way, to get through one mountain. When they reached Nevada, they were laying 3 miles (5 km) of track a day. Then they got up to 4 and then to 5 miles (8 km) a day.

Work trains carried tools and work teams in the race between the Union Pacific and Central Pacific railroads to lay the most track.

At the same time, the Union Pacific Railroad was being laid westward. Most of their workers were Irish Americans. They, too, were laying up to 5 miles (8 km) of track a day. Then one day they laid 6 miles (10 km) of track.

The leaders of both railroads were in a race. Each day, by telegraph, they learned how much track the other group had laid. Crocker heard that the Union Pacific workers had laid 6 miles (10 km) of track. So he talked to his workers. Soon afterward they laid 7 miles (11 km) of track. And later they set a record. In one 12-hour day, Crocker's workers laid over 10 miles (17 km) of track.

The golden spike   Finally on May 10, 1869, the two railroads met in Promontory (prom′ ən tôr ē), Utah. On that day hundreds of people came to see the last spike driven.

The last spike was made of gold. Each time the spike was struck, a signal went out on the telegraph. People all over America rang bells and celebrated.

The race is over! Locomotives from the Union Pacific and Central Pacific railroads meet at Promontory, Utah, on May 10, 1869.

COMPLETION OF THE PACIFIC RAILROAD—MEETING OF LOCOMOTIVES OF THE UNION AND CENTRAL PACIFIC LINES: THE ENGINEERS SHAKE HANDS.
[PHOTOGRAPHED BY SAVAGE & OTTINGER, SALT LAKE CITY.]

On that historic day a St. Louis newspaper, the *Missouri Democrat*, reported:

> Let everybody listen to the fire bells today, and hear the last spike of the Pacific Railroad driven home. . . . Soberly [seriously] considered, this transcontinental highway is the most marvelous work of human hand. . . .

At the place where the spike was driven, two locomotives were facing each other. The engineers drove them forward until they touched. It was time for a celebration. The transcontinental railroad was finished. California was now linked to the rest of America.

CHECKUP

1. What problems did Charles Crocker face when building the Central Pacific Railroad?
2. How did the workers know how much track each railroad laid daily?
3. What special happening took place in Promontory, Utah, on May 10, 1869?

The Farming and Livestock Industries

VOCABULARY

agriculture	drought
industry	

Fertile land   In the middle and late 1800s, most people made their living from **agriculture**—that is, growing crops and raising farm animals. They bought a few things such as salt, sugar, and coffee from a store. But most of what they ate was from their farms.

After the transcontinental railroad was built, many people came to California. They were looking for fertile land.

Farm workers   The Japanese began coming to California in the early 1890s. They learned farming quickly and started saving money. With the money, they bought farmland. Other farmers felt threatened. They felt the Japanese were doing too well.

In 1905 the farmers who feared the Japanese held a meeting in San Francisco. In 1913, California passed a law to keep the Japanese from buying land. It was called the Webb Act.

Workers were needed to help the California farmers. So the farmers started hiring Mexican workers. But the farmers wanted them only when it was time to pick the crops. The rest of the year they were sent back to Mexico.

Wheat in the Central Valley   The Central Valley has some of the most fertile land in the United States. Farmers discovered that they could grow wheat there without irrigation. From the 1860s to the 1890s, wheat became the most important farm crop in California.

There were many small wheat farms in the Central Valley. But as the years went by, things changed. Rich farmers bought the small farms and formed large farms. They grew thousands of acres of wheat. To plow and harvest such crops of wheat, 20 or 30 horses were often used at one time. It was not until the late 1800s that steam-powered tractors began to replace horses. By 1890, California was second among all the states in wheat production.

California's fertile land makes it an important farm state. At one time wheat was the most important crop.

Wheat farming declines   By the middle of the 1890s, a smaller amount of wheat was being grown in the Central Valley. This was partly because of the actions of England and Italy. They had been buying a lot of California wheat. But these countries found they could buy wheat cheaper from the Middle West and Russia.

A second problem was the land in the Central Valley. Over the years it had become less fertile. Fertilizers and some irrigation were needed. These added to the cost of farming wheat. So farmers started growing other crops that made more money than wheat.

Livestock   At the time of the early missions, cattle raising was California's most important business. In those days, cattle were valuable mostly for their hides and for tallow made from beef fat. As you learned in Chapter 5, the hides were used to make leather. And the tallow was used to make candles.

In the mid-1800s, livestock raising was still the major **industry** (in′ də strē) in California. *Industry* means "a business or trade." There were millions of cattle and many large ranches. During the 1800s the sheep industry also began to grow. This caused problems for both cattle raisers and sheep raisers.

Cattle and sheep were selling for high prices in California. Many cattle and

Raising cattle became an important California industry in the 1800s.

The Wine and Citrus Industries

Getting started   The California livestock industry got its start at the first missions. The same is true for two other major industries in California. The padres in the early missions were the first to grow grapes and **citrus fruits**. Citrus fruits are fruits such as lemons, limes, oranges, and grapefruits.

Every mission had a **vineyard**, a place where grapes are grown. The grapes were used to make wine for the missions. But the wine was not sold to people outside the missions.

The wine industry   Los Angeles was the center of the early wine industry. More vineyards were later planted in northern California. Many new varieties of wine grapes were brought over from Europe.

The wine industry grew rapidly during the last half of the 1800s. Sonoma Valley was the first northern valley to produce wine grapes. Later the Napa, Santa Clara, and Livermore valleys also began to grow excellent grapes. The climate and soil in the northern valleys proved to be almost perfect for growing grapes. The wines produced from these

sheep were driven there from other places where the prices had dropped. But there was only so much grassland where the animals could feed. Soon cattle and sheep raisers were fighting.

Another problem was the dry weather. The grasslands of California become very dry during the summer months. Sometimes the dry periods go on through the winter. These are called **droughts** (drouts). One drought happened in 1863–1864. It was so dry that thousands of cattle and sheep died of hunger or thirst.

CHECKUP

1. What were many of the people who came to California after the building of the transcontinental railroad seeking?
2. What caused wheat farming to decline in California between 1890 and 1895?
3. What kinds of problems did the California livestock industry face in the 1860s?

In the 1800s, grapes were crushed in a hand-turned wine press in many California vineyards.

grapes became well liked across the United States. By 1900, California was producing 19 million gallons (72 million L) of wine per year. Eight out of every 10 gallons produced in the United States were produced in California.

The orange industry   The padres in the early missions also planted orange trees. But the oranges were not very good.

In 1873 a new type of orange tree was planted in California. It was from the South American country of Brazil. This type of orange was called a **navel orange**. Because the Brazilian trees were first sent to Washington, D.C., they were called Washington navels.

The Washington navel is a high-quality orange. It is large, juicy, sweet, and seedless. As the people found out about this orange, thousands of trees were planted. Orange growing became a major industry in southern California.

The Washington navel was a winter-ripening fruit. The growers also planted the Valencia (və len′ shē ə) orange, which ripens in the summer. The California growers grew both the Washington navel and the Valencia oranges. They were able to supply fruit throughout the year.

Problems   In the late 1800s, people in the United States were not used to eating oranges. An orange was something special that might be bought for Thanksgiving or other special days.

California growers were growing millions of excellent oranges. But they had to get the American people to buy and eat oranges more often. And they had to find a way to transport the oranges across the nation. Most of the people in the country lived in the East.

Oranges were advertised in many places across the nation. Speeches were made telling how oranges were good for a person's health. The orange growers used the railroads to transport the oranges. They used refrigerated cars that kept the fruit cool while it was being shipped. The first trainload of oranges was sent to St. Louis in 1877.

DELICIOUS
JUICY
TREE-RIPENED
PERFECT

THIS IS
ORANGE
WEEK
IN IOWA

Orange Day In California, March 1st

For Years March 1st Has Been Celebrated as "Orange Day" in Southern California and the Festivities Embrace a Period of One Week. -o- -o-

Price
Within
the Reach
of
Everyone
and
Everyone
Should
Use
Them

California
Oranges
Were
Never
So
Good
and
Cheap
as
Now

Now, Iowa Will Celebrate "Orange Week"

March 1st to 7th, by Receiving Direct from the Beautiful Groves of California, Hundreds of Carloads of the Choicest Oranges Grown in the World. -o- -o-

This Is Orange Week In Iowa---Cheapest Now---Best Now

Advertisements like this one got many people throughout the United States to buy California oranges.

1. Washing the fruit

2. Sorting the fruit

3. Filling the containers

4. Sealing the containers

5. Processing with heat

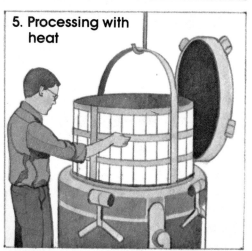

6. Labeling the containers

Most of the lemons in the United States come from lemon groves like these in California.

The lemon industry   The California citrus industry also included lemons. The Eureka (yù rē′ kə) lemon was brought to Los Angeles about 1870. And the Lisbon (liz′ bən) variety of lemon also became popular in California. The state became the leading grower of lemons. It grew nine out of every ten lemons that were sold in the United States. Today California remains the leading grower of lemons in the United States.

More industry   Olive growing in California also began at the first missions. An olive grove in the San Fernando Valley became the largest in the world.

Plums were also grown in California by the Spanish padres. Around 1853 a Frenchman brought prunes, or dried plums, to California. Then he brought seeds and cuttings from France to plant plum trees. They became popular, and planting was increased.

Walnuts and almonds were also grown at the missions. The English walnut became the most popular walnut. It was brought to California in the 1860s. By the 1860s almonds were common in California.

California became the major producer of all these products. And as a result of the growth of the fruit industry, the canning industry also grew.

CHECKUP

1. Who were the first to grow California grapes and citrus fruits?
2. What city was the center of the early California wine industry?
3. How was the navel orange tree first started in California?
4. How were the American people encouraged to buy and eat oranges in the late 1800s?

California for Health and Wealth

A slogan for California   To sell the California oranges, much money was spent in advertising. One statement was used often. It said: "Oranges for health; California for wealth." This became a **slogan**. A slogan is a saying that everybody knows.

Health seekers   Many doctors believed that fresh air and a dry climate could cure various diseases. So thousands of people with diseases went to southern California seeking the warm, dry climate. This caused a new kind of rush. It was a health rush instead of a gold rush.

A railroad price war   Another thing caused southern California to **boom.** *Boom* means to "grow very fast." In the 1880s a new railroad was built. This was the Atchison, Topeka, and Sante Fe. It connected the midwest with California along a southern route. When this new railroad arrived in southern California, it had to win customers away from other railroads.

To try to win customers, a **price war** began. In a price war, businesses cut their prices to get customers. In the railroad price war, the cost of a train ticket dropped greatly. A ticket to California from a midwestern state cost about $125 before the price war. In 1887 the Atchison, Topeka, and Sante Fe dropped the price to $5 and then to only $1.

Soon the trains were crowded with people going to southern California. They were going there to get healthy or wealthy.

The boom in real estate   It is estimated that more than 200,000 people came to southern California in 1887. This was the year of the price war. Many of the people stayed, and this created a new kind of boom. This was a boom in **real estate**.

Real estate is property that includes houses and land. With thousands of new people needing houses and land, there was a sudden growth in the sale of real estate. Within a short time there were 60 to 100 new towns near Los Angeles.

Electric railways and suburbs   Life in Los Angeles began to change. This was partly because of the electric railways that were built. The electric railways ran in various directions from the center of the city. The fares on the trains were cheap.

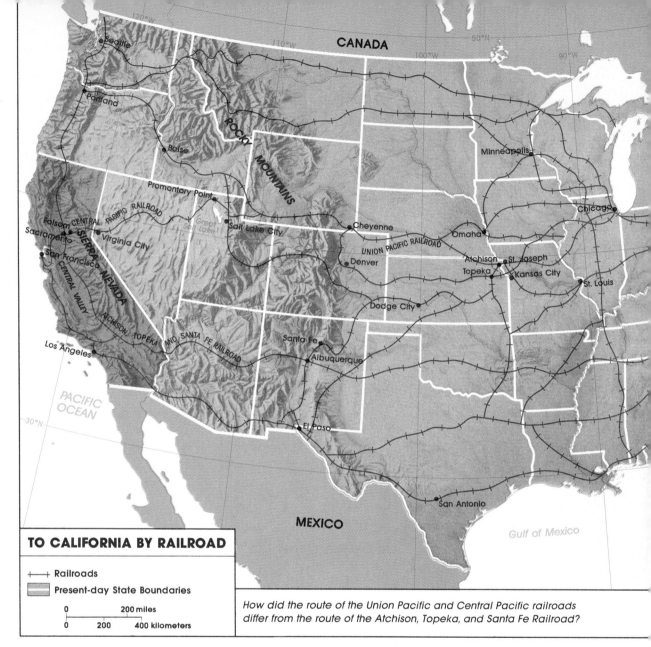

TO CALIFORNIA BY RAILROAD

┼┼ Railroads

▭ Present-day State Boundaries

```
0          200 miles
0    200    400 kilometers
```

How did the route of the Union Pacific and Central Pacific railroads differ from the route of the Atchison, Topeka, and Santa Fe Railroad?

The electric railways helped create a new way of life. Some people who worked in Los Angeles began to live in small towns outside the city. These towns are called **suburbs** (sub′ ərbz).

Looking ahead   In the next chapter you will learn about California at the beginning of the 1900s. You will learn about the San Francisco earthquake, early automobiles, the oil boom, and the saving of California's water and land.

CHECKUP

1. In the late 1800s, why did many people with diseases go to southern California?
2. What caused the railroad price war of 1887?
3. What caused the 1887 real-estate boom?

9/CHAPTER REVIEW

KEY FACTS

1. Before the transcontinental railroad, California's distance from the eastern part of the United States was a problem.

2. In 1855 a railroad was completed across Panama that connected the Atlantic Ocean with the Pacific Ocean.

3. The Pony Express and the telegraph both provided faster means of communication in the early 1860s.

4. The Central Pacific Railroad and the Union Pacific Railroad met in Promontory, Utah, in 1869.

5. Farming and raising livestock were both major industries in California in the mid-1800s.

6. By 1900 California was producing 8 out of every 10 gallons of wine produced in the United States.

7. In the late 1800s California's oranges were advertised across the nation.

8. In 1887 thousands of people came to southern California. This was mainly a result of the railroad price war and people's interest in California's climate.

VOCABULARY QUIZ

Write the numbers 1 to 10 on a sheet of paper. Match these words with the definitions.

a. vineyard   f. citrus fruits
b. drought   g. real estate
c. suburbs   h. transcontinental
d. clipper ships   i. industry
e. slogan   j. price war

1. Property that includes houses and land
2. Crossing a continent
3. A place where grapes are grown
4. Fruits such as lemons, limes, oranges, and grapefruits
5. A business or trade
6. Happens when businesses cut their prices to get customers
7. A long period of time with little or no rain
8. A common saying that everybody knows
9. Fast sailing ships
10. Small towns located outside of a city

REVIEW QUESTIONS

1. What were some of the ways that messages were sent across the country before the transcontinental railroad?

2. What were people's reactions when the Central Pacific Railroad and the Union Pacific Railroad met on May 10, 1869?

3. What are some products that were grown in California in the 1860s and today?

4. What were some of the causes of the California real-estate boom of 1887?

ACTIVITIES

1. Bring in some California farm products to show the class. Label them and show where in the state each was grown.

2. Put yourself in the place of a stagecoach driver or a Pony Express rider in 1860. Keep a diary. Describe what you see and what your life is like as you travel between Missouri and California.

9/SKILLS DEVELOPMENT

USING CONTEXT CLUES

MORE THAN ONE MEANING

You have learned how to use a dictionary to find the meaning of words. Sometimes a dictionary is not close at hand. Sometimes, too, a dictionary gives more than one meaning for a word. Take the word *leaf*, for example, as it is used in these three sentences.

1. The last dead leaf on the tree fluttered in the winter wind.
2. Before our cousins came for dinner, we put another leaf in the old dining-room table.
3. Each leaf of the old book was brown and faded.

WHAT ARE CONTEXT CLUES?

In each sentence above, the word *leaf* has a different meaning. Yet you probably knew what the word meant each time it was used differently because of the other words in the sentence. The words that are around another word are called *context*. In each sentence above, these words helped you to know the meaning of the word *leaf*. A *clue* is something that helps you figure out the answer to a problem. Words that you know in a sentence and that help you get the meaning of one or more words in a sentence are called *context clues*.

SKILLS PRACTICE

In the exercise that follows, look for context clues for the underlined word in each sentence. On a sheet of paper write what you think is the meaning of each underlined word. Then look up the word in a dictionary. See if the meaning you wrote was correct in the context of the sentence.

1. The stagecoach driver's <u>ambition</u> caused him to travel with great speed and determination across the plain.
2. The stagecoach riders became <u>accustomed</u> to riding day and night.
3. A <u>throng</u> of people gathered in Utah at Promotory on May 10, 1869, to see the last railroad spike driven.
4. In the late 1800s and early 1900s, people across the nation saw <u>numerous</u> advertisements for orange sales.
5. The orange growers discovered that they could use the railroads to <u>transport</u> oranges.
6. During 1887 thousands of people with various <u>ailments</u> traveled to southern California because of the warm, dry climate.
7. Many people who had <u>hesitated</u> to travel west because of the cost were able to do so during the railroad price war of 1887.
8. Around 1887 many people from the East looked for homesites and <u>invested</u> in California land.

3/UNIT REVIEW

1. The discovery of gold in 1848 changed the history of California. — *Why did California merchants like Sam Brannan want people to come and hunt for gold?*

2. In the 1850s it took months for people to travel to California. There was no fast way to get there. — *What were the two sea routes to California? How long did each take? How did people usually travel overland? How long did it take for Sarah Eleanor Royce and her family to get to California?*

3. Hunting for gold in California was slow, hard work. — *Imagine you are living in a gold-mining camp. Write a letter to your cousin in Ohio telling how you pan for placer gold.*

4. In 1849 the military governor of California called for a constitutional convention. In 1850 California became the thirty-first state. — *What is a constitution? What do we celebrate on September 9?*

5. Studying California's history helps us to understand the present, to learn from the past, and how to be good citizens. — *What can we learn from California's history in the 1850s? What kinds of things do good citizens do? Draw a picture or cartoon showing people being good citizens.*

6. Before the completion of a transcontinental railroad, one of California's biggest problems was its distance from the eastern part of the country. — *How long did it take people to travel across the country by stagecoach?*

7. Four San Francisco merchants helped Theodore Judah build the transcontinental railroad. They became known as the "Big Four." — *Look up information on these four men in an encyclopedia or other reference book and write a short paragraph about each. Can you name and locate four places or buildings in California named after these four men or their families?*

8. Today California leads all the other states in the production of farm products. — *List at least four important farming industries or crops in California today.*

California in the New Century

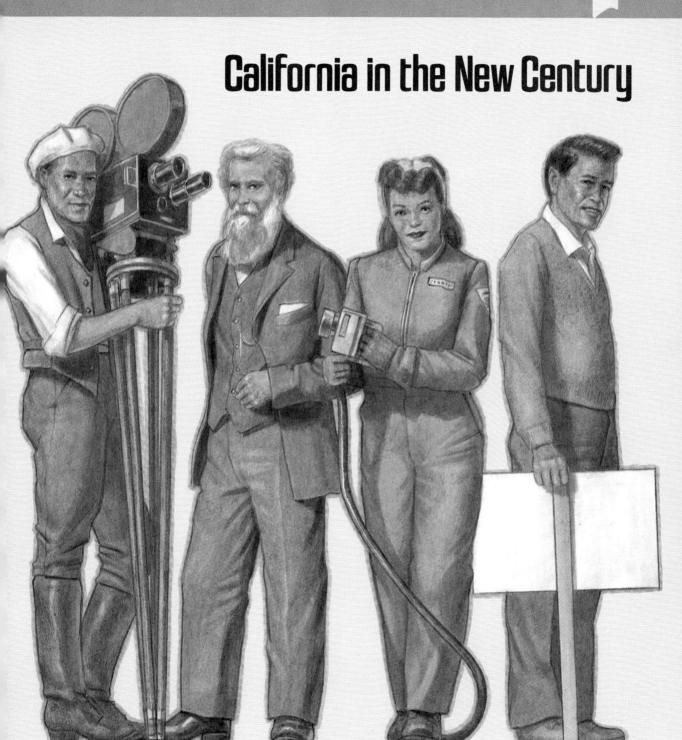

10 California Grows

The Twentieth Century Begins

VOCABULARY

earthquake	exposition
fault	

San Francisco earthquake The day was April 18, 1906. In the early morning hours the horses had become restless. But most of San Francisco had had a quiet night. At 5:12 A.M. the earth suddenly began to shake. A Los Angeles newspaper told about it this way: "The first shock came while still the mighty city lay deep in slumber [sleep]. Then came the rumble of deep thunder from . . . the . . . earth. The city shook like an aspen leaf. . . ." A person who worked for a San Francisco newspaper said, "It seemed as though my head were split with the roar that crashed into my ears."

On that terrible morning the San Andreas Fault slipped and moved. The earth split. The first shock of the **earthquake** lasted 40 seconds. The second shock lasted 25 seconds. And in that sum of 65 seconds, a large part of San Francisco had crumbled. People were running everywhere. Buildings were falling apart. Little pieces of glass showered down onto the streets.

But the worst damage was to come. Electric wires fell and their sparks started fires. Wood stoves and fireplaces fell apart and started more fires. Fire soon spread through a large part of the city. But there was no water to put out the fire. The water pipes had been broken apart by the earthquake.

The fire did not stop burning for 3 days. By the time it stopped, 478 people were dead and 250,000 were homeless. The earthquake and fire cost San Francisco at least $500 million.

Outside San Francisco The earthquake started under the ocean north of San Francisco. That morning two ships, the *John A. Campbell* and the *Argo*, suddenly began to shake. But the ocean looked peaceful!

The earthquake moved toward land at 2 miles (3 km) per second. It hit the coastline in Humboldt County, 200 miles (322 km) north of San Francisco. Whole forests of giant redwood trees snapped.

The earthquake and fire destroyed so many homes in San Francisco that camps, like the one in the bottom picture, were set up for thousands of homeless people.

At Point Reyes Station a train flipped into the air as the track buckled. In the city of Santa Rosa, buildings crumbled and fires broke out. Much of the city was destroyed, and 75 people died.

The earthquake shook places south of San Francisco also. Fourteen buildings at Stanford University fell apart. The Agnew State Hospital crumbled, killing 100 people. And in San Jose, thousands of people were left homeless.

Earthquakes Why did the earthquake happen in California? Look at the picture of the San Andreas Fault on page 195. Find it on the map, too. A **fault** is a break in the solid rock layer of the earth. The earth moves slowly along either side of a fault. The San Andreas

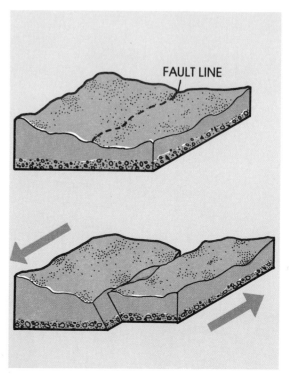

FAULT LINE

The arrows show in what direction the earth moves on either side of a fault line.

In what year did Californians see the first Pasadena Tournament of Roses parade?

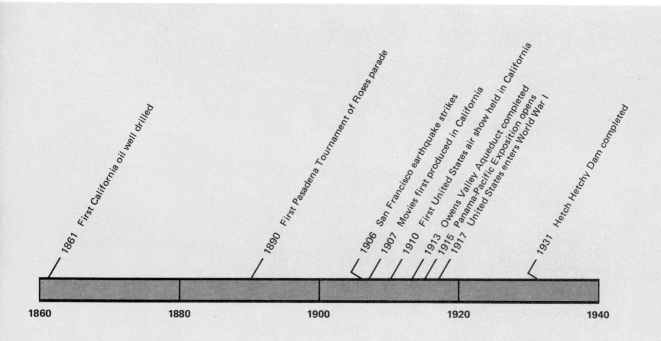

1861 First California oil well drilled

1890 First Pasadena Tournament of Roses parade

1906 San Francisco earthquake strikes

1907 Movies first produced in California

1910 First United States air show held in California

1913 Owens Valley Aqueduct completed

1915 Panama-Pacific Exposition opens

1917 United States enters World War I

1931 Hetch Hetchy Dam completed

1860   1880   1900   1920   1940

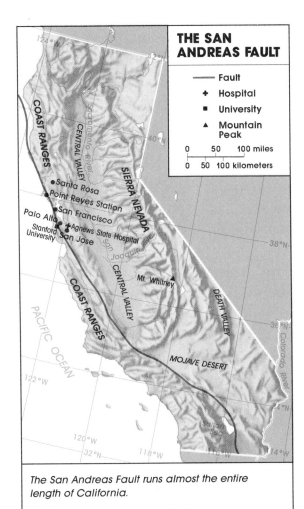

THE SAN ANDREAS FAULT

— Fault
+ Hospital
■ University
▲ Mountain Peak

0   50   100 miles
0   50   100 kilometers

The San Andreas Fault runs almost the entire length of California.

This photograph shows an aerial view of part of the San Andreas Fault.

Fault is more than 750 miles (1,210 km) long. The land along the fault moves about 2 to 2½ inches (5 to 6 cm) each year.

When there is a strong and sudden movement along a fault, it is called an earthquake. Sometimes during an earthquake, mountains are moved to a different position. Because of an earthquake, hills can become flat, and flatland can change into cliffs.

San Francisco recovers The San Francisco earthquake and fire of 1906 was the worst tragedy that had ever happened in California. But it did not stop the people of San Francisco. They started to rebuild right away. People from other parts of the United States and the world sent help. They sent food, medicine, blankets, and money. By 1915 the city had been rebuilt. That year San Francisco proudly welcomed people from all over the world to an **exposition** (eks′ pə zish′ ən), or large fair.

CHECKUP

1. What do the words "while still the mighty city lay deep in slumber" from the Los Angeles newspaper mean?
2. What words from the Los Angeles and San Francisco newspapers tell you that the earthquake must have been very loud?
3. Name five things that happened to San Francisco because of the earthquake.
4. What causes an earthquake?

California on the Move

Panama exposition   The Panama Canal had been opened in 1914. It greatly shortened the trip for ships coming from the East Coast and Europe to California. The map on page 145 shows the difference between this new route and the old one around Cape Horn. This meant the port city of San Francisco would be much busier. So San Francisco held the Panama–Pacific International (in' tər nash' ə nəl) Exposition to celebrate the opening of the canal that linked the Atlantic and Pacific Oceans.

Today the Palace of Fine Arts has a science museum.

In 11 palaces, people showed new art, new books, and all kinds of plants and flowers. There were new kinds of machines and other **inventions,** and lots of fun rides. There was even a huge model of the Panama Canal that worked! About 19 million people visited the exposition. It was a great hit. One of the palaces, called the Palace of Fine Arts, can be seen today in San Francisco.

The important automobile   Can you think of a time when there were no automobiles in California? Can you think of a California without freeways and traffic? The automobile opened up the huge lands of California. Distances between points in the state were great. The car helped people to travel these distances faster and more easily.

The early automobiles cost a lot of money. By 1908 the cost had dropped from $1,000 or more to $850. By 1914 the Model T automobile was $490. More Californians were able to buy autos. Auto touring clubs formed. Groups of people would travel in long lines of automobiles to places like Yosemite. In 1910 there were about 43,210 automobiles in the state. By 1930 there were more than 2 million.

Look at the early California road map on page 197. Old road maps used landmarks for directions. Would they be easier to follow than our road maps?

These automobiles were known as "tin lizzies." Their owners drove them along this new highway to celebrate its opening.

The first road maps used landmarks such as schools and houses to guide people.

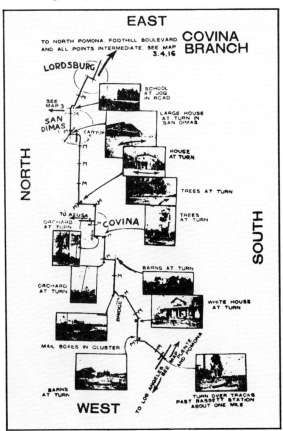

California started two important new ideas for highways. The center line that divides highways in the middle was first used in California. The automatic traffic light also started in our state.

The car brought many businesses to California. There were factories where cars were put together. The need for glass, batteries, and roads meant work for thousands of people.

The oil boom   The discovery of oil helped California boom in the early 1900s. And California grew very fast. The first oil well was drilled in 1861 in Humboldt County. All through the 1860s there was an oil rush like the gold rush of 1848 and 1849. Tar, made from oil, was used to protect roofs from leaking. Kerosene (ker′ ə sen), also made from oil, was burned in lamps wherever there was no electricity. Oil was used to keep

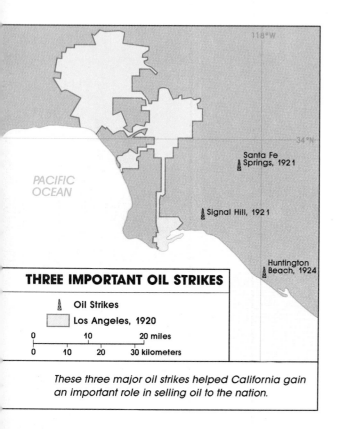

THREE IMPORTANT OIL STRIKES

⚓ Oil Strikes
▢ Los Angeles, 1920

0		10		20 miles
0	10	20	30 kilometers	

118°W

34°N

PACIFIC
OCEAN

⚓ Santa Fe
Springs, 1921

⚓ Signal Hill, 1921

⚓ Huntington
Beach, 1924

These three major oil strikes helped California gain an important role in selling oil to the nation.

machine parts running smoothly. But even then there was too much oil and not enough uses for it in the 1860s. Many oil companies went out of business.

The real growth in selling oil came after many people bought automobiles. In the early 1900s more oil was discovered. In 1910 oil companies filled 77,697,568 barrels of oil! A lot of the oil was used to make gasoline for autos.

When oil is found, it is called an **oil strike.** One of the biggest oil strikes was made at Huntington Beach in 1920. More oil strikes were made at Santa Fe Springs and Signal Hill in 1921. By 1924 California was first in the oil business. Today it ranks fourth after Texas, Louisiana, and Alaska.

These towers, called derricks, sprouted all over Signal Hill once oil was discovered there.

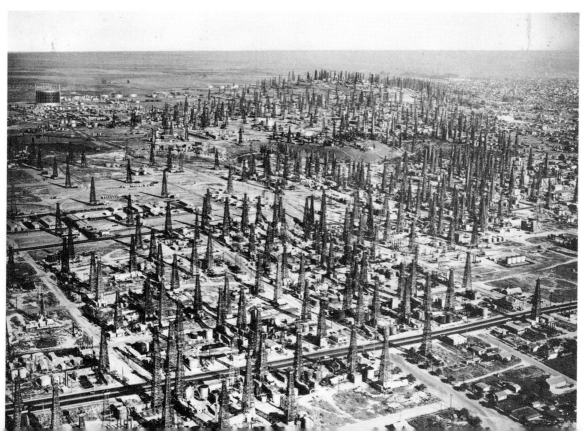

Building airplanes in California
"Viva aviation." These words started a *Los Angeles Times* news story in 1910. *Viva* means "long live." **Aviation** (ā′ vē ā′ shən) means "the flying of heavier-than-air airplanes." As early as 1883 John J. Montgomery flew a **glider** near San Diego. A glider is a plane without a motor. But the first motor-powered flight in California was in 1910.

The flight was made by a French airman named Louis Paulhan. During this first air show ever, another airman, named Glenn Curtiss, did tricks in his **biplane**. A biplane has two sets of wings. Wood is used to make the frames for the wings. The frames are covered with cloth. About 200,000 people watched the show. It was very exciting.

Curtiss not only flew planes, but he also drew plans to make them. In 1911 he developed the first successful **hydroplane** (hī′ drə plān), a plane that can land on water. He landed it in San Diego Bay. He also made the first plane that could land safely on the deck of a ship. Curtiss started the flight-training school near San Diego. During World War I hundreds of pilots trained there.

The climate of California made it the perfect place to build and test airplanes. The names Glenn Martin, Donald W. Douglas, and T. Claude Ryan became well-known in California and across the United States.

At this first aviation meet in the United States, Louis Paulhan set two world records for flying—height and length of time.

The first airplane made in California was built by Glenn Martin in 1907. He turned an old church in Santa Ana into an airplane factory. His airmail service from Compton to Santa Ana may have been the first in the United States.

Donald Douglas drew plans for airplanes. He started by working for Glenn Martin. In 1921 he formed his own company. In 1924 his company built the first army planes to travel around the world.

Lindbergh helped to draw up the plans for **The Spirit of St. Louis.** Ryan's airplane factory built the plane in 60 days.

T. Claude Ryan had been an army pilot. He started building planes in 1923. His airplane factory built *The Spirit of St. Louis* for Charles Lindbergh. In *The Spirit of St. Louis*, Lindbergh became the first man to fly alone across the Atlantic Ocean. California's airplane builders were helping to improve travel by air everywhere.

World War I   World War I also helped California to grow. In 1917 the United States began to fight in the war. More goods had to be made to supply the soldiers. Harbors in San Francisco and Los Angeles were used to ship goods to the war sites.

California did a lot to help win World War I. More than 150,000 soldiers from California fought in the war. Californians built airplanes that were used during the war. California farmers sent large amounts of grains, fruits, meats, and vegetables to the war sites. They also increased their cotton crops. Cotton was used to make soldiers' uniforms. There were millions of men fighting in the war. Some farmland was replanted for growing cotton to supply enough of this crop.

One of the areas to change to cotton growing was the San Joaquin Valley. A new type of cotton was perfect for the California climate. This was the start of one of the biggest crops in California. Today California is the second leading state in growing cotton.

CHECKUP

1. What was the main reason for having the Panama–Pacific International Exposition?
2. How did the automobile bring work to Californians?
3. Name at least two people who started the important airplane business in California.

Water and Land Conservation

—VOCABULARY—

crisis   dam

aqueduct conservation

The Salton Sea is a shallow saltwater lake.

Importance of water Have you ever thought about where water comes from and what it does for you? Water is one of California's most important resources. Without it large parts of California would be desert. Irrigation solved many of California's water problems in the early 1900s. You learned that irrigation is a way of bringing water to crops through ditches and canals. Irrigation is also a way of bringing water to people through a set of pipes.

Imperial Valley water Look at the map on page 202. Find the Imperial Valley. In the 1800s the Imperial Valley was part of the Colorado Desert. By 1900 a man named George Chaffey had built a canal. It brought water from the Colorado River to the desert. Chaffey renamed the desert Imperial Valley. His canal brought many farmers to the valley.

Crops can be grown in the Imperial Valley all year. They include alfalfa, cotton, sugar beets, and a variety of fruits.

By 1905 there were 14,000 people living there. Over 100,000 acres (40 ha) were farmed. But a terrible thing happened. The Colorado River broke through the banks of the canal and flooded the valley. The flooding lasted almost 2 years. There was so much water that it filled in a very low part of the land. That body of water is now called the Salton Sea.

The farmers did not want to give up their land. The Southern Pacific Railroad helped them. Everyone worked hard to repair the break in the canal. The trains hauled in rock and gravel for 52 days. They hauled over 2,057 carloads of rock, 321 carloads of gravel, and 203 of clay. Finally the rock, gravel, and clay closed the break. The Imperial Valley was saved. In just a few years it became known as the Winter Garden of the World.

Los Angeles needs water   In 1904 Los Angeles faced a water **crisis**, or turning point. Many people had been moving to the city. There was not enough water for all the people. There had also been several droughts since 1892.

The leaders of Los Angeles began to look for more water. They found water in the Owens River. The river is in the Owens Valley on the eastern side of the Sierra Nevada. City leaders decided to build an **aqueduct** (ak′ wə dukt) to bring the water to Los Angeles. An aqueduct

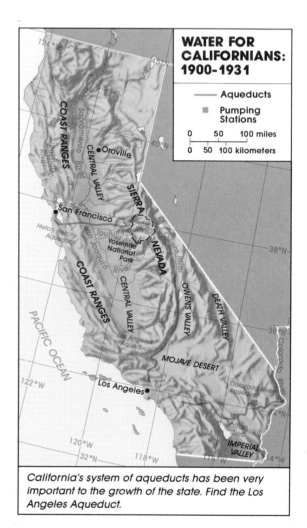

California's system of aqueducts has been very important to the growth of the state. Find the Los Angeles Aqueduct.

has large open or closed pipes for carrying water. The aqueduct had to be about 240 miles (386 km) long. The workers cut 142 tunnels into the mountains. That was a very big project in those days.

Work on the aqueduct started in 1908. Five years later 15 million people watched water flow down the aqueduct for the first time. Los Angeles had a new supply of water.

It cost the city of Los Angeles more than $24 million to build the Owens Valley Aqueduct.

The north's water San Francisco needed water. The leaders of the city decided to get water from the Sierra Nevada. They wanted to put a **dam**, or wall, across the Tuolumne River. The dam would be called the Hetch Hetchy Dam.

The place where the dam would be built was called the Hetch Hetchy Valley. It was also called Little Yosemite. It had many beautiful waterfalls and cliffs.

A man named John Muir was very unhappy about the dam. He thought Little Yosemite should be saved for use as a national park. Many people joined Muir in the fight to save Little Yosemite. They went all the way to the United States government to fight the building of the dam. The fight went on for years, but San Francisco leaders won. The dam was finally finished in 1931. Today Little Yosemite is under water.

This is what the Hetch Hetchy Valley looks like today, filled with water.

Keeping California beautiful   Have you ever visited a national park? John Muir helped to start three national parks in California. Muir talked to President Theodore Roosevelt about some of the beautiful land and forests in California. President Roosevelt agreed to save some of those places for parkland. They are Yosemite, Sequoia, and Kings Canyon national parks.

President Theodore Roosevelt (left) and John Muir (right) are overlooking Yosemite National Park.

John Muir was a very important **conservation** leader in California. Conservation is the wise use of natural resources. Without conservation many beautiful forests, deserts, and mountains of California might have been destroyed. Wildlife might have died.

Many other Californians joined Muir to save some of the state's naturally beautiful places. Did you know that the hills north of San Francisco were covered with redwood trees at one time? By 1903 there was only one stand of redwoods left. Just as loggers were about to cut this last stand of redwoods, a man named William Kent saved them. Kent borrowed money to buy the land where the trees stood. Then he turned it over to the federal government. The woods were named Muir Woods to honor John Muir.

The California State Division of Beaches and Parks also was started in the early 1900s. When you visit Big Basin Redwoods or Morro Bay, you are visiting state parks started in the early 1900s.

CHECKUP

1. Why did California need a lot of irrigation?
2. How did water from the Owens River in the Sierra Nevada get to the city of Los Angeles?
3. Why was there a fight over Little Yosemite? Who led the fight to save Little Yosemite?
4. How does the work of John Muir, William Kent, and other conservationists help Californians today?

Californians and the Arts

This San Francisco building, known as the Veteran's War Memorial, houses the Museum of Modern Art.

Music   In the early 1900s the Grand Opera House in San Francisco was one of the finest in the nation. On the night before the 1906 earthquake, Enrico Caruso, a well-known opera singer, sang there. He was very frightened by the earthquake on April 18. He thought he had lost his singing voice. After the earth stopped shaking, Caruso opened his hotel window and tried to sing. His voice was all right!

A woman named Artie Mason Carter helped to bring music to Los Angeles. She collected money from people who liked music. In 1921 she started an outdoor theater called the Hollywood Bowl. People still enjoy going to the Hollywood Bowl today.

Newspapers   Newspapers became an important part of California life in the late 1800s and early 1900s. Los Angeles had a newspaper called the *Los Angeles Times.* Harrison Gray Otis bought the *Times* in the late 1800s. He built it into the largest daily newspaper in Los Angeles.

The newspapers for Sacramento, Modesto, and Fresno were started by the McClatchy family. Their newspaper stories helped the small farmers fight the powerful, large ranchers.

Two newspapers were started in San Francisco in the late 1800s. The *Chronicle* was started by two brothers, Charles and Michael de Young, in 1865. In 1887 William Randolph Hearst's father bought the *Examiner* for him. Hearst became known all over the world for his success with newspapers. His huge home, called San Simeon, looks like a castle. It is near San Luis Obispo. The castle and some of its land became a state park in 1958.

The Mutt and Jeff comic strip first appeared in the *Chronicle* in 1908. Mutt and Jeff are still in some of our country's newspapers today. A man named Bud Fisher created Mutt and Jeff.

The *Eagle* was the first black-American newspaper in southern California. It was started by Charlotte Bass.

Early movies   When you think of movies, you might think of Hollywood. However, movies were not always made in California. The first movies were made in New York and New Jersey.

It was not until 1907 that movies began to be made in California. Then **producers**, or the people who make the movies, came to California. They decided California was a better place to make movies. Movies could be filmed outdoors all year long.

Three producers had their first big success in Hollywood in 1913. These men were Samuel Goldwyn, Jesse Lasky, and Cecil B. DeMille. They used low-cost cameras and filmed in an old barn. Their first movie was a western. All three men became very well-known because of their movies. By 1914 there were 73 other movie companies in California.

Hollywood fame   Hollywood soon became known for its movies everywhere in the United States. Thousands of people dreamed of going to Hollywood. Because of Hollywood, some actors and actresses became movie stars. Stars were the most well-liked actors and actresses. Most people wanted to see their movies.

The first "talkie"   Adding sound to movies was an exciting discovery. In 1927 *The Jazz Singer* changed the movie industry. This was the first **talkie**, or movie with sound. It starred a singer named Al Jolson. Al Jolson also wrote and sang a song about California. It is on page 207. Have you ever sung this song?

People enjoyed the talking movie. The talkie started a new boom in the movie business.

Al Jolson and May McAvoy are shown in this scene from **The Jazz Singer**.

CALIFORNIA HERE I COME

Al Jolson
Bud DeSylva
Joseph Meyer

Cal - i - forn - ia, here I come___

Right back where I start - ed from.___

Where bow - ers of flow - ers bloom in the sun.___

Each morn - ing at dawn - ing, bird - ies sing an'

ev - 'ry - thing. A sun - kist miss said, "Don't be late."

___ That's why I can hard - ly wait.___

___ O - pen up that Gold - en Gate.___

___ Cal - i - forn - ia, here I come.

Writers There were many fine writers in California in the early 1900s. Frank Norris wrote *The Octopus*. It told about the battle between the farmers and the powerful railroad owners. The two groups fought over the right to land and over the cost of shipping crops.

Jack London was most well-known for his book *The Call of the Wild*. It is about Buck, a dog from the Santa Clara Valley. Buck is stolen, sold as a sled dog, and taken to Alaska. In the early 1900s many dogs were stolen from their California homes. They were sold to people who explored Alaska.

Mary Austin, another writer, traveled from Illinois to settle in California. She liked to write about the California Indians who lived near her home.

Even today many children enjoy reading Jack London's exciting stories.

Do you think you could carve the shape of an animal in wood or stone?

Art and parades Arthur Putnam was one of the most well-known **sculptors** of the early 1900s. A sculptor carves shapes out of wood or stone. Putnam was praised for his statues of animals. He was also in charge of the sculpture for the Panama–Pacific Exposition in San Francisco.

The Pasadena Tournament (tėr′ nə mənt) of Roses parade was started in 1890. In the early 1900s football games were added to the day's happenings. Today many Americans watch the parade and football game every New Year's Day.

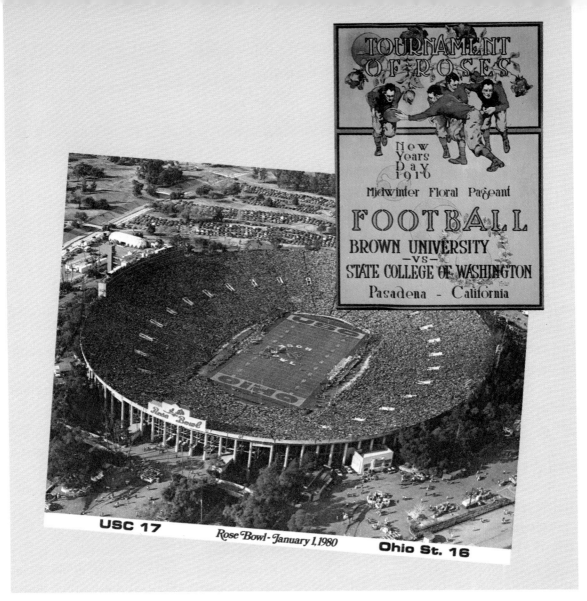

TOURNAMENT OF ROSES

New Years Day 1916

Midwinter Floral Pageant

FOOTBALL
BROWN UNIVERSITY
—vs—
STATE COLLEGE OF WASHINGTON

Pasadena - California

USC 17   Rose Bowl - January 1, 1980   Ohio St. 16

These posters announce the Tournament of Roses parade and football game.

Looking ahead   The early 1900s were good years for Californians. California had grown a lot during that time. In Chapter 11 you will learn about California in the 1930s and 1940s. In those years California played an important part in solving some very big problems faced by all Americans.

CHECKUP

1. Why did the movie business come to California?
2. How did Artie Mason Carter bring music to Los Angeles?
3. How did William Randolph Hearst get started as the owner of the San Francisco *Examiner*?
4. What parade do Americans watch today that was started in the early 1900s?

KEY FACTS

1. The San Francisco earthquake and fire of 1906 was the greatest tragedy in the state's history.

2. The opening of the Panama Canal in 1914 greatly shortened the trip from the East Coast and Europe to California.

3. The nation's first aviation meet was held near Los Angeles in 1910.

4. Water is one of California's most important resources.

5. Californians worked hard to keep California beautiful.

6. The movie business became very important in California in the early 1900s.

VOCABULARY QUIZ

Fill in each blank with the word or words that best complete the sentence.

1. When there is a strong and sudden movement along a fault it is called an _____.

2. A large fair is sometimes called an _____.

3. When oil is found it is called an _____.

4. Glenn Curtiss built a _____ which can land on water.

5. When people fly heavier-than-air airplanes it is called _____.

6. People build _____ to move water from one place to another.

7. The wise use of natural resources is called _____.

8. People who make movies are called _____.

9. Movies with sound were called _____.

10. Arthur Putnam was a well-known _____ of animals.

REVIEW QUESTIONS

1. Why was the San Francisco earthquake a great tragedy?

2. List three reasons automobiles became popular in California.

3. What new businesses became important in California in the early 1900s?

4. List three areas of California that needed water in the early 1900s. How did each area get its water?

5. What did John Muir and other conservation people do for California?

ACTIVITIES

1. Look for information about old autos or airplanes in the library. Write a report about either one. Cover the years from 1900 to 1930 in the United States.

2. Imagine that you were a star in the movies in the 1920s. What would your life have been like? Pretend you are being interviewed by a reporter. Write down what you would say about how you remember your life as a star.

3. Write a poem or draw a picture about what you think California was like in the early 1900s.

READING FOR UNDERSTANDING

Telegraph Heroes   The world learned about the San Francisco earthquake because of the bravery of a few telegraph operators. On April 18, 1906, they stuck to their posts at the telegraph office. When they were driven out by fire, they worked from the islands in the harbor.

The Bulletins   These are some of the messages sent by the telegraph operators during the earthquake. Read them carefully.

BULLETIN.
The Postal-Telegraph-Cable Company.
To Po.
To answer to query [question] as to what caused damage, S.F. says the greatest damage done by fire [on] account [of] no water, they are getting at it now, as it has such headway can not control it. The damage by earthquake very severe, and considerable [great] loss of life by falling buildings. The Call Building is in full blaze now and it is only question of minutes for us in Postal here.
10:30 A.M. 18th April.

BULLETIN.
    The city practically ruined by fire. . . .
The Call Building is burned out entirely, the Examiner Building just fell in a heap. Fire all around in every direction. . . . Destruction by earthquake something frightful. The City Hall dome stripped and only the frame work standing. . . . Lots of new buildings just recently finished are completely destroyed. They are blowing standing buildings, that are in path of flames, up with dynamite. No water. It's awful. . . .
    "I want to get out of here or be blown up."
Chief Operator Postal Telegraph Office,
    San Francisco, Cal. 2:20 P.M.
    April 18, 1906.

SKILLS PRACTICE

On a piece of paper, answer these questions about the telegraph messages.
1. Why did fire cause the greatest amount of damage?
2. Which building must have been very close to the telegraph office?
3. "The city practically ruined by fire." What word is missing from the telegraph operator's sentence? Why, do you think, did the telegraph operators leave some smaller words out of their messages?
4. Why, do you think, was dynamite used to fight the fire?

11 The Depression Years and World War II

California Feels the Depression

```
VOCABULARY
depression          Dust Bowl
tourists
```

Hard times   The boom of the 1920s ended with a **depression** in the 1930s. A depression is a time when many people have no jobs and very little money. Since they do not have much money, stores do not sell much. Many factories close because stores do not buy their goods. In those factories that stay open, workers may have to take a cut in pay.

The depression of the 1930s hit all parts of our country. People had less money to spend. They bought fewer of California's products. In 1929, Californians sold $750 million worth of fruits, vegetables, and other foods. In 1932, during the depression, they sold only $32 million worth.

Before the depression, large numbers of **tourists** came to California. A tourist is one who makes a trip for pleasure. Tourists came to enjoy California's scenery and sunshine. But in the 1930s fewer tourists could afford to come.

Some companies in California went out of business. Many others made fewer products. Then they needed fewer workers, so some people lost their jobs. In a depression many people suffer.

Was California better off?   At the same time that people in California were suffering from the depression, many people continued to move there. Why did they do this?

For many years, advertisements had told people to come to California. The ads said that California was a land of promise. Maybe the depression is not so bad in California, people thought. They believed that whatever they found in California would be better than what they were leaving. California was their hope for a better future.

More than a million people moved to California in the 1930s. Many of them were from the states of Oklahoma and Kansas. There had been a long drought in those states. The fields were so dry that crops could not grow. Then the wind started blowing. With no crops to hold the soil in place, there were huge dust storms. The air was so thick with

Millions of Americans suffered from hard times in the 1930s.

dust that sometimes it hid the sun. It was hard for people to breathe. The area where these storms took place became known as the **Dust Bowl**.

On to California   Many farm families decided to leave their homes in the Dust Bowl. They stuffed into their old cars as many things as they could. Mattresses were tied on top of the cars. Then the children piled in, and the families began the long trip to California.

When these families reached California weeks later, very few found what they had hoped for. By the time they arrived, they were almost out of money. They had to work or starve. But thousands of people already in California also needed jobs.

The Dust Bowl people found they were not welcome. Californians called the Dust Bowl people Okies, but not all of them came from Oklahoma. Many Cal-

With all of its belongings, a family from the Dust Bowl heads for California during the depression.

ifornians who still had jobs feared losing them to the newcomers. Many of the newcomers would work for very low pay. A state law was passed to keep people from moving to California unless they already had jobs there.

When did World War II begin? About how many years was the United States at war?

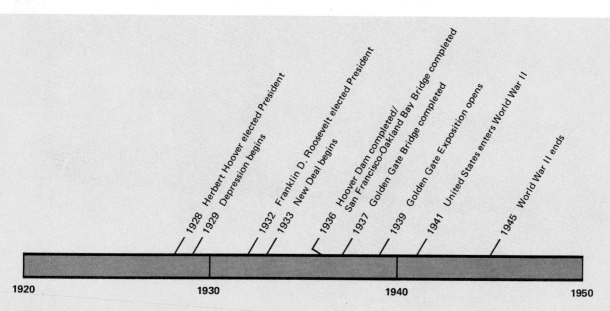

1920   1930   1940   1950

1928 Herbert Hoover elected President
1929 Depression begins
1932 Franklin D. Roosevelt elected President
1933 New Deal begins
1936 Hoover Dam completed/San Francisco-Oakland Bay Bridge completed
1937 Golden Gate Bridge completed
1939 Golden Gate Exposition opens
1941 United States enters World War II
1945 World War II ends

Most of the Dust Bowl people stayed on. Somehow they got along, but making a living during the depression years was very hard. Later, many of these people and their children would find the better life they were seeking.

In search of a better life   The Dust Bowl families were not the only people who came to California in search of a better life. As you know, Mexico is California's neighbor to the south. For years Mexicans had been coming across the border, looking for jobs. Many found work on farms and in orchards. They worked hard but received very little pay. Whole families had to work just to make enough money to eat.

Some other people who had to work long hours for little money were the Filipinos. They had come from the Philippine Islands, located across the Pacific Ocean from California. The United States got those islands from Spain in 1898 and held them until 1946. Most of the Filipinos who came to California held low-paying jobs. They worked on farms and in restaurants and homes.

Like the Dust Bowl people and the Mexicans, the Filipinos had a hard time during the depression. Some Californians were afraid they would lose their jobs to the Filipinos. For a time, the state even offered to pay Filipinos to return to the Philippines if they would agree not to come back.

Mexican farm workers gather melons in the Imperial Valley of California.

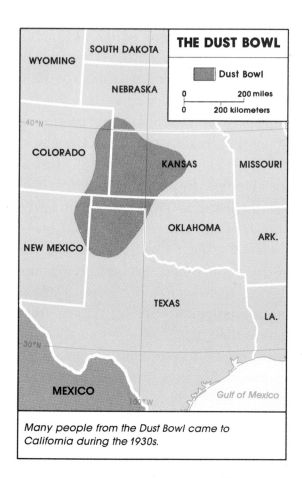

THE DUST BOWL

Dust Bowl

0   200 miles
0   200 kilometers

WYOMING

SOUTH DAKOTA

NEBRASKA

40°N

COLORADO

KANSAS

MISSOURI

NEW MEXICO

OKLAHOMA

ARK.

TEXAS

LA.

30°N

MEXICO

100°W

Gulf of Mexico

Many people from the Dust Bowl came to California during the 1930s.

California Fights the Depression

The depression gets much worse
Americans had never known a depression so bad. By 1932, millions of Americans were without work. When the depression began, the President of the United States was Herbert Hoover. He was the first resident of California to become President. Hoover had helped millions of people in Europe during and after World War I. At that time he was in charge of providing food and money

Herbert Hoover, the first United States President from California, poses with Mrs. Hoover on a train platform.

The 1930s were not good times for any groups moving into California. Not until the depression came to an end would there be jobs for all who wanted them.

CHECKUP

1. What happened to factories in the 1930s?
2. Why did many people come to California during the depression of the 1930s?
3. Why did they not find what they hoped for when they arrived in California?
4. Besides the Dust Bowl people, what other people sought a better life in California?

A welder works on pipes that will bring water to the city of San Francisco. This water system was built under one of the New Deal programs for fighting the depression.

for the war-torn countries. Now, as the depression worsened, he worried about Americans.

Hoover believed that people in need should be helped. However, he did not think the United States government should hand out money to them. He believed help should come from the governments of the cities and states where the needy lived. He also believed the help should come from groups that help the poor.

Hoover thought, too, that the country would get over the depression in time. But the depression kept getting worse. The states and cities and the groups that help the poor did not have enough money. More and more people needed help.

A new President In 1933 the United States got a new President. He was Franklin D. Roosevelt. Most people in California voted for him. So did most of the rest of the country.

Roosevelt wanted the United States government to help the needy people at this time. He had many different plans, or **programs**, for fighting the depression. He called all these programs together the **New Deal**.

Fighting the depression One program gave money to people out of work. They could use the money for food, clothing, and other things. By 1934 more than a million Californians were getting this help each week. So were millions of other Americans.

The lake behind Hoover Dam is many miles long. For what purposes is the water used?

Other New Deal programs made jobs for people. Workers were hired to build schools, hospitals, and playgrounds. Hundreds of Californians worked at such jobs as did people in the other states. The things they built would be used by thousands of people.

Under one New Deal program, young men were hired to work in forests and parks. They planted trees and built mountain trails. They stocked streams with fish. In California they helped to set up six new parks.

These and other New Deal programs did not bring the depression to an end. But they gave many people the help they needed to get food and other things. And they gave people hope that better times would come.

Hoover Dam   One very important project for Californians in the 1930s was the building of Hoover Dam. A dam is a wall built across a river to hold the water back. Hoover Dam is on the Colorado River, between Nevada and Arizona. It is about 60 miles (97 km) east of the California border. Behind the dam a huge lake formed. Today the lake supplies water for people in southern California. An aqueduct, or pipeline, carries great quantities of the water each day to Los Angeles. The city is 242 miles (387 km) from the lake! Water from the lake also makes much land usable for farming.

The water behind Hoover Dam is used in making electricity as well. Water falling from high behind the dam makes wheels turn. As the wheels turn, they drive machines that make electric power. Electric power made by falling water is called **hydroelectric power**. This power is sent through lines to southern California. It is used to light buildings, run machines, and do many other things.

San Francisco's bridges   Two other big building projects in the 1930s were the bridges of San Francisco.

The first bridge was built to connect San Francisco and Oakland, cities on opposite sides of the bay. The bridge is more than 8 miles (13 km) long. At the time it was built, it was the longest bridge in the world.

The narrow opening from the Pacific Ocean into San Francisco Bay has long been called the Golden Gate. A year after the San Francisco–Oakland Bay Bridge was opened, the Golden Gate Bridge was finished.

The Golden Gate Exposition   In 1939, Californians held a big fair to celebrate the building of the two bridges. They even built an island in San Francisco Bay as a place to hold the fair. The island was nearly a mile long and two thirds of a mile wide. It was named Treasure Island. The fair, called the Golden Gate Exposition, went on for almost a year.

This picture was taken during the building of the Golden Gate Bridge across the entrance to San Francisco Bay. What part of the bridge was yet to be put in place?

The Golden Gate Exposition on Treasure Island brought visitors from all over America to San Francisco.

Some 30 countries and 350 industries took part. They had many kinds of things to show. Millions of visitors came to see the sights and to have fun.

The Golden Gate Exposition did more than celebrate the two bridges. It also told the world that California was recovering from the depression.

CHECKUP

1. Who was the first California resident to become President of the United States?
2. In what ways did the New Deal help people in California?
3. How did Hoover Dam help California?
4. Why was the Golden Gate Exposition held?

Californians in World War II

America at war   In 1941 the United States went to war. It did so after Japan attacked Pearl Harbor in the Hawaiian (hə wī′ yən) Islands. Those Pacific islands were owned by the United States. Many ships of the American navy were stationed at Pearl Harbor.

On December 7, 1941, Japanese war planes bombed Pearl Harbor. They sank many ships. More than 2,300 Americans were killed.

In 1941, Japan had already been at war with China for several years. And on the other side of the world, war was raging in Europe. Two of Japan's partners—Germany and Italy—were fighting against their neighbors. Japan, Germany, and Italy all wanted to take land from other countries.

Americans did not like what Japan, Germany, and Italy had been doing. But we had stayed **neutral** (nü′ trəl). A neutral country is one that does not join with either side in a war. However, after the Pearl Harbor attack, the United States was no longer neutral. We went to war against Japan, Germany, and Italy.

Would Japan attack California? Japan is straight across the Pacific Ocean from California. After the attack on Pearl Harbor, people feared that Japan might next attack California and the other states lying along the Pacific Coast.

Alarms were set up in California cities to warn people in case of an attack. If an alarm sounded at night, people were to turn off all lights. It would be hard for Japanese pilots to find the darkened cities.

No California city was ever attacked by Japanese planes. But in the first weeks of the war, there were false alarms in several cities. And early in 1942 a Japanese submarine (sub′ mə rēn) did attack. Surfacing in the ocean off Santa Barbara, it fired at an **oil refinery** (ri fī′ nər ē). An oil refinery is a place where gasoline and other products are made from oil taken out of the ground. The submarine did no harm, but the attack made Californians nervous.

The United States was at war until 1945. The war touched the life of nearly every American. It brought great changes to California.

The armed forces   During the war years, 1941–1945, about 700,000 men and women from California joined the armed forces. They served on battlefields all over the world.

California was one of the leading states for training the armed forces. In 1941 the state had a few training camps and

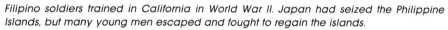

Filipino soldiers trained in California in World War II. Japan had seized the Philippine Islands, but many young men escaped and fought to regain the islands.

bases. These were made larger, and new ones were set up. Treasure Island, where the Golden Gate Exposition had been held, became a naval base during the war.

Most of those who took part in the Pacific fighting sailed from California. San Francisco, Los Angeles, and San Diego were busy ports.

War industries   California was a leader, too, in making many of the things needed to carry on the war. In 1939 the value of goods made in California's factories was about $3 billion. By 1943 the value was up to $10 billion.

The building of airplanes became a big industry in California during the war. Lockheed Aircraft in Burbank built 20,000 planes. Thousands more were built by the company founded in 1922 by Donald Douglas in Santa Monica.

Shipbuilding was another big industry. Ships were needed for carrying troops and supplies and for fighting the war at sea. Before the war started, only 4,000 people worked at the shipyards in California. But 282,000 people were doing this work by 1943. During the war years Californians built 100,000 ships.

One shipbuilder was a man named Henry Kaiser (kī′ zər). It took a lot of steel to build ships. Yet very little steel was made in California. So Kaiser built California's first complete steel mill. It

was at Fontana (fän tan′ ə), east of Los Angeles.

California's oil industry grew also. Large amounts of gasoline and oil were needed for tanks, trucks, airplanes, and ships. Many new oil wells were drilled, and old wells were made deeper. Oil output shot upward.

During World War II, a skilled worker at a California aircraft factory rivets part of an airplane.

Kaiser's ships were made in sections. This picture shows the stern of a ship.

The depression ends The coming of war ended the depression. There were thousands of jobs in the war industries. Anyone who wanted a job could get one. Women took over many jobs once held only by men.

Wages went up. In 1939 the average weekly wage for a factory job was $27.80. By 1944 it was $55.21. The wealth of Californians increased three times during the war years.

Most people who had had a hard time during the depression could now make a good living. The people from the Dust Bowl at last had a better life. Thousands of blacks from the South moved to California to take jobs in the factories and on the farms. Workers were brought in from Mexico to plant and harvest crops. Between 1940 and 1945 the number of people living in California went up by about 2 million.

But not all people in California had it better during the war. For the Japanese Americans the war years were a very bad time.

The Japanese Americans In 1941 about 112,000 Japanese Americans were living in states on the Pacific Coast. Most of them were in California. They were honest and hardworking, but some other people were jealous of their success.

After the Pearl Harbor attack, many people turned against the Japanese Americans. There was fear that Japan might attack the Pacific Coast states. Some people thought the Japanese Americans would be more loyal to Japan than to America.

This fear led our government to move the Japanese Americans into camps that were much like prisons. They had to leave their homes and businesses. Some Japanese Americans lost everything they had.

More than two thirds of these people were American citizens. Many of them had been born in the United States. These sons and daughters of Japanese immigrants were called **Nisei** (nē sā′). They had grown up and gone to school in America. Many of the young men wanted to fight for America in World War II. The army finally agreed to put them in a special group that was sent to Europe.

There the Nisei fought hard for America. Many were killed. The Nisei group won more medals for bravery than any other group of the same size in the American army.

The Nisei were proving their loyalty to the United States though their families were being held in camps. Today we can see how fear can make people do unfair things. We can hope that loyal American citizens will never be treated so unfairly again.

The war ends   In 1945 the United States and the countries fighting with us won the war. The last country to **surrender**, or give up, was Japan.

There must never be another world war, people said. So at the end of the war, leaders from 50 countries met in

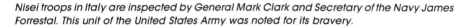

Nisei troops in Italy are inspected by General Mark Clark and Secretary of the Navy James Forrestal. This unit of the United States Army was noted for its bravery.

At San Francisco in 1945, an American official signs the agreement that forms the United Nations. The person standing directly behind the table is President Truman.

San Francisco. There they formed the **United Nations**. This group, it was hoped, would keep countries from going to war in the future. The United Nations would try to have countries solve their differences peacefully.

California's future   From 1941 to 1945, Californians had played a big part in winning the war. Many had served in the armed forces. Many others had made the products and raised the crops needed for victory.

Now, with the war over, Californians wondered what the future held for their state. Would it go back into a depression? Or would the growth of the war years continue?

Looking ahead   In the next chapter you will learn about California after World War II. You will be reading about California's growth, good times, new industries, and much more.

CHECKUP

1. What made America go to war in 1941?
2. In what ways did California supply help for the armed forces?
3. What industries in California were important in winning the war?
4. What happened to Japanese Americans in the Pacific states during World War II?

II/CHAPTER REVIEW

KEY FACTS

1. During the depression of the 1930s, many Californians were without jobs.
2. Though times were hard everywhere, people continued to move to California in the depression.
3. The New Deal of President Franklin D. Roosevelt gave money to those in need and made jobs for many people.
4. Californians helped win World War II by joining the armed forces and by building ships, planes, and other products.
5. Japanese Americans were treated unfairly in World War II. They were forced to live in camps that were much like prisons.

VOCABULARY QUIZ

Write the numbers 1 to 5 on a sheet of paper. Match these words with the definitions below.

a. Nisei
b. depression
c. neutral
d. hydroelectric power
e. tourist

1. Electric power produced from falling water
2. A person who travels for pleasure
3. Japanese immigrants' sons and daughters, born and educated in America
4. A country that does not take sides in a war
5. A time when many people do not have jobs and business is poor

REVIEW QUESTIONS

1. What is a depression?
2. Who were the Dust Bowl people? Why were Californians unhappy about those people coming to California?
3. How did President Roosevelt try to help California and the nation in the 1930s?
4. Why was the building of Hoover Dam important to California?
5. Why did the United States enter World War II?
6. What industries grew larger during World War II? Why?
7. Why were Japanese Americans relocated during World War II? How did many Nisei show their loyalty to America?
8. Why did leaders from 50 countries meet in San Francisco in 1945? What was the purpose of the organization set up by these leaders?

ACTIVITIES

1. On an outline map of the United States, color the states of the Dust Bowl yellow. Then draw lines showing routes that people from the Dust Bowl may have traveled to California.
2. Your grandparents lived during World War II. They can probably tell you many interesting stories about the war years. Ask about their jobs, where they lived, what they did for entertainment, and other questions. Write down what they tell you, and turn in your report to your teacher.

KEEPING A DIARY

A WRITTEN RECORD

In a diary you keep a written record of what you do and how you feel about things that are important to you. Usually you keep this written record in a little book with blank pages. There is a space on the pages for you to write something every day for a year or more.

Here are three entries that José wrote in his diary.

April 27

Dear Diary,

Tomorrow we are going to visit Auntie Lupe. Mom says that it will take about 4 hours to drive there. Auntie's house is near Disneyland. I am so excited!

TO AUNTIE LUPE'S HOUSE

April 28

Dear Diary,

We saw Auntie Lupe today. We left home early this morning. Dad drove, and I rode in front with him. Mom and my sister, Maria, were in the back seat.

After driving for 2 hours, Dad asked, "Is anyone hungry?" Maria and I shouted, "Yes!" We stopped at a diner, and Maria and I each had a muffin and a glass of milk.

Auntie was happy to see us. She made a very good lunch. Then we all went to a park. Maria and I had lots of fun there. We are staying overnight at Auntie's house. To-morrow we go to Disneyland.

April 29

Dear Diary,

I was so excited last night I could hardly sleep. We went to Disneyland early this morning and stayed all day.

My favorite ride was Space Mountain. Maria and I went on it twice. It's a very scary roller-coaster ride. The Haunted House and Pirates of the Caribbean were fun, too. The whole park was fun! At night there was even a parade. We were really tired, and Maria and I fell asleep on the way back to Auntie Lupe's. I can't wait to go to Disneyland again.

SKILLS PRACTICE

Now use your imagination to prepare some diary entries. Pretend that you and your family are moving to California during World War II. Your dad will be working at an airplane factory near Los Angeles. Write diary entries for your first two days in California. Tell what you did, where and how you traveled, and what you saw. In writing your diary entries, make use of what you learned from this chapter. You may want to get more information from books in your library.

Remember to use a date for each entry. You may begin your diary entries with the following sentences.

First entry What a busy day this has been since we arrived in California.
Second entry Today we saw many interesting things in Los Angeles.

12 California After World War II

A Time of Growth

┌─VOCABULARY─────────────────┐
│ electronics   aerospace │
│ computers   satellite │
│ convenience │
│   foods │
└──────────────────────────────┘

No depression   When World War II ended in 1945, Californians wondered what would happen to their state. In the last chapter you read about the Great Depression before the war. After the war, people were afraid there might be another depression. They knew that factories would no longer be making war goods. If the factories closed, many workers would lose their jobs.

These fears never came true. California did not have another depression. Nor did the rest of the United States. Instead, California entered into the greatest years of growth in its history.

Good times   During the war, Californians had earned lots of money. Now they were ready to spend it on the things they needed, such as cars, stoves, and refrigerators. During the war, they had not been able to buy these things. The factories had then been making goods for the armed forces. Now the factories could turn to the making of peacetime goods.

In the years after the war, factories were busier than ever. And there were more of them. In 1947 there were 215 new factories built in the Los Angeles area. Another 392 were built in the San Francisco Bay area. These factories made chemicals, building supplies, metal products, and many other things. The aircraft and oil industries continued to be strong.

Oil companies in California began to look for new supplies of oil. They found them off the coast, beneath the floor of the Pacific Ocean. To get the oil, engineers at Long Beach built an island. Then they drilled down through the island into the pools of oil below. Off the beach at Santa Barbara, they tried something different. They built big platforms on long, steel legs that stood on the ocean floor. The platforms had to be strong to stand up against ocean storms. To get the oil, the companies drilled from the platforms into the ocean floor.

California's growth after the war created a need for more housing.

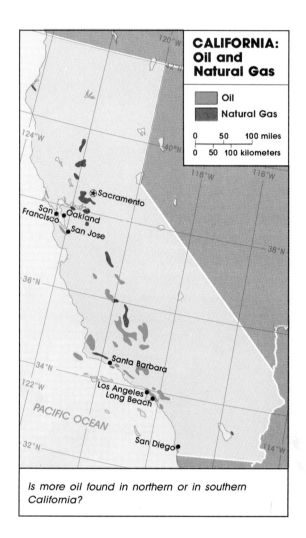

**CALIFORNIA:
Oil and
Natural Gas**

Oil

Natural Gas

0   50   100 miles
0   50   100 kilometers

*Is more oil found in northern or in southern
California?*

New industries Some important new industries were started at this time. One was the **electronics** (i lek tron′iks) business. Electronics makes use of electricity to give us many wonderful things. Without electronics we would not have our TV sets, radios, and **computers**. Do you know what a computer is? It is a machine that can do many kinds of tasks, from steering airplanes to running factories.

Another business that grew quickly was the making of **convenience** (kən vēn′ yəns) **foods**. These foods are partly prepared or cooked before they are sold in the stores. Among these foods are instant potatoes, frozen vegetables, and even whole dinners. How many of these have you eaten?

All over California, business boomed. By the middle of the 1950s, Los Angeles was the third largest industrial and

About how long did the Korean War last? When did astronauts first land on the moon?

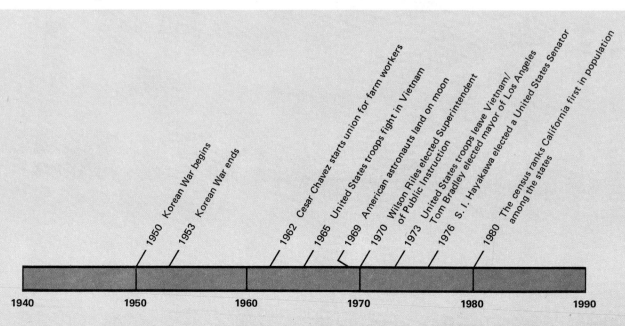

1940   1950   1960   1970   1980   1990

1950 Korean War begins
1953 Korean War ends
1962 Cesar Chavez starts union for farm workers
1965 United States troops fight in Vietnam
1969 American astronauts land on moon
1970 Wilson Riles elected Superintendent of Public Instruction
1973 United States troops leave Vietnam/ Tom Bradley elected mayor of Los Angeles
1976 S. I. Hayakawa elected a United States Senator
1980 The census ranks California first in population among the states

marketing center in the United States. And a few years later, it became the second largest!

The space industry   In the late 1950s, Americans became interested in exploring space. California soon became a leader in the **aerospace** industry. Aerospace factories make airplanes and spacecraft.

The Jet Propulsion Laboratory in Pasadena and the Ames Research Center south of San Francisco have planned many spacecraft. A kind of spacecraft that moves around the earth is called a **satellite** (sat′ ə līt). It can pick up telephone messages or television programs from stations on the earth. It sends these messages and programs to other parts of the earth. Some satellites gather information about the weather.

The spacecraft Columbia rests on a runway at Edwards Air Force Base following a seven-day journey into space.

Despite the loss of a hand, this man is as skillful as any other worker in fitting electronic parts together.

Other spacecraft fly far out from the earth. Some gather information by machines and send it back. Other spacecraft carry people. In 1969, American astronauts were the first people to land on the moon.

Edwards Air Force Base in Antelope Valley has played an important part in our country's space program. Spacecraft have landed there on their return to earth. Millions of Americans have watched these landings on television.

Goods for the armed forces   After World War II the orders to California factories for war planes, weapons, and other war goods dropped. But in 1950 the United States became involved in a war in Korea (kô rē′ ə). That war lasted 3

Some electronic equipment for a submarine is being made in this California factory.

A rising population   In 1941 about 7 million people lived in California. By 1961 the population was more than 16 million. And in 1980, California, with more than 23 million people, had the biggest population among the 50 states.

What brought so many people to California? Many came to get jobs in the state's growing industries. Many were attracted by California's beautiful beaches and mountains and its pleasant climate. Some people compared these years after World War II to the gold rush 100 years earlier. Now, as then, people came to California to seek their fortunes.

years. Then in the 1960s and 1970s, the United States was at war in Vietnam (vē et' näm) for several years.

Both Korea and Vietnam are in Asia, across the Pacific Ocean from California. As in World War II, California was the place from which many of the American armed forces left on their way to the war fronts.

America's part in these wars brought new orders for war goods in California. Airplane factories that had closed after World War II were now opened again. Many new kinds of weapons were made. In the years that have followed, California has become a leader in making goods for the United States Army, Navy, and Air Force.

Homes, schools, and highways When a state's population grows quickly, many things are needed. One of the things that people need is a place to live. During World War II the government had not allowed houses to be built. The things that houses are made of, such as lumber and concrete, were used by the armed forces. Now, thousands of houses and apartments were needed. Many were built on what had once been farmland. Fields, orchards, and pastures were cleared to make room for the houses. New hospitals, libraries, and shopping centers were also built.

To get from their homes to their jobs, people needed highways. By the middle of the 1950s, more than $1 million was

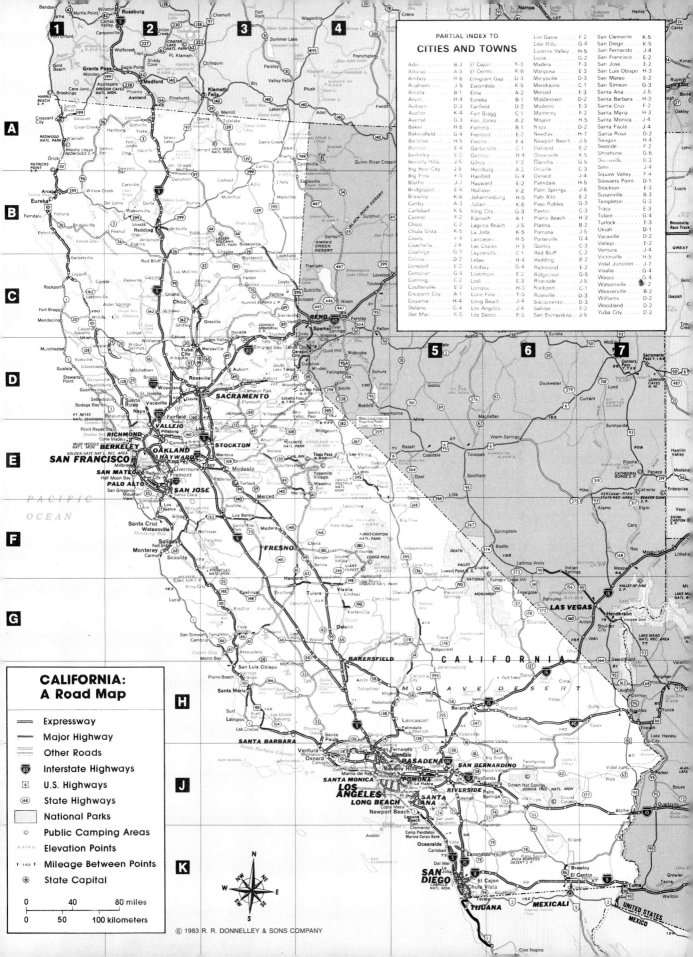

CALIFORNIA: A Road Map

being spent in California every workday for new highways. In the 1960s and 1970s more than 12,500 miles (20,112 km) of highway were added. They connected every city in the state that had a population of more than 5,000.

Another great need was schools. Many families that moved into California had children. There was a great increase in the number of children in school. For a while 121 new classrooms were needed each week. Hundreds of new schools had to be built.

Water The rise in population and the building of new homes, schools, and factories meant that more water was needed. It was especially needed in the Los Angeles area.

New dams, reservoirs, and tunnels were added. They controlled the flow of water so that it could be sent where

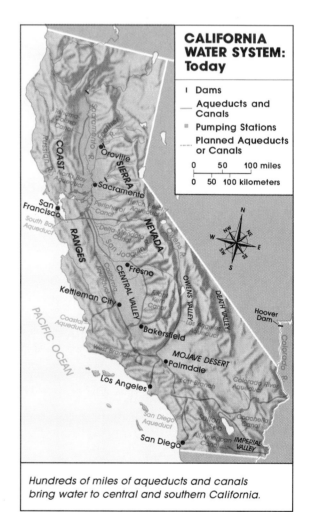

CALIFORNIA WATER SYSTEM: Today

ı Dams
___ Aqueducts and Canals
■ Pumping Stations
... Planned Aqueducts or Canals

0   50   100 miles
0   50   100 kilometers

Hundreds of miles of aqueducts and canals bring water to central and southern California.

Water from the lake behind Oroville Dam irrigates farmland many miles to the south.

it was needed most. They also prevented the flooding of towns in the Central Valley of California. Farmers were now able to grow crops in the southern and western parts of the San Joaquin Valley.

The biggest project for controlling water was the building of Oroville (ōr′ ō vil) Dam on the Feather River. This is the highest dam in the United States, rising 771 feet (235 m). The dam holds back water for irrigating thousands of acres of farmland. The dam also helps control floods. And the water is used in making hydroelectric power.

The building of Oroville Dam was a big step forward in California's goal to control the flow of water. But it will be many years before the job of controlling water is completed.

Another possible way of dealing with water shortages is to use ocean water. However, ocean water contains salt that must be removed. To remove it costs so much that this way of getting fresh water is not often tried.

CHECKUP

1. Why was there no depression after World War II?
2. What were some of the industries that did well after the war?
3. Why did so many people come to California at this time?
4. What were some of the problems caused by the rise in population?

Seeking Equality for All

VOCABULARY

mayor	boycott
Chicanos	ancestors
union	legislature
strikes	

Many different peoples   As you learned earlier, many different peoples came to California. These peoples had different backgrounds. Sometimes they had different beliefs. Because of their differences, some peoples were not always treated fairly.

It is the goal of our government that all Americans be treated fairly and equally. Since the end of World War II, Californians and other Americans have moved closer to that goal. Let us see how some of the different peoples in California have helped make the spirit of freedom stronger in our state.

Black Californians   There were few blacks in California before World War II. Many came during and after the war. They settled mainly in the cities, especially in Los Angeles. A thousand black people a month moved into Los Angeles in the 1960s.

Few blacks had lived in cities before. Most were unskilled workers who worked for low wages. And many were not able to find jobs at all. They had to live in run-down neighborhoods.

Mayor Thomas Bradley of Los Angeles puts forth his views to a group of Californians before election day.

C. Riles. In 1970 he was elected super-intendent of public instruction. From 1973 to 1979 Yvonne Brathwaite Burke served in the United States Congress.

In 1973 Thomas Bradley was elected **mayor** of Los Angeles. A mayor is the chief officer of a city. Bradley was re-elected in 1977 and 1981. Los Angeles is the largest city in California and one of the largest in the United States.

Mexican Americans   As you know, California was once owned by Mexico. People of Mexican background are among the oldest families in California. No group in the state has grown more rapidly in recent years than the Mexican Americans, or **Chicanos** (chi kä′ nōz). *Chicanos* is the name some Mexican Americans call themselves.

In 1960 there were 1.4 million Mexican Americans in California. Today there are more than 4 million. Many of them have come to find jobs and make a better life for themselves.

Most of the state's Mexican Americans live in southern California. Many of them live in poor neighborhoods in cities. Los Angeles has the largest Mexican population of any city in the United States.

Though many Mexican Americans live in cities, a large number are farm workers. They work hard picking fruits and vegetables at harvest time.

For these black people, life was hard. The future seemed hopeless. This feeling of despair caused much trouble in some black areas in the 1960s. One of these areas was the Watts neighborhood in Los Angeles. There were many fires and shootings. Lives were lost and much property was destroyed.

The troubles of the 1960s brought the needs of blacks to public attention. Greater care was now taken to meet these needs. More jobs were opened up. In Watts a new hospital was built, as well as a cultural center.

While many blacks have found it hard to better their way of life, other blacks have done well. Some have become public officials and are now in high positions. The first black to win a state-wide election in California was Wilson

In 1962 Cesar Chavez (sē′ zər chä′ vez), a young Mexican American, started a **union** for farm workers. A union is a group formed within an industry to help the group's members. Wages for farm workers were very low. Chavez wanted to get better wages for the members of his union. He led **strikes** against the growers of roses, lettuce, grapes, and other crops. A strike takes place when workers try to get what they want by staying away from their jobs.

During some strikes Chavez called for a **boycott**. A boycott takes place when people will have nothing to do with a particular group. Chavez asked people to stop buying the food raised by the growers against whom his union was striking. Chavez also led a march of farm workers up the Central Valley of California. There he met the governor of

California, who agreed to help him. The strike against the grape growers lasted 3 years. Finally the growers agreed that the workers could have a union. Some years later a new law gave farm workers the same rights as factory workers.

Mexican Americans joined in marches and strikes in the 1960s to get better treatment. The people of California began to elect more and more Mexican Americans to school boards and other posts. Mexican Americans, proud of their background, are playing a bigger part in California life.

Asian Americans   More than 1 million Asian Americans live in California today. Asian Americans are people who came from China, Japan, and other Asian countries, or whose **ancestors** came from those lands. An ancestor is a person from whom one is descended—for example, a father, mother, grandfather, grandmother, and so on.

The Chinese and Japanese are the largest groups of Asian Americans in California. Other groups include people from Korea and the Philippines. After the war in Vietnam ended, many people came to California from Vietnam and Cambodia. A number of Asians who have recently come to California have settled in Orange County.

The first Chinese people in California came at the time of the gold rush. They

Under the leadership of Cesar Chavez, the working conditions for farm workers improved.

were not welcomed and were not treated fairly. Chinese workers labored hard to help build the first railroad line that crossed the continent. But then a law was passed that for many years kept the Chinese from entering the United States.

Most of the earliest Japanese in California were farm workers. They also were treated unfairly. Do you remember reading in Chapter 11 about the Japanese Americans who were placed in camps during World War II? After the war some came back to California. Others settled elsewhere.

In recent years Japanese Americans have been asking for payment for the property taken from them. The 314 Japanese Americans who worked for the state of California in 1942 were fired. In 1982 the government of the state of California agreed to pay each of them $5,000 for lost wages. One lawmaker said that the payment "will let the world know we made a sad mistake." Other Japanese Americans have not been paid for their losses.

Despite the way Japanese Americans were treated, they have made great progress. They have worked hard to get ahead. Many have started their own businesses. Some have risen to high positions.

One such Japanese American is S. I. Hayakawa. He studied hard and became a college professor. Then he be-

As a child, Norman Mineta was one of 110,000 Japanese Americans who were placed in camps during World War II. In 1971, he was elected mayor of San Jose. Today he is a member of the United States Congress.

came president of San Francisco State College. In 1976 the people of California voted him into the United States Senate. He retired in 1983.

American Indians   The first people in California were the Indians, or Native Americans. More than 90,000 Indians still live in California today.

Indians have also known unfair treatment over the years. To draw attention to their call for equal treatment, one group of Indians took over Alcatraz (al' kə traz) Island in 1969. On this island in San Francisco Bay, there had once been a prison. The Indians stayed on Alcatraz Island from 1969 to 1970. They wanted the government to make the island into an Indian cultural center.

They did not get the center they asked for. But they did succeed in letting people know about some of their troubles in gaining equality. This led to a greater understanding of Indian problems.

Women Another group that wanted equal treatment was women. Women had not had the same rights as men. Now, just as other groups tried to get equal treatment, so did women.

Women were able to get laws passed that helped in getting equal treatment. They worked at jobs that had not been open to them before. They did work that only men had done before. Many women had the chance to get better jobs.

The story of one woman shows the gains that California women were making. Romana Acosta Bañuelos became a successful businesswoman in Los An-geles. She owned a plant that processed Mexican food. In 1969 she was chosen treasurer of the United States.

It was a great honor to be chosen for this post. But she was not the first woman to hold that job. During the 1950s another California woman was treasurer of the United States. She was Ivy Baker Priest. Later she became treasurer of California.

Other women have held important government posts in California. In 1974, March Fong Eu, a Chinese American, was elected secretary of state. Before that she had been in the state **legislature**. The legislature is the group that makes laws for the state. In 1978, Dianne Feinstein was the first woman elected mayor of San Francisco.

Looking ahead In the next chapter you will learn about California's state and local governments. You will also learn how California plays an important part in our national government.

A San Francisco fire fighter explains to Mayor Dianne Feinstein the steps being taken to halt a blaze.

CHECKUP

1. What problems did blacks face after coming to California?
2. How did Cesar Chavez try to improve life for Mexican Americans?
3. What was the goal of the Indians who seized Alcatraz Island? To what extent did they help their people?
4. In what ways have women made gains in recent years?

KEY FACTS

1. After World War II, industries boomed in California and many people moved there.

2. After World War II, Californians built many roads, schools, houses, shopping centers, and water projects needed by the growing population.

3. Much military equipment needed to fight the wars in Korea and Vietnam was produced in California.

4. In recent years various groups in California have demanded equal treatment with other Americans. Among these groups are blacks, Mexican Americans, Asian Americans, American Indians, and women.

5. In recent years, conditions have improved for these groups.

VOCABULARY QUIZ

Match the terms with their definitions. Use a separate sheet of paper.

a. satellite

b. mayor

c. union

d. legislature

e. strike

1. The chief officer of a city

2. When workers try to get what they want by staying away from their jobs

3. A kind of spacecraft that moves around the earth

4. The group that makes laws for the state

5. A group formed within an industry to help the group's members

REVIEW QUESTIONS

1. Why did California not have a depression after World War II?

2. What were the effects on our state when so many people moved to California after World War II?

3. What were some important new industries in California after the war?

4. How did the Korean and Vietnamese wars affect California?

5. What action did blacks take to get equal treatment?

6. What action did Mexican Americans take to get equal treatment?

7. What other groups have sought equal treatment? In what ways have they made progress?

ACTIVITIES

1. On a map of California, show all the cities of 100,000 or more in 1950. On another map, mark all the cities of 100,000 or more in 1980. You will need to use an almanac of California to do this.

2. On a map show the locations of Korea, Vietnam, and California. Color Korea red, Vietnam green, and California blue.

3. Imagine that someday your children ask you about what happened in California following World War II. What would you tell them? Write down what you would say in the form of a dialogue. (For writing a dialogue, use directions in the Skills Development exercise on the opposite page.)

WRITING A DIALOGUE

WHAT IS A DIALOGUE

Do you know what a dialogue is? It is when two or more people talk with each other. Dialogues can be written. When a dialogue is written, a new paragraph is begun for each speaker. The first word is indented. A speaker's words are enclosed in quotation marks.

The following dialogue is between Theresa, who lives on a farm near Modesto, California, and her cousin Laura from West Virginia. Laura's family is visiting Theresa's family during the summer. On a windy August day, Theresa and Laura come in the house after taking a walk. They have picked some grapes from the vines in the backyard.

A DIALOGUE

"These grapes are good," said Laura. "So sweet."

"They're Thompson seedless," said her cousin Theresa.

"It sure is hot out there today," Laura said. "I don't know how you can stand it."

"Oh, you get used to it," said Theresa. "It's only 100°F today. And it gets cooler in the winter."

"It was fun learning how raisins are made out of grapes," said Laura. "I didn't realize you just dried the grapes on paper laid down between the rows of grapevines."

"Do you like raisins in bread and cake, Laura?" asked Theresa.

SKILLS PRACTICE

Note where quotation marks are placed in this dialogue. Now, on a sheet of paper, copy the sentences below and place quotation marks in the right places.

Wasn't your aunt's party fun last night? asked Laura.

Not really, replied Theresa. I had to do a lot of work. You were lucky. You were a guest.

I liked it, but I wish we could have gone swimming in her pool. Don't you, Theresa?

Yes, that would have been a lot of fun, said Theresa.

Now write a dialogue of your own in which two people who live in California are talking. They are talking about certain things in the state. Before you start writing, read again the first paragraph in column 1. Follow the directions given in that paragraph.

You may want to start your dialogue with one of the sentences below.

a. "I really like living in California. It's a neat place," said Yasuko to her friend.

b. "My dad really has a terrific job," said Ron to his friend Steve.

c. "We're going to visit Los Angeles this summer," Dawn told her friend Kathleen. "You've been there before. What are the best things to see?"

4/UNIT REVIEW

1. The early 1900s in California have often been referred to as the "boom" years. — *Why can these years be called the "boom" years?*

2. Water and land are two of California's most important resources. — *Why are these resources so important? What does your region of California do today to help conserve land and water? Are there other resources in your part of the state that need to be protected?*

3. The boom of the 1920s ended with a depression in the 1930s. The depression hit California hard. — *What were some of the problems in California that were created by the depression?*

4. Franklin D. Roosevelt had some different ideas about the role of the United States government. — *What did President Roosevelt think the role of the United States government should be during the depression? How did the programs he introduced during the depression help California?*

5. In 1941 the United States went to war. California helped the United States to win World War II. — *How did California help the United States to win the war?*

6. The population of California is made up of people of varying ancestry. — *Name one minority group that was not always treated fairly in California. What problems did that group face? How has that group worked for equal treatment in the state?*

7. In 1941 about 7 million people lived in California. By 1980 more than 22 million people were living in California. — *What brought so many people to California? What kinds of problems were created by so many people moving to California? Does your part of the state still have any of these problems?*

8. Many different groups of people with different backgrounds and beliefs came to California. Each group helped the state to grow into what it is today. — *Cut out pictures from magazines and newspapers that show examples of many different Californians. Paste these pictures on a piece of posterboard and label it "Californians All."*

California: Today and Tomorrow

State Government

VOCABULARY
- state government
- local governments
- amendments

Kinds of governments   The government of California is the government of all the people in California. It is called our **state government**. People from all parts of California choose people to represent them in Sacramento, our state capital. A person must be at least 18 years old to vote in California.

The people also choose representatives to the county and the city governments. These governments are called **local governments**.

In this chapter you will study California's state and local governments. You will learn how these governments work. You will learn how they serve the people of California.

Our constitution   You may remember from Chapter 8 that a constitution is a set of laws by which a state or country is governed. We have a United States Constitution, and each of the 50 states has a constitution.

You also learned in Chapter 8 that California's first constitution was written in 1849. It gave California citizens a number of rights and freedoms.

In 1879 the constitution was rewritten. This second constitution was longer and more detailed than the first one. Over the years the constitution of 1879 became very long. Many additions were made. These additions are called **amendments**. By the 1960s hundreds of amendments had been added to the state constitution.

In 1963 a group of 60 citizens was picked to suggest changes in the state constitution. This group finished its work in 1972. The group had revised over half the constitution. This revised constitution is the basic law by which California is governed today.

Capital city   Sacramento became the capital city of California in 1854. Most of the state's official business takes place there. The most noticeable building in the city is the state capitol. Its copper dome can be seen from miles away.

California is proud of its restored capitol building in Sacramento.

244

Many visitors view the beautifully restored interior of the dome at the capitol.

The capitol was finished in 1874. It is in a large park. The park has lawns, plants, and many trees. Through the years, people worked to make the building up-to-date. This caused the inside and outside of the building to lose the look it had when it was first built.

A big challenge   In 1976 a plan was started to restore the capitol. *Restore* means "to put back in original condition." This plan was not easy to carry out. Over 2,000 workers were on the job. People used pictures and read books and newspapers to know how the capitol looked.

Each room was rebuilt to its original look. As much of the original material as possible was used in restoring the rooms. People had to try to find the things that had been removed from the original building.

A big job was the removal of the original roof of the dome on the capitol. The old roof was replaced with a new copper roof.

The project took 6 years and cost over $65 million. It was completed in 1982. A celebration was held for the reopening of the capitol.

CHECKUP

1. What kinds of governments make up the local government?
2. What is the purpose of California's constitution?
3. What happened to our state constitution in 1879?
4. What is the capital city of California?
5. What kind of project was begun on the capitol in 1976 and was completed in 1982?

Three Parts of the State Government

Branches of state government Our state government has three parts. One is the **legislative branch**. Another is the **executive branch**. The third is the **judicial branch**.

The legislative branch The laws of California are made by the legislative branch. This branch is divided into two parts.

One part of the legislative branch is the **Assembly**. It has 80 members. This is because the state is divided into 80 parts. Each part is almost equal in population. These parts are called districts. Each assembly district chooses a person to the Assembly. A member is chosen for a 2-year term. The Assembly Speaker runs the meetings of the Assembly. The Speaker is chosen by the members of the Assembly. The Assembly has a special room in the state capitol.

The other part of the legislative branch is the **Senate**. The Senate has 40 members called **senators**. Each senator represents a senatorial district. Each district is almost equal in population. A senator is elected for a 4-year term. The Senate also has a special room in the state capitol.

The members of both the Assembly and the Senate must approve a **bill**. A bill is a possible law. The bill can then be sent to the governor for a signature. If the governor signs the bill, it becomes a law. However, the governor may decide not to sign the bill. This is called

Can you name the two parts of the legislative branch of government?

BRANCHES OF STATE GOVERNMENT

Legislative Branch

Executive Branch
(Governor)

Judicial Branch

Assembly
(80 members)

Senate
(40 members)

Supreme Court
(Chief Justice)
(Six Associate Judges)

How a Bill Becomes a Law

1. A member of the Assembly or Senate writes a bill.

2. The Assembly and Senate approve the bill.

3. The governor signs the bill, and it becomes a law.

4. If the governor vetoes the bill, it goes back to the Assembly and Senate.

5. The Assembly and Senate vote again. If the bill gets ⅔ of the votes, it becomes a law.

a **veto**. If this happens, both the Assembly and the Senate must vote on the bill again. Each must pass the bill by a two-thirds vote for the bill to become a law.

The executive branch   The governor is the head of the executive branch of government. This part of government is in charge of carrying out the laws. The governor is chosen for a 4-year term.

The governor may sign or veto a bill. This person also appoints people to important jobs in the state government. The governor is the leader of the state.

The **lieutenant governor** takes over the governor's duties when the governor is not able to do the job. The lieutenant governor is the leader of the Senate.

The judicial branch   The branch of government that interprets, or explains, the laws is called the judicial branch.

As secretary of state, March Fong Eu keeps all the state's records.

This branch of government decides if a law has been broken.

The state **supreme court** is the highest court in the state. It is made up of a chief justice, or judge, and six associate justices. A justice is appointed by the governor and approved by the voters. A justice serves a term of 12 years.

Other state officers   There are a number of other officers in the state government. The attorney general is the chief legal advisor to the state. The secretary of state keeps all the state records and directs state elections. The controller controls and accounts for the state's income and spending. The state treasurer is the banker of the state's money. The superintendent of public instruction is the chief school officer of California.

The members of the California Assembly meet in this chamber hall.

Former Chief Justice Earl Warren and President Ronald Reagan were both former governors of California.

Federal officers from California
One President of the United States is a former governor of California. Ronald Reagan was governor from 1967 until 1975. Another governor of California, Earl Warren, became head of the United States Supreme Court. He was governor of California from 1943 until 1953.

Two other Presidents were from California. They are Herbert Hoover and Richard M. Nixon. Hoover was President of the United States from 1929 until 1933. Nixon was President of the United States from 1969 until 1974.

CHECKUP

1. Into how many parts is the legislative branch divided? Name the parts.
2. What happens when the governor signs a bill?
3. Why is the judicial branch of government important?

Local Government

——VOCABULARY——
county seat
county board of supervisors

Kinds of local government   Local governments were set up by the state to give services to the people. These public services include schools, roads, and police and fire protection. They also include public health service. Local governments affect our lives daily. County government and city government are the two basic kinds of local government.

County government   As you learned in Chapter 2, California is divided into 58 counties. Each Californian lives in a county.

The **county seat** is the town or city within the county that is the center of the county government. The county courthouse and office buildings are located in the county seat. Where is the county seat for your county? Is it the largest city in your county?

If you live in San Francisco, you have a special form of local government. San Francisco has a combined city and county government. Only a few places have this form of government.

The **county board of supervisors** is the law-making body for the county. This board is also in charge of carrying out the law.

Many public services are provided for the people by the county. Public records of marriages, births, and deaths and a local system of courts are provided by the county. It also provides for voter registration. Police service, fire service, and road upkeep are county services. Some counties run airports, parks, and libraries.

City government   Cities are located within counties. Over 90 percent of the people in California live in cities.

City governments are made to provide services. These services are in addition to county services. They include more police and fire protection. They also include parks, libraries, road repair, street lightning, and garbage collection.

California has two kinds of city governments. One is the mayor-council. The other is the council-manager.

Loretta Glickman, the mayor of Pasadena, is the first black woman to hold this position.

With a mayor-council, a mayor is elected by the voters of the city. The mayor's job is to run the city government. A council is elected by the people of the city. The council makes laws for the city. Los Angeles, San Francisco, and San Diego all have this kind of local government.

The most common kind of city government in California is the council-manager. It also has an elected city council. The council hires a city manager to run the city government. Often the city manager is a trained expert in how to run a city.

Fire protection is one of the many services provided by city governments.

CHECKUP

1. What is the purpose of local governments?
2. Where are the county courthouse and office buildings located?
3. What kinds of services are provided by city governments?

California and the National Government

National attention   California plays an important part in our national government. This is because it has so many people. In the United States House of Representatives, California has more representatives than any state. The number of representatives a state has is based on population. The larger the state's population, the more representatives it has. Based on the 1980 population, California has 45 representatives. Each one represents a part of the state called a **congressional district**.

In the United States Senate, California, like all states, has two senators. Each senator represents the whole state.

California is also very important to the election of our nation's President. California has more votes than any other state. People running for President spend a lot of time in California trying to win votes. As a result, much national attention is given to the state.

A state with many differences
California is a **diverse** state. That means it is made up of differences. The state has diverse geography, industry, and population. These differences make California a challenge to govern.

There are many special-interest groups in the state. Sometimes these groups try to get the government to act on their concerns. The concerns are many and they are changing. Some of them are listed below.

- Social justice
- Crime
- Welfare programs
- Water problems
- Dirty air
- Dirty water
- Crowded population
- Educational needs
- Energy crisis
- Taxes

Looking ahead   In the next chapter you will learn about some of the major cities in California. You will learn about their diversity, population, industry, history, recreation, tourist attractions, and much more.

CHECKUP

1. Why does California have a large number of representatives in the United States House of Representatives?
2. What are some things that make California a diverse state?
3. How is the government affected by special-interest groups?

252

California's State Seal

Have you ever seen the seal of the state of California? Look at the picture of the seal on page 159. The seal appears on all official documents.

The seal of the state of California has pictures that show important things about the state. It has 31 stars to show that California was the thirty-first state to join the United States. The word *Eureka* (yú rē′ kə) on the seal is a Greek word. It is the state motto and it means "I have found it." The mountains shown on the seal are the Sierra Nevada. They represent the beauty of the state. The ships stand for trading between California and other places.

A man shown digging in the ground stands for a gold miner. Look closely below this man. Do you see the drawing of some wheat? This shows that California produces many farm products. The bear reminds us of the time when California was called the Bear Flag Republic.

The woman dressed like a Roman warrior is Minerva (mə nėr′ və). She is from an old Roman legend. The Romans had many gods. They told stories about their gods. One story was that the king of the gods, Jupiter, had a headache one day. Suddenly, from his head jumped his daughter Minerva, full-grown. And his headache went away. Minerva reminds us that California suddenly became a state.

The Great Seal of the state of California appears on all official California documents.

KEY FACTS

1. California's first constitution was written in 1849 and was rewritten in 1879.

2. Sacramento became the capital city of California in 1854.

3. The government of California has three branches. They are the legislative branch, the executive branch, and the judicial branch.

4. The governor is chosen for a 4-year term.

5. The state supreme court is the highest court in the state.

6. County government and city government are two basic kinds of local government.

7. California plays an important part in our national government.

8. In the United States House of Representatives, California has more representatives than any other state.

VOCABULARY QUIZ

1. The government of all the people in California is called our (a) state government, (b) city government, (c) county government, (d) local government.

2. The branch of government that makes the laws of California is called the (a) legislative branch, (b) executive branch, (c) judicial branch, (d) associate branch.

3. The members of both the Assembly and the Senate must approve a (a) senator, (b) bill, (c) governor, (d) term.

4. The highest court in the state is called the (a) general court, (b) original court, (c) supreme court, (d) executive court.

5. The town or city within the county that is the center of the county government is called the (a) county police, (b) county board, (c) county part, (d) county seat.

REVIEW QUESTIONS

1. What is the basic law by which California is governed today?

2. What are the three branches, or parts, of the government of California?

3. If a bill is vetoed, what must then happen for the bill to become a law?

4. What are some of the public services provided by local governments?

5. In what way does California play an important part in our national government?

ACTIVITIES

1. Get a copy of the California constitution from your school library or the state office of publications. Find the part of the constitution that provides for the number of senators and the number of Assembly members.

2. Watch for articles in newspapers or news magazines about a concern or concerns of special-interest groups in California. Select an article to bring to class. Tell your classmates in your own words about the concern or concerns mentioned in the article.

13/SKILLS DEVELOPMENT

MAKING AN OUTLINE FOR A REPORT

THE PURPOSE OF AN OUTLINE

A good report requires organization. The purpose of an outline is to help you organize your ideas. An outline is your plan for writing. An outline may be written in question form. The answers to the questions will help you make your report.

Below is an outline for a report about a California political leader. Her name is March Fong Eu.

OUTLINE

The topic is March Fong Eu.

I. What is March Fong Eu's background?

II. What statewide political offices has March Fong Eu been elected to?

III. What are March Fong Eu's duties in her present position?

Now read this report written from the outline. Notice how the outline and the report are similar.

March Fong Eu is of Chinese-American ancestry. She was born in Oakdale, California. She is a graduate of the University of California. She also has a master's degree from Mills College and a doctor's degree in education from Stanford University. Dr. Eu was elected to three terms on the Alameda County School Board. She also served four terms in the California Assembly.

On November 6, 1974, March Fong Eu was elected secretary of state. She was the first person of Chinese-American ancestry to be elected to a statewide office in California.

As secretary of state, Dr. Eu keeps all the state's records. She manages the state's archives. This is where all the state's records are kept. She also works with county election officials to supervise elections. Another duty of the secretary of state is to represent California in foreign affairs.

SKILLS PRACTICE

In the exercise above, notice that the answers to the questions make up the paragraphs in the report. Now you can try to write an outline about one of these topics.

Lawmaking in California
Earl Warren: Governor of California, 1943–1953

Follow these steps.

1. Ask yourself, What do I want to know about my topic?

2. Write down what you want to know in question form. Number your questions with Roman numerals.

3. Look for books or other material that will help you answer the questions.

4. Under each question, write some information that will help you answer the question.

You now have an outline. From your outline you will be able to write a report on your topic.

14 California's Cities

The San Diego Urban Area

VOCABULARY
urban areas	endangered
stucco	species
ethnic	
aquarium	

Why people live in cities   Where do you live? Do you live in a large city or in one of its suburbs? Do you live in an apartment or in a house? Maybe you live on a ranch or a farm.

California has many different kinds of places where people live. But most Californians live in cities or in **urban areas**. An urban area is made up of a large city and its suburbs. California is the most urban state in the nation. Over 90 percent of Californians live in or near a city.

Can you think of reasons why people live in cities? If you said there are many jobs in cities, you are right. But there are other reasons, too. In cities there are many things to do. You can visit museums, tall buildings, parks, and zoos. You can watch professional sports. You can see plays and hear concerts. You are close to shopping and schools.

According to the 1980 census, there are 323 cities in California that have 5,000 or more people. Many of California's cities are among the largest in the country.

A trip through California's cities
A car trip through some of California's cities would be interesting. Starting in the south, the first great city we will visit is San Diego.

The beautiful city of San Diego   San Diego is a great seaport. It has beautiful beaches. It has a world-famous zoo, and many museums. There are golf courses, boating areas, and other places for recreation in the city.

San Diego is in southern California. It is close to the Mexican border. It was founded in 1769 by Spanish soldiers as a presidio, or fort. Father Junipero Serra started the first California mission there the same year. Today San Diego is among the 20 fastest-growing cities in the nation. It is the second most populated city in California. San Diego is also the eighth most populated city in the United States.

The city of San Diego has one of the world's finest natural harbors.

The city of San Diego is located on San Diego Bay. It has one of the world's finest harbors. Tuna boats use this harbor. Fishing is an important business in San Diego.

Along San Diego Bay there are many large navy ships in the harbor. San Diego has one of the largest United States naval bases on the Pacific coast.

Industries   All along the bay and around the edges of the city are airplane factories. San Diego has had important aerospace industries since the late 1920s. These factories make all kinds of airplanes, and spacecraft.

Electronics is another growing industry in the San Diego area. There are over 1,000 manufacturing plants. Different kinds of computers and other electrical machinery are made in many of them.

Strong Spanish-Mexican influence
Spanish-Mexican influence is everywhere in San Diego. You can see it in the city's buildings. Many houses and businesses have red tile roofs and white **stucco** walls. Stucco walls are made of a mixture of cement, sand, and lime. You see Spanish-Mexican influence in the bright paintings and decorations on walls and buildings. You find it in the many good restaurants that serve Spanish and Mexican food.

Many boats like the *Sea Quest above* fish for tuna off California's Pacific coast.

About 15 percent of San Diego's population is Mexican American. Like most of California's large cities, San Diego has many other **ethnic** groups. An ethnic group is made up of people who share many common traits and customs. San Diego has a large black community. About 10 percent of the population is black. Asian Americans make up nearly 7 percent of the population. San Diego also has large neighborhoods of Americans whose ancestors were from Portugal, Italy, and Germany.

Culture and recreation   There are many places in San Diego to have fun and learn things. San Diego has over 100 parks. The two largest are Balboa Park and Mission Bay Park. Balboa Park is the home of San Diego's famous zoo. The zoo is one of the largest in the world. It has over 5,000 animals.

Mission Bay Park on San Diego's Pacific coast is San Diego's main recreation area. The park has fine beaches and sailboats and the world's largest **aquarium**, Sea World. Do you know what an aquarium is? It is a place where plants and animals that live in the sea are kept for people to see. Turn to page 37 to see the map of Sea World.

San Diego has many museums. In Balboa Park there are museums of fine art, aerospace, and natural history. There is even a Hall of Champions. It honors San Diego athletes. Another museum has exhibits on American Indians.

San Diego's Wild Animal Park

Almost every tourist in San Diego visits its world-famous zoo. Another place to

Flamingos in San Diego's zoo are much photographed.

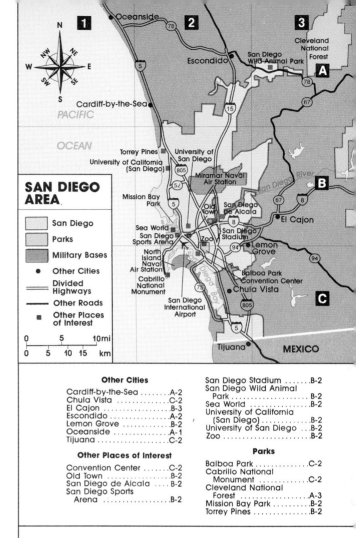

SAN DIEGO AREA

	San Diego
	Parks
	Military Bases
●	Other Cities
══	Divided Highways
—	Other Roads
■	Other Places of Interest

0   5   10mi
0 5 10 15 km

Other Cities

Cardiff-by-the-Sea	A-2
Chula Vista	C-2
El Cajon	B-3
Escondido	A-2
Lemon Grove	B-2
Oceanside	A-1
Tijuana	C-2

Other Places of Interest

Convention Center	C-2
Old Town	B-2
San Diego de Alcala	B-2
San Diego Sports Arena	B-2

San Diego Stadium	B-2
San Diego Wild Animal Park	B-2
Sea World	B-2
University of California (San Diego)	B-2
University of San Diego	B-2
Zoo	B-2

Parks

Balboa Park	C-2
Cabrillo National Monument	C-2
Cleveland National Forest	A-3
Mission Bay Park	B-2
Torrey Pines	B-2

Use the key to find Balboa Park on the map. Can you locate Sea World on the map?

Zoological Society of San Diego

visit is the San Diego Wild Animal Park. It opened in 1972 and covers 1,300 acres (92,000 ha). It is about 30 miles (48 km) north of the business district.

Many kinds of wild animals roam free among plants and trees like those found in their native lands. There are places in the park for Asian and African animals. Visitors ride a train through the different parts of the park. Guides talk about the animals that can be seen.

The Wild Animal Park provides more than entertainment. Important work is done here to help save **endangered species**. Animals that are becoming scarce out in the wild are called endangered species.

San Diego's sports teams   If you like to see sports events, San Diego has three professional teams. The San Diego Chargers play in the National Football League. The San Diego Padres play in baseball's National League. And the San Diego Clippers play in the National Basketball Association.

Each year there are water-skiing championships on San Diego and Mission bays. Hang-gliding events are held in Torrey Pines in the northern part of the city. The San Diego golf tournament is one of the most famous in the United States.

With its fine year-round climate and many attractions, San Diego continues to draw people. Over 2 million tourists visit San Diego each year. And thousands of people have retired there because of the fine weather.

CHECKUP

1. Why do many people live in cities?
2. What is San Diego's rank among the cities of California?
3. Name some important industries in San Diego.
4. Why does San Diego attract so many visitors each year?

The Los Angeles Urban Area

VOCABULARY

| freeways | planetarium |
| commute | |

California's fastest growing cities Driving north along California's coast we enter Orange County. We are likely to see many new houses being built. Orange County is the home of some of California's fastest-growing cities. The city of Anaheim is about 90 miles (145 km) northwest of San Diego. Anaheim is also about 15 miles (25 km) from the Pacific Ocean.

Anaheim has many airplane, automobile, and electronics factories. Millions of people come to Anaheim every year to visit Disneyland. The city is also home to two professional sports teams. The California Angels are an American League baseball team. The Los Angeles Rams are in the National Football League. Both teams play their games in Anaheim Stadium.

Los Angeles   On the Pacific coast, about 30 miles (50 km) northwest of Anaheim, we come to Los Angeles. It is the most populated city in California. It is the third most populated city in the country. About 3 million people live in Los Angeles. Another 4.5 million people live around the city.

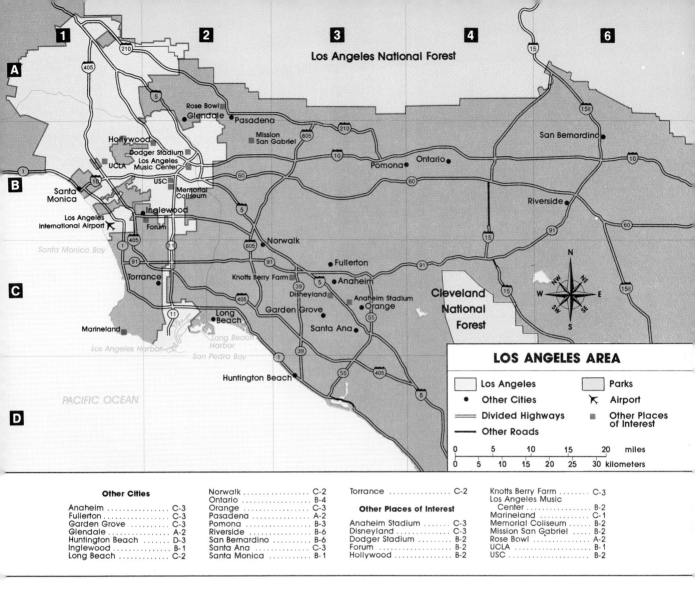

Map legend:

LOS ANGELES AREA

▢	Los Angeles	▢	Parks
●	Other Cities	✈	Airport
═══	Divided Highways	■	Other Places of Interest
───	Other Roads		

0   5   10   15   20   miles
0   5   10   15   20   25   30   kilometers

Other Cities

		Norwalk	C-2	
		Ontario	B-4	
Anaheim	C-3	Orange	C-3	
Fullerton	C-3	Pasadena	A-2	
Garden Grove	C-3	Pomona	B-3	
Glendale	A-2	Riverside	B-6	
Huntington Beach	D-3	San Bernardino	B-6	
Inglewood	B-1	Santa Ana	C-3	
Long Beach	C-2	Santa Monica	B-1	

Torrance	C-2

Other Places of Interest

Anaheim Stadium	C-3
Disneyland	C-3
Dodger Stadium	B-2
Forum	B-2
Hollywood	B-2

Knotts Berry Farm	C-3
Los Angeles Music Center	B-2
Marineland	C-1
Memorial Coliseum	B-2
Mission San Gabriel	B-2
Rose Bowl	A-2
UCLA	B-1
USC	B-2

Can you locate the Los Angeles International Airport on the map above? How is it pictured?

Los Angeles covers a very large area. It has 465 square miles (1,204 sq km). The city reaches from the Pacific Ocean to the San Gabriel Mountains, 30 miles (48 km) to the northeast. It has over 50 miles (81 km) of shoreline.

Los Angeles started as a small pueblo. It was founded in 1781 about 30 miles (48 km) from the Mission San Gabriel. You can still visit San Gabriel and the restored pueblo.

In 1850, the same year California became a state, Los Angeles became a city. When the railroad reached the city in 1876, the population of Los Angeles began to grow.

261

A Visit to Olvera Street

To the northeast of the Los Angeles Civic Center is the restored Pueblo de Los Angeles, the Spanish town that was founded in 1781. Running north from the Pueblo plaza is Olvera Street. This brick-paved, colorful street brings back the original Spanish-Mexican feeling of early Los Angeles.

The rebuilding of Olvera Street began in 1929 and was finished the next year. In those days, however, the street did not have all the outdoor stalls and visitors it has today.

At the entrance to Olvera Street is a carved wooden cross that marks the founding of Los Angeles. A visit to the street is much like a visit to a Mexican town. Shops on both sides of the street sell serapes, or wool blankets worn as cloaks, food, furniture, and baskets. Down the middle of the street, which is closed to cars, are stalls offering bargains in Mexican pottery and silver jewelry.

At night Olvera Street seems even more full of life and color. Music comes from the restaurants and in the street. Colored lights sparkle.

Festivals and holidays are especially exciting times on Olvera Street. At Christmastime the ceremony of *Los Posadas* takes place. *Los Posadas* means "the lodgings" in Spanish. Each evening for 8 days, players reenact the journey of Mary and Joseph to Bethlehem for the birth of their son Jesus. Another holiday celebration is the traditional blessing of animals that takes place in the spring.

Olvera Street's shops and outdoor stands draw many visitors.

A trade and industrial center Los Angeles is an important business and trade center. It has many aerospace factories and electronics businesses. Los Angeles is the home of some motion picture companies and many television production companies. People like to visit these studios to see how movies and TV shows are made. Driving through the city, you can see oil wells pumping. Oil and gas fields are found in the city and in the nearby countryside.

Los Angeles has the busiest and most important port on the Pacific coast. Its harbor handles much of our country's trade with Australia, Japan, and Southeast Asia. The port of Los Angeles is also the home of a large fishing fleet.

Los Angeles freeways The Los Angeles urban area spreads in all directions. Only the New York urban area has more people, jobs, businesses, and industries. Linking Los Angeles and the nearby towns and cities is a large system of **freeways**. Freeways are express highways with limited entrances and exits. Many people in Los Angeles **commute** on the freeways to and from work in private cars. *Commute* means "to travel back and forth regularly."

Los Angeles attractions There are miles of beautiful beaches in and around Los Angeles. You can visit museums as

A network of freeways links the Los Angeles urban area.

well as amusement parks. Griffith Park, in the center of the city, has a zoo. It also has a **planetarium**. This is a building that has a cameralike machine that shows how the planets and the stars look in the sky.

In the heart of the downtown area is the Los Angeles Civic Center. It includes a 32-story city hall that is a city landmark. Nearby is the Los Angeles Music Center for the Performing Arts. It is one of the finest in the nation.

There are many colleges and universities in Los Angeles. Two of the largest are the University of California at Los Angeles (UCLA), and the University of Southern California (USC).

Sports events In the fall in Los Angeles you can see the college football games of the USC Trojans and the UCLA Bruins. There are also many professional sports teams in Los Angeles. The

Dodgers play baseball at Dodger Stadium north of the downtown area. The Lakers of the National Basketball Association play their games in nearby Inglewood, a suburb of Los Angeles. The Kings of the National Hockey League also play in Inglewood. The newest professional team in Los Angeles is the Raiders (formerly the Oakland Raiders).

Flowers and plants make up Tournament of Roses floats.

The people of Los Angeles Los Angeles has many ethnic groups. Over 815,000 Mexican Americans live there. That is 28 percent of the city's people. There are large groups of people whose ancestors came from Japan, China, and the Philippine Islands. People from many countries live in Los Angeles.

The black community in Los Angeles grew rapidly during World War II. Black workers came to work in the airplane and shipbuilding factories. Today over 500,000 blacks live there. They form about 17 percent of the population of the city of Los Angeles.

Long Beach, Pasadena, San Bernardino Just to the south of Los Angeles is the city of Long Beach. Long Beach has a large oil industry. It also has shipbuilding and aerospace companies. The harbor at Long Beach is the third busiest in the United States.

About 10 miles (16 km) northeast of Los Angeles is the city of Pasadena. It is the home of the Rose Bowl stadium. Two leading college football teams play there every New Year's Day. On that day Pasadena also has a parade called the Tournament of Roses. It has beautiful floats made of flowers and plants.

The city of San Bernardino is located at the foot of the San Bernardino Mountains. It is about 60 miles (95 km) east of Los Angeles. It is the center of a large mining and farming area. San Bernardino has many manufacturing plants, including steel mills. Resorts in the mountains attract skiers in the winter and hikers in the summer.

CHECKUP

1. Why do many people visit Anaheim each year?
2. Name three important industries of Los Angeles.
3. Why are the Los Angeles freeways important?
4. Name four ethnic groups in Los Angeles.

The Cities of the Central Valley

Bakersfield   North of Los Angeles we enter California's Central Valley. About 80 miles (130 km) from Los Angeles we come to Bakersfield. The population of the city of Bakersfield is more than 100,000.

Acres of farmland surround Bakersfield. Grapes, cotton, and citrus fruits are the main crops. You also see many oil wells. The discovery of oil in 1899 opened the way for Bakersfield's development.

Fresno   About 180 miles (290 km) north of Los Angeles is the city of Fresno. The name *Fresno* is the Spanish word for "ash tree." The city has a population of about 220,000. Fresno is the center of one of the fastest-growing urban areas in California. The city of Fresno is in the valley of the San Joaquin River. Fresno County has the highest production of farm products in the United States. The city of Fresno is often called the raisin capital of the world. About 60 percent of the United States raisin crop is grown there.

Fresno has many **food-processing** plants. Food processing is the preparation of farm products, such as fruits and vegetables, for the marketplace. It includes the freezing, canning, and packaging of foods. A food-processing factory is sometimes called a **cannery.**

Modesto-Stockton   Leaving Fresno, we drive northwest through the northern part of the San Joaquin Valley. About 110 miles (175 km) from Fresno we come to the cities of Modesto and Stockton. Modesto has a population of about 100,000. Stockton's population is about 150,000. The two cities are the center of a growing urban area.

Stockton was founded in 1848, and Modesto in 1870. Stockton was one of the first settlements in the San Joaquin Valley.

Raisins drying in the sun are a common sight in the vineyards around the city of Fresno.

Stockton's industry grew with the arrival of Benjamin Holt. He set up a tractor manufacturing company with his brother in 1883. Today, industry in the Modesto-Stockton area is centered on farm products. But lumber, paper goods, and machinery are also produced.

What may surprise you are the large ships docked at Stockton's waterfront. A deepwater channel, dug in 1933, connects Stockton with San Francisco. Stockton is an inland seaport. Freighters take fruit crops, coal, and grain down the channel to San Francisco Bay. They return with materials and parts for Stockton's factories.

Stockton is the home of the University of the Pacific. It has 6,000 students. The Holt Atherton Library in Stockton has one of the finest collections of California history in the state.

Sacramento   Our state capital, Sacramento, is in the Central Valley. It is about 150 miles (240 km) north of Fresno. It is located at a point where the Sacramento and American rivers meet. The Sacramento River is the largest waterway in California. It drains all the northern part of the Central Valley.

Sacramento has a population of about 275,000. It has been the state capital since 1854. The city was founded in 1849 by the son of John Sutter. John Sutter was the Swiss pioneer who built Sutter's Fort.

Old steam engines and cars make Sacramento's Railroad Museum a wonderful place to visit.

The oldest part of the city is on the east bank of the Sacramento River. It has been restored to look the way it did in the 1860s. There are wooden sidewalks and brick streets. The Railroad Museum in Sacramento has one of the best railroad collections in the nation.

With the discovery of gold at Sutter's sawmill in 1848, Sacramento became a mining center and a boom town. In 1860 it became the last stop of the Pony Express. By 1869 Sacramento had become the western end of the first cross-country railroad in the United States.

The city today   Along the Sacramento River in the city are large ships. Since 1963 a deepwater channel has linked the city with San Francisco Bay. There are many interesting places to see in Sacramento. As you know, the beautiful state capitol has been restored to look much like it did in the early 1900s. In Sutter's Fort State Historical Park, you can visit a rebuilt Sutter's Fort. On weekends the fort comes alive with people reenacting the days of the 1840s.

The main work of Sacramento is government. Industries include food-processing companies and factories that make rocket engines. The country's largest almond factory is also there.

At the end of August or the first part of September, the state fair is held in

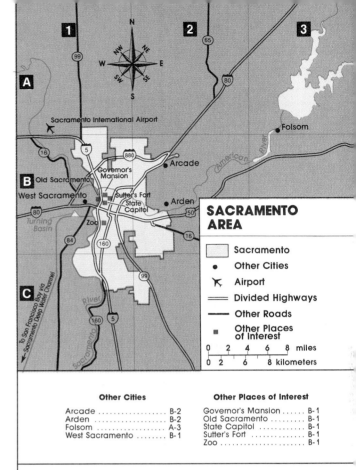

SACRAMENTO AREA

▢	Sacramento
•	Other Cities
✕	Airport
═	Divided Highways
──	Other Roads
■	Other Places of Interest

0   2   4   6   8 miles
0   2   6   8 kilometers

Other Cities		Other Places of Interest	
Arcade	B-2	Governor's Mansion	B-1
Arden	B-2	Old Sacramento	B-1
Folsom	A-3	State Capitol	B-1
West Sacramento	B-1	Sutter's Fort	B-1
		Zoo	B-1

Sacramento is located where the American and Sacramento rivers meet. Find the capitol building on the map.

Young people play basketball in the National Basketball Tournament at the Sacramento State Fair.

Sacramento. The amusement park at the fairgrounds is open all year.

Sacramento puts us in touch with both the old and the new. Much of California's history began in this city. And the city continues to make history as the state capital.

CHECKUP

1. Why is the city of Fresno an important agricultural center?
2. Why is Stockton called an inland seaport?
3. What are some of the attractions that bring tourists to Sacramento?

The Cities Around San Francisco Bay

—VOCABULARY—
greenbelts

The San Francisco Bay area Driving from Sacramento to San Francisco, we cross the hills that separate the Central Valley from the San Francisco Bay area. At the top of the hills, you can look down on the bay. It is one of the most beautiful sights in the world. All along its shores are cities and towns. At night these places become groups of twinkling lights.

The San Francisco Bay region has many people. Its three most populated cities are San Francisco, Oakland, and San Jose.

San Francisco The city of San Francisco lies on a narrow peninsula between the Pacific Ocean and San Francisco Bay. There are three routes into San Francisco. From the east you cross the bay on the Oakland–San Francisco Bay Bridge. This bridge opened in 1936. It is about 8 miles (13 km) long.

Coming from the north through Marin County, you cross the Golden Gate Bridge, which opened in 1937. It is one of the most beautiful bridges in the world. Its roadway is 250 feet (75 m) above the water. And its twin towers reach 750 feet (225 m) into the sky. Coming from the south you drive through Santa Clara and San Mateo counties.

San Francisco is a city of hills. Some hills are small and easy to climb. Many others are steep. One of the most famous hilly streets is Lombard Street. For one block this brick-paved street zigzags down a hill. It is called the crookedest street in the world.

A cable-car system was started in 1873 to move people up and down San Francisco's hills. Over the years no visit to San Francisco was complete without a cable-car ride. In 1982 the system was shut down for rebuilding. After the overhauling, the cable cars are sure to be popular again.

Bay, ocean, and hills make San Francisco a beautiful place. Here a trolley climbs one of the many hills.

Bushes and flowers border both sides of Lombard Street.

San Francisco is one of the most interesting cities in the United States. People from almost every country in the world have come to live in San Francisco. This mix of people has made the city a very exciting place in which to live.

History of the city   San Francisco was first settled by the Spanish in 1776. In that year a mission was founded there. It was called *Mision San Francisco de Asís*. It was named for St. Francis of Assisi. Later the mission came to be known as the Mission Dolores. The small Spanish settlement was first called *Yerba Buena*. In Spanish this means "good herb" or "good grass." The name was changed to San Francisco in 1877.

During World War II the city became one of the largest shipbuilding centers in the world. Today when we visit many docks along the waterfront, we see gift shops and tourist areas. San Francisco is still a busy port. But much shipping has moved to the city of Oakland, across San Francisco Bay.

Chinatown   One of San Francisco's most popular places is Chinatown. It has one of the largest Chinese communities outside of Asia. Thousands of Chinese Americans live and work in this part of the city.

Many Chinese Americans have moved from Chinatown to the suburbs of San Francisco. They live and work in different ways than their parents and grandparents did. Yet they are still proud of their rich Chinese heritage.

Many of Chinatown's buildings have roofs that curve up.

A tourist and business center San Francisco is an important banking center. It is the home of the world's largest bank, the Bank of America. Over 1,500 factories produce a wide variety of goods in San Francisco. There are clothing, food-processing, and publishing companies. Metal products are also made.

Over 2 million tourists come to San Francisco each year. The city has many fine museums. One of the most beautiful is the Palace of Fine Arts. You read about it in Chapter 10.

San Francisco has many parks and playgrounds. One of the largest and most famous is Golden Gate Park. Visitors can see a Japanese tea garden, the San Francisco Academy of Sciences, and an art museum.

This pagoda is in Golden Gate Park.

Willie Mays bats for the San Francisco Giants.

More than 100 festivals are held in San Francisco each year. Many of these festivals are in honor of one of the many ethnic groups in the city. One of the most famous is the Chinese New Year celebration in late January or in the early part of February.

Two professional sports teams, the San Francisco 49ers and the San Francisco Giants, play in Candlestick Park stadium. The 49ers won football's Super Bowl in 1982. For many years Willie Mays, a popular sports hero, played for the Giants, a National League baseball team.

There are other places in San Francisco that tourists want to see. Alcatraz was a federal prison. It was on an island in the bay. Two other popular places to visit are the Golden Gate National Recreation Area and the Muir Woods National Monument, a forest of giant redwoods north of San Francisco.

Oakland   Just across the bay from San Francisco is the city of Oakland. It has a busy harbor. Goods from all over the world are handled here.

The Oakland area was settled by the Spanish in the 1770s. Most of Oakland was once part of a huge ranch. It was called the Rancho San Antonio. Oakland became a city in 1850. Lake Merritt, in the heart of downtown Oakland, is a large natural saltwater lake.

After the 1906 earthquake, many people from San Francisco came to Oakland. The city began to grow during World War II. Today it is an important and busy city. Two large shipbuilding industries are here.

Most goods shipped into and out of Oakland's port travel in very large boxes called containers.

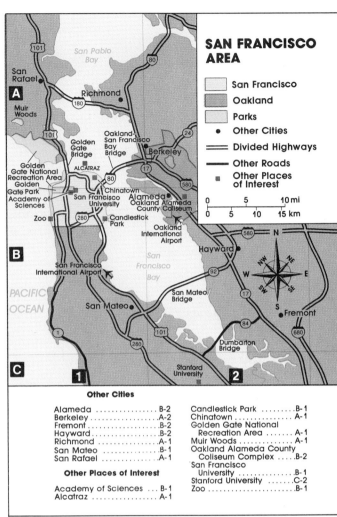

SAN FRANCISCO AREA

	San Francisco
	Oakland
	Parks
•	Other Cities
=	Divided Highways
—	Other Roads
▪	Other Places of Interest

0   5   10 mi
0   5   10   15 km

Other Cities

Alameda	B-2	Candlestick Park	B-1
Berkeley	A-2	Chinatown	A-1
Fremont	B-2	Golden Gate National	
Hayward	B-2	Recreation Area	A-1
Richmond	A-1	Muir Woods	A-1
San Mateo	B-1	Oakland Alameda County	
San Rafael	A-1	Coliseum Complex	B-2
		San Francisco	
Other Places of Interest		University	B-1
		Stanford University	C-2
Academy of Sciences	B-1	Zoo	B-1
Alcatraz	A-1		

The Oakland-San Francisco Bay Bridge links San Francisco and Oakland.

Sports   Oakland has become known for its professional sports teams. The Oakland A's won baseball's World Series three straight years in the 1970s. The Oakland Raiders (now the Los Angeles Raiders), a football team, also won two Super Bowl championships. The Golden State Warriors basketball team also plays in Oakland.

271

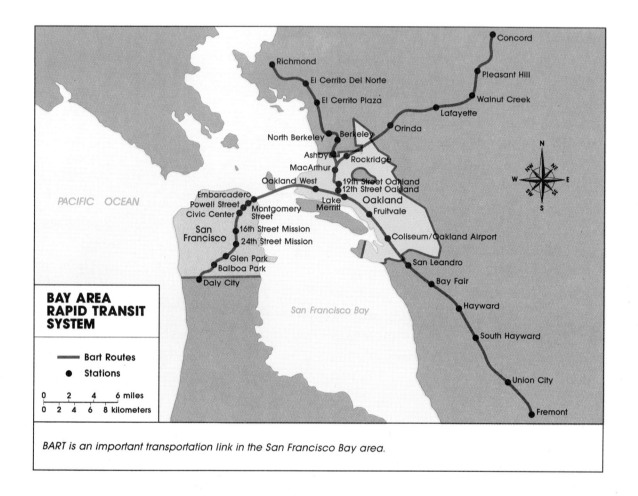

BART is an important transportation link in the San Francisco Bay area.

BART   The Bay Area Rapid Transit (BART) system connects Oakland, San Francisco, and many of their suburbs. This modern electric rail system was opened in 1972. BART travelers can ride through a tunnel under the bay to San Francisco. They can ride to Concord in Contra Costa County to the east, or north to Richmond. BART has 71 miles (114 km) of track. Someday this transportation system will link all the cities around San Francisco Bay.

Berkeley   No visit to the East Bay area would be complete without a visit to the city of Berkeley and the University of California there. Like Oakland, Berkeley was also a part of the Rancho San Antonio.

The University of California at Berkeley is the main branch of the state university. The university is located to the east of the city. It is in the hills overlooking San Francisco Bay and the Golden Gate Bridge.

Around Berkeley, Oakland, and the other East Bay cities are **greenbelts**. A greenbelt is a large area of open land on the edge of cities. Greenbelts are used for parkland and hiking trails. In the 1920s, people decided to preserve some land in the eastern hills around San Francisco Bay. This has become the East Bay Regional Park District.

San Jose   In the southern part of the San Francisco Bay area is the city of San Jose. It is about 50 miles (80 km) south of San Francisco. It is the fourth most populated city in California. About 636,000 people live in San Jose.

San Jose was founded by the Spanish in 1777. It was the first state capital of California. The first state legislature met there. California's first public college, San Jose State University, was founded there in 1871.

Today San Jose is one of the fastest growing cities in the United States. It is a major industrial center. It has important electronics and aerospace companies.

Tour's end   Our journey through some of California's largest cities is finished. There are many other cities and towns in the state that are well worth visiting and knowing. As we said at the beginning of the chapter, California is a land of cities.

Many of California's cities have grown at a fast rate. Some have become very large. This growth has created problems. In many cities there are not enough houses for the number of people. Sometimes there are slums. In some urban areas transportation systems are not large enough to move people quickly. The building of freeways has cut up other cities and separated people from one another.

Industry has caused problems of air pollution in many California cities. Smog often fills the air over San Francisco and Los Angeles. Smog is now found in some of the cities of the Central Valley.

Californians are working on all these problems. And they have begun to find answers to many of them.

Looking ahead   In the next chapter you will read about some of the ways in which California is a leader among the states. You will learn, too about some of the problems that California is trying to solve.

CHECKUP

1. What bridge would you cross if you entered San Francisco from the east?
2. How is BART important to the San Francisco Bay area?
3. Where is San Jose located?
4. What are three problems that California cities face?

14/CHAPTER REVIEW

KEY FACTS

1. More people in California live in or near cities than in any other state.
2. San Diego has a number of electronics industries and a large naval base.
3. Orange County, California, has some of the state's fastest-growing cities.
4. Los Angeles is an important business, financial, and trade center.
5. Fresno has many food-processing plants.
6. With its ethnic groups and beautiful location, San Francisco is one of the most exciting cities in the world.

VOCABULARY QUIZ

Fill in each blank with the word or words that best completes the sentence.

1. A large city and its suburbs make up an _____.
2. With their red tile roofs and _____ walls, many of San Diego's houses show Spanish-Mexican influence.
3. People who share many common traits and customs are said to make up an _____ group.
4. An _____ is a place where plants and animals that live in the sea are kept for people to see.
5. Express highways with limited entrances and exits are called _____.
6. To _____ means to travel back and forth regularly.
7. Freezing, canning, and packaging farm products is called _____.

8. A _____ is a large area of open land used for parks on the edge of a city.

REVIEW QUESTIONS

1. Give some reasons why San Diego has become California's second most populated city.
2. Why are many canneries found in the city of Fresno?
3. Name the three largest cities in the San Francisco Bay area.
4. What are some of the problems faced by California's cities?

ACTIVITIES

1. Find out about the city or town in which you live. If you do not live in a city or town, find out about one near you. Write a brief report about your city or town. Your report should (1) locate your city or town on a map of California, (2) list the cities and other landmarks around it, and (3) briefly tell some important things about your city or town.

2. If you could design a city, what would it be like? Pretend that you have been asked to design a city. Your plan or map should include the following: (1) a business center, (2) a transportation system, (3) freeways, (4) parks and greenbelts, (5) neighborhoods of houses, (6) schools, and (7) sports stadiums and museums. Draw your city plans on a big piece of paper.

READING A SCHEDULE

HOW TO READ A SCHEDULE

When you want to take a train, bus, or plane, it is helpful to know how to read a schedule. On this page is a simplified BART schedule. It tells you how long it takes—in minutes—to go between 15 stops on the BART system.

Suppose you want to find out how long it will take you to go from Berkeley to Fremont. Find Berkeley on the left side of the chart. Put a finger on Berkeley. Now find Fremont on the bottom of the chart. Put a finger of your other hand on Fremont. Move both fingers, one across and the other up, until they meet. They should meet at 50 minutes. That is the time it takes to go from Berkeley to Fremont on the Bay Area Rapid Transit system.

SKILLS PRACTICE

1. How long would it take you to travel from Berkeley to Coliseum?
2. How long would it take you to travel from Berkeley to Hayward?
3. How long would it take you to travel from Concord to Richmond?

BART TIME SCHEDULE (In Minutes)

	Daly City	24th St. Mission	Civic Center	Embarcadero	Oakland West	Concord	Walnut Creek	Richmond	El Cerrito Plaza	Berkeley	19th St. Oakland	Lake Merritt	Coliseum	Hayward	Fremont
Daly City		10	15	21	28	68	58	59	48	45	34	33	42	55	69
24th St. Mission	10		5	11	18	57	48	48	41	34	24	23	31	44	59
Civic Center	15	5		6	13	53	43	43	36	29	19	18	27	40	54
Embarcadero	21	11	6		8	47	38	38	30	24	14	13	21	34	49
Oakland West	28	18	13	8		40	30	30	23	16	7	5	14	27	41
Concord	68	57	53	47	40		10	51	44	37	34	39	47	59	74
Walnut Creek	58	48	43	38	30	10		42	35	28	25	30	38	50	65
Richmond	59	48	43	38	30	51	42		8	15	25	30	37	50	64
El Cerrito Plaza	48	41	36	30	23	44	35	8		7	17	22	30	42	57
Berkeley	45	34	29	24	16	37	28	15	7		11	16	23	36	50
19th St. Oakland	34	24	19	14	7	34	25	25	17	11		6	13	26	40
Lake Merritt	33	23	18	13	5	39	30	30	22	16	6		8	21	35
Coliseum	42	31	27	21	14	47	38	37	30	23	13	8		13	27
Hayward	55	44	40	34	27	59	50	50	42	36	26	21	13		15
Fremont	69	59	54	49	41	74	65	64	57	50	40	35	27	15	

15 California: A Leader Among the States

A Growing Giant

```
┌─VOCABULARY────────────────────┐
│  manufacture      foreign trade │
│  silicon          exports       │
│  commerce         imports       │
│  consumer         minerals      │
│  retail trade                   │
└─────────────────────────────────┘
```

Past, present, and future   In this book you have learned how California has grown and changed. Today it is a state made up of homes, farms, and factories. About 24 million people live in California. More people live in California today than in any other state.

Manufacturing   To **manufacture** is to make something by hand or by machine. California leads the 50 states in manufacturing. It makes more goods than most countries of the world. In fact, if California were a country, it would be the seventh among all countries in the world in the worth of its manufactured goods!

California leads all the rest of the states in making machines and electronic equipment. It is also the leader in the American aerospace industry.

California is a world leader in making computers. A great deal of this work is done in Santa Clara County. This area is known as Silicon Valley. The material **silicon** is something formed in nature and used in making computers.

Farming   As you know, California is the leading farming state. You may want to review the graphs on pages 304–305.

California produces almost all the almonds, apricots, avocados (av′ ə kä′ dōz), broccoli (brok′ ə lē), dates, figs, nectarines, olives, safflower, and walnuts grown in the United States. It is first among the states in raising grapes, lettuce, strawberries, peaches, tomatoes, carrots, lemons, melons, and many other crops. Grapes are the crop that brings the most money into California. No other state produces so many different farm products.

Commerce   The buying and selling and shipping of goods is known as **commerce**. When a business sells a product to a **consumer**, or user, it is called **retail trade**. Californians spend billion's of dollars on retail trade.

Factories making parts for electronic games, calculators, and computers line the streets in Silicon Valley.

California is also the leading state in **foreign trade**. This is buying products from other countries and selling them products. California's leading trade partner is Japan.

Products sold to other countries are called **exports**. Among the important exports of California are aerospace and electronics equipment, food products, and machines. Selling these products to foreign countries brings money into California. It also provides jobs.

Products bought from foreign countries are called **imports**. Among the important imports for California are oil, automobiles, motorcycles, and bicycles.

This ship at a dock in Sacramento is ready to load a cargo of rice to be exported from California.

Transportation   For a state to carry on trade, it must be able to move goods and people from place to place. Our state has more cars and trucks than any other state.

In 1941 the Pasadena Freeway was opened. It was the first high-speed highway in California. Today the state has more than 5,400 miles (8,688 km) of high-speed highway.

There is much airplane travel in California. Some of the busiest airports in the United States are in California. More than 13 million people board planes each year at Los Angeles International Airport.

Mines and forests   California is third among the states in producing **minerals**. Minerals are natural resources found in the earth. The most important mining product is oil. More than 40 different minerals are mined in the Sierra Nevada.

California has more forests than any state except Alaska. Look at the graph on page 305. How does California rank in lumber production?

CHECKUP

1. What are some of the products that make California a leader in manufacturing?
2. In what crops is California a leader?
3. What are exports and imports?
4. How do transportation, mining, and forestry make California stronger?

Setting the Pace

─VOCABULARY─
| economic | trend |

A leader in many other ways   From what you have read in this chapter, you can see the **economic** importance of California. *Economic* means "having to do with the production and selling of goods and services." California is an economic leader in the United States and in the world.

The tourist industry   Every year millions of people come to California. They come from other states. They also come from countries all over the world. They spend money for meals, places to stay, and sightseeing. Taking care of visitors makes jobs. Name some jobs that are needed because of tourists.

Sports   Californians are very active in sports. These sports range from archery and badminton to surfing and volleyball. What is your favorite sport?

Californians like to take part in sports. They also like to watch their favorite teams play. California has more than a dozen professional sports teams. These sports teams include baseball, football, basketball, hockey, and soccer.

The Los Angeles Dodgers and the Oakland A's have both been World

A toothy, mechanical beast greets some camera-carrying tourists in California.

Californians enjoy all types of sports, including backyard games of basketball. This game is being played by some boys in the Los Angeles area.

Both the UCLA and USC football teams are widely known. Their game creates much excitement for those watching.

Series winners. The Oakland (now Los Angeles) Raiders and San Francisco 49ers won Super Bowl championships. The Los Angeles Lakers and Golden State Warriors have been National Basketball Association champions.

California college teams also have fine records. UCLA (the University of California at Los Angeles) has often been a national champion in college basketball. Stanford University, the University of Southern California, and UCLA all have great football teams.

The arts California has many museums, theaters, and concert halls. The beauty of California makes artists want to paint pictures of it. It is not strange to see an artist at work beside a country road or a city street.

There are hundreds of theaters in California. Many famous actors and actresses began working in one of these theaters.

Music of all types is popular throughout the state. The Los Angeles Philharmonic Orchestra and the San Francisco Symphony have performed throughout the world. The Monterey and Sacramento jazz festivals attract people from all over the United States.

Hollywood has long been a world center for making motion pictures. Thousands of motion pictures have been made there. Many of the shows that we see on national television are made in California.

California colleges and universities rank among the best in the world.

Schools and colleges   California has more schools than any other state. The first colleges in California were founded in the 1850s. Among them were California Wesleyan (now the University of the Pacific) and Santa Clara College (now the University of Santa Clara). Today California has some of the best colleges and universities, both public and private schools.

California: a trendsetter   A **trend** is an idea that is put forth and accepted by many people. Many trends started in California. From skateboards to computers and clothes, California is a trendsetter. It is said many times that new ideas and trends begin in California and move eastward across the country.

One of the many reasons why California is a trendsetter is because it has so many talented people. They are leaders in many different fields. You have read about and seen pictures of some of these people in this book.

CHECKUP

1. Why is the tourist industry important to California?
2. Name some of the sports teams that Californians like to watch.
3. In what ways is California a leader in the arts and in education?
4. What is meant when we say that California is a trendsetter?

281

California's Problems

Air pollution   Making the earth's air, soil, and water dirty is called **pollution**. Almost all of California has some air pollution. The air is polluted by smoke and gases from open fires, factories, and from the many cars on California's roads.

Smog is a name given to polluted air. Smog is a mix of smoke, gases, and fog. It is often very bad in and around Los Angeles. It makes the eyes burn and the nose and throat hurt. The smog hurts growing plants. It even harms paint on houses.

California has tried to cut down on its smog. All cars sold in the state have had to reduce the pollution they give off. Groups have been set up to check on pollution caused by factories. But California's population continues to grow. There are more cars and more factories. It will be hard to solve the smog problem.

Not enough water   As the number of people keeps growing, California must have more water. It is needed in homes, in factories, and on farms.

California needs water all year. Yet almost all rainfall is between November and April. More than two thirds of California's water supply is north of Sacramento. But three quarters of the water is needed south of Sacramento.

Do you remember reading about the Owens Valley Project, the Feather River Project, and the California Aqueduct? These have been some of the steps taken to supply water where it is needed. But much more must be done.

Using the land wisely   As the number of people in California went up, much farmland was taken to build homes, factories, shopping centers, and freeways. Now many people are worried that the farmland and green parts of the state will be used up.

Today towns and cities are looking more closely at the way the land is used. In some places there are rules on the use of land. The goal is to allow some growth to take place, while keeping some of the natural beauty that still is found in the state.

A shortage of electricity   Making enough electricity for everyone who needs it in California will be a big problem in the years ahead. Electric companies are trying to make more electric power. One way of doing this is to burn coal. But this causes air pollution. Another way of making electricity is by using waterpower. This means building

A ramp is used by people to board this train in San Francisco. Providing for the handicapped is one of the social problems that California and the nation are trying to solve.

big dams. There are not many good places left for big, new dams. Another way to make electricity is to use **nuclear** (nü′ klē er) **power**. But people do not agree that this way of making electricity is safe. Because of safety fears, not many nuclear plants are being built.

Social problems   California has many of the same **social problems** that other states have. Social problems are people problems. They come up when people live close together. Living close together means all of us must think not only of our own well-being but also of the well-being of others. Here are some questions about social problems.

1. How can California provide equality for everyone in schooling, in getting jobs, and in protection under the law?
2. How can California best help those out of work, the ill, and the handicapped?
3. How can California cut crime and protect its citizens?
4. How can California raise the money to pay for the services that its citizens need?

These are some of the social problems that California must try to solve. California will continue to have problems. But with its scientists, engineers, and scholars, it will lead the way in solving these problems. And in doing so, California will remain a model for the rest of the world. It will be a place where millions of people with different backgrounds can live together in harmony and can enjoy a high quality of life.

CHECKUP

1. Why is air pollution a serious problem?
2. What are some of the steps taken to meet the water problem?
3. What other problems face California?
4. What might the future bring to California?

EMBLEMS OF OUR STATE

State Seal

State Bird—*California valley quail*

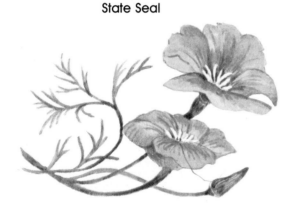

State Flower—*Golden poppy*

State Tree—*California redwood*

State Flag

KEY FACTS

1. Among the 50 states, California ranks at or near the top in manufacturing, agriculture, and commerce.

2. California's natural beauty and many other attractions bring millions of tourists to the state.

3. California is a leading state in the arts, in sports, and in education.

4. Many trends start in California and then move eastward across the United States.

5. Among the problems that Californians must deal with are air pollution, water and electricity shortages, and the misuse of land.

6. California has many of the same social problems that other states have.

VOCABULARY QUIZ

Match these terms with the definitions. Use a separate sheet of paper.

a. consumer   f. mineral
b. smog   g. import
c. manufacture   h. pollution
d. export   i. commerce
e. nuclear power   j. agriculture

1. One way to make electricity

2. The production of food crops and farm animals

3. A product sold to a foreign country

4. The buying, selling, and shipping of goods

5. To make something by hand or by machine

6. Making something dirty

7. A mixture of smoke, gases, and fog

8. A product that is bought from a foreign country

9. The user of a product

10. A natural resource found in the earth

REVIEW QUESTIONS

1. What are California's leading manufactured goods?

2. Why is foreign trade very important for California?

3. In what ways does California rank high in meeting transportation needs?

4. What are some of the California sports teams that have attracted attention?

5. In what ways is California a leader?

6. What are the pollution and water problems that face Californians?

7. What social problems does California have in common with most other states?

8. In what ways does the future seem bright for California?

ACTIVITIES

1. Your cousins, who live in another state, are going to make their first visit to California. They write, asking what sights they should see in your part of the state. Write a letter to them, answering their question.

2. At the top of a sheet of paper, write the words *California Products*. Below the title, make two columns. Label the columns *Farm Products* and *Factory Products*. Below each label, list as many products as you can.

FINDING INFORMATION IN A LIBRARY

WHAT IS A CARD CATALOG?

A library is a source of much information. You know that a library has many books. Do you know how to find the one that has the information you need?

One way is by using the card catalog. A card catalog is a listing of all the books in the library. The books are listed on cards that are kept in drawers. Each book is listed alphabetically by the subject, the title, and the author's last name.

In this book you have learned much about California. Now you might want to find a book that will tell you more about California. How can you use the card catalog to find such a book?

USING A CARD CATALOG

First, you will look in the card catalog under C for the subject *California*. You will find many cards under this heading. These are subject cards. A subject as broad as *California* will be broken down further into smaller subjects. You will probably see subheadings for cities, climate, geography, government, and so on. These subheadings help narrow the subject. One subheading, History, lists a book entitled *California Heritage* by Oscar Lewis. The card tells you on what shelf in the library you will find the book. Write the number down and find the book.

You may already know the title of the book you want. Perhaps someone told you *Six Months in Gold Mines* is a good book about life in the goldfields. You will look under the letter *S* for the first word of the title, *Six*. The complete title of the book will be on a title card.

A friend of yours may say, "A book by Jackson has many good pictures about life in the mining camps, but I have forgotten the title." Then you will look under the letter *J* to find *Jackson*. You may find several books by authors named *Jackson*. These cards are author cards. If you do not know the author's first name, you may have to look through the titles until you find a title that seems to be right. If you find *Gold Rush Album*, that is probably the right book.

SKILLS PRACTICE

Now see how well you can use the card catalog. Write down the type of card and the letter under which you will find the following:

a. A book about Los Angeles

b. A book written by John Steinbeck

c. A book about the U.S. Senator Hiram Johnson

d. The book with the title *Ranchos Become Cities*

e. A book written by the author Upton Sinclair

f. A book about deserts

Much information can be found in the library. Each time you use the card catalog, it will be easier. If you have questions about the use of the library, the librarian is there to help.

5/UNIT REVIEW

1. The governor of the state of California is head of the executive branch of government. Study the table of governors on page 311. — *How many governors has the state of California had? Who was the first governor? What were the dates of his term? Who was governor in 1949? In what year did his term start?*

2. County government and city government are the two basic kinds of local government. — *Where is your county seat located? If you live in a city, what kind of government does it have? If you do not know these facts, how could you find out about them?*

3. California's cities, with their fine year-round climate and many attractions, draw millions of tourists from all over the country. — *Suppose you are going to visit the cities of San Diego and Los Angeles. Make a list of places in each city that you want to visit.*

4. San Francisco is one of the most beautiful and exciting cities in the world. — *What are three attractions that bring thousands of visitors to San Francisco each year?*

5. California is a state with many natural resources. — *What are some of California's natural resources?*

6. More people live in California than in any other state. California is important to the United States and to the whole world. — *Give three reasons why California is so important to the United States and to the world.*

7. California is a leader among the states in arts, sports, and education. — *What are some of the reasons why California sets the pace in these three areas?*

8. Like all the other states California has problems. If it is to keep on being a leader, these problems must be solved. — *What are some environmental problems in the state? What are some social problems? Can we hope that California will continue to find answers to these problems?*

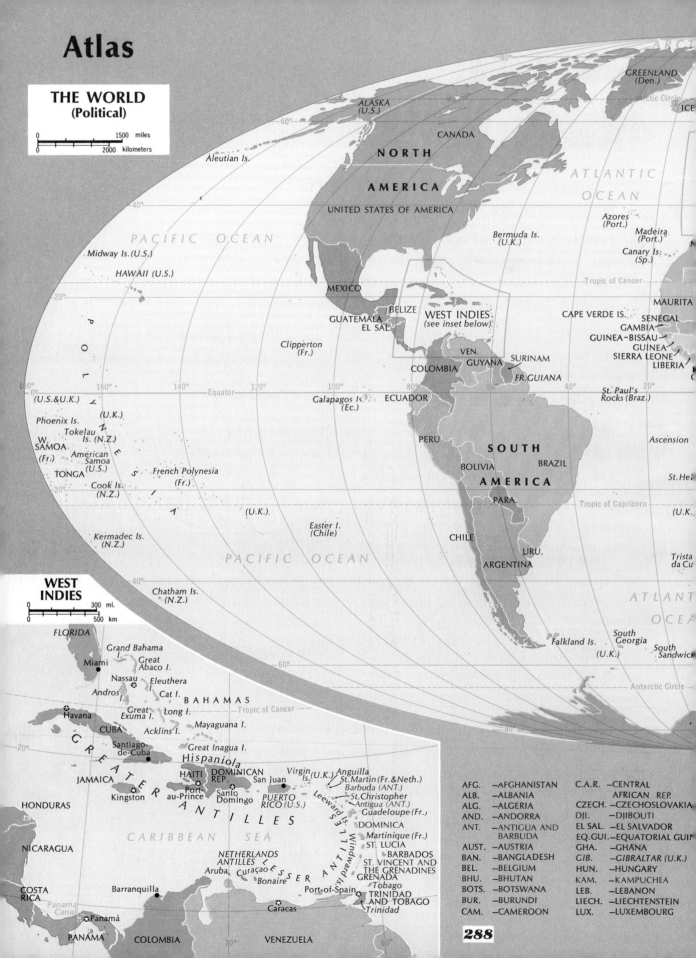

Seattle
Olympia
WASHINGTON
Spokane
Mount St. Helena
CASCADE RANGE
Portland
Bonneville Dam
Salem
Eugene
OREGON
COAST RANGES
Great Falls
Missouri River
Helena
MONTANA
Billings
ROCKY MOUNTAINS
IDAHO
Boise
Idaho Falls
Snake River
Pocatello
WYOMING
Casper
SIERRA NEVADA
Reno
Carson City
NEVADA
Great Salt Lake
Ogden
Salt Lake City
Provo
Laramie
Cheyenne
GREAT PLAINS
Sacramento
Oakland
San Francisco
San Jose
UTAH
CALIFORNIA
Fresno
COAST RANGES
Las Vegas
ROCKY MOUNTAINS
COLORADO
Denver
Aurora
Colorado Springs
NEBRASKA
Grand Island
Lincoln
KANSAS
Wichita
Los Angeles
Long Beach
Anaheim
Santa Ana
San Diego
PACIFIC OCEAN
ARIZONA
Phoenix
Mesa
Tucson
Colorado River
Albuquerque
Santa Fe
NEW MEXICO
Las Cruces
El Paso
Rio Grande
OKLAHOMA
Oklahoma City
Lawton
Fort Worth
TEXAS
Austin
Cat Spring
Brazos River
San Antonio
Corpus Christi

NORTH DAKOTA
Grand Forks
Bismarck
Fargo
SOUTH DAKOTA
Pierre
Rapid City
Sioux Falls
Missouri River
Arkansas River
Omaha
Topeka

160°W
Honolulu
Kailua
HAWAII
PACIFIC OCEAN
Hilo
155°W
22°N
20°N
0   100 miles
0   150 kilometers

U.S.S.R.
ARCTIC OCEAN
BROOKS RANGE
Arctic Circle
ALASKA
Fairbanks
ALASKA RANGE
Anchorage
CANADA
PACIFIC OCEAN
Juneau
0   200 miles
0   200 kilometers

290

CANADA

MINNESOTA

Duluth

MICH.

Lake Superior

St. Paul

apolis

WISCONSIN

Green Bay

Lake Michigan

MICHIGAN

Lake Huron

Lake Ontario

Rochester

MAINE

Augusta

Lewiston

Burlington
Montpelier

VT. N.H.

Portland

Rutland
Concord

Manchester

Nashua

Boston

NEW YORK

Albany

MASS.
Springfield

Worcester
Providence

Madison

Grand
Rapids

Lansing

Buffalo

Scranton

CONN.
Hartford

R.I.

Cranston
Warwick

Milwaukee

Detroit

Bridgeport

New Haven

Rockford

MOUNTAINS

Yonkers
Newark

Jersey City

New York

IOWA

Cedar
Rapids

ines

Davenport

Chicago

Gary

Toledo

Cleveland

Lake Erie

Akron

PENNSYLVANIA

Harrisburg

Trenton

NEW
JERSEY

Fort
Wayne

OHIO

Columbus

Dayton

Pittsburgh

Philadelphia

Newark
Wilmington

Mississippi River

ILLINOIS

INDIANA

Indianapolis

Wheeling

Baltimore

Dover

DELAWARE

Springfield

Cincinnati

Rockville

MD.

Annapolis

Washington,
D.C.

sas

River

WEST VIRGINIA

Charleston

Richmond

as City

St. Louis

Huntington

Louisville

Frankfort

Lexington

Jefferson City

VIRGINIA

Norfolk

Virginia Beach

MISSOURI

Ohio

APPALACHIAN

KENTUCKY

Nashville

Knoxville

Greensboro

Raleigh

ATLANTIC
OCEAN

ARKANSAS

Memphis

TENNESSEE

Charlotte

NORTH CAROLINA

ort Smith

North
Little Rock

Little Rock

Mississippi River

SOUTH CAROLINA

Columbia

Birmingham

Atlanta

North
Charleston

MISSISSIPPI

ALABAMA

GEORGIA

Charleston

Meridian
Jackson

Montgomery

Columbus

Savannah

Shreveport

LOUISIANA

Mobile

Tallahassee

Jacksonville

Biloxi

Baton Rouge

New Orleans

Morgan City

on

Gulf of
Mexico

FLORIDA

Tampa
St. Petersburg

N
NW   NE
W   E
SW   SE
S

Miami   Miami Beach

THE UNITED STATES
OF AMERICA

Key

Rivers

Mountains

National Capital

State Capitals

Other Cities

0   100   200 miles

0   100   200   300 kilometers

291

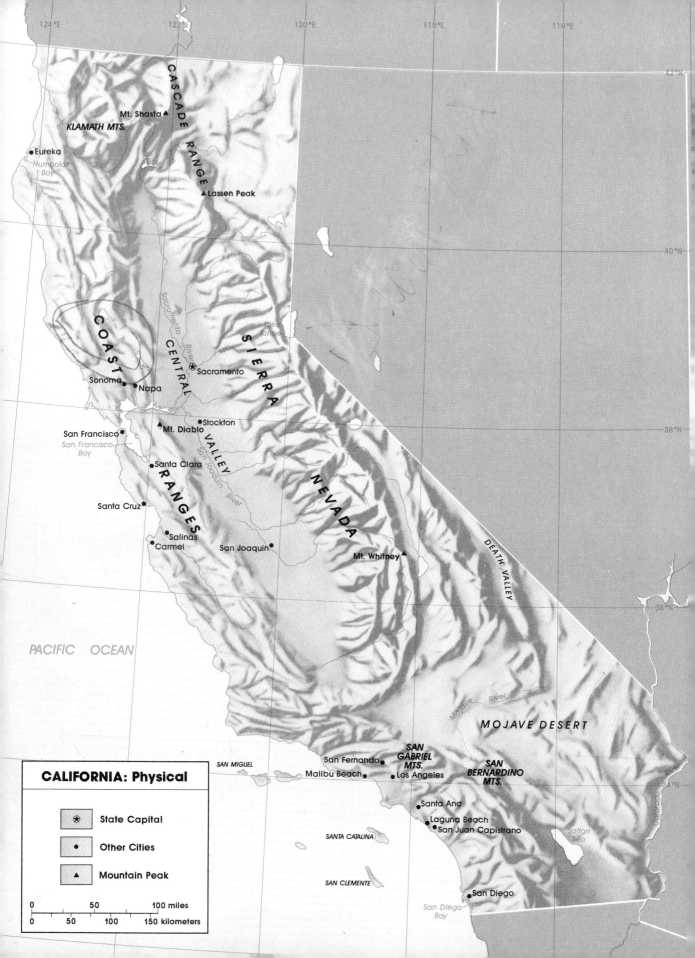

CALIFORNIA: Physical

124°E   122°E   120°E   118°E   116°E

42°N
40°N
38°N
36°N
34°N

CASCADE RANGE

KLAMATH MTS.

▲ Mt. Shasta

• Eureka

Humboldt Bay

▲ Lassen Peak

COAST

CENTRAL

Sacramento River

Lake Tahoe

SIERRA

• Sonoma   • Napa
⊛ Sacramento

RANGES

VALLEY

NEVADA

• Stockton
▲ Mt. Diablo

San Joaquin River

San Francisco •
San Francisco Bay

• Santa Clara

Santa Cruz •

• Salinas
• Carmel

• San Joaquin

Mt. Whitney ▲

DEATH VALLEY

PACIFIC OCEAN

Mojave River

MOJAVE DESERT

SAN GABRIEL MTS.

SAN BERNARDINO MTS.

SAN MIGUEL

San Fernando •
Malibu Beach •

• Los Angeles

• Santa Ana

Colorado River

SANTA CATALINA

• Laguna Beach
• San Juan Capistrano

Salton Sea

SAN CLEMENTE

• San Diego

San Diego Bay

Legend

⊛ State Capital

• Other Cities

▲ Mountain Peak

0   50   100 miles
0   50   100   150 kilometers

GAZETTEER

The Gazetteer is a geographical dictionary. It shows latitude and longitude for cities and certain other places. Latitude and longitude are shown in this form: (36°N/118°W). This means "36 degrees north latitude and 118 degrees west longitude." The page reference tells where each entry may be found on a map.

Africa. The earth's second largest continent. p. 35.

Alcatraz. Rocky island in San Francisco Bay. A prison was once located on this island. p. 271.

American River. Rises in the Sierra Nevada. Flows into the Sacramento River at Sacramento. In 1848 John Marshall discovered gold in this river. p. 267

Anacapa. Small island off the southwest coast of the state. It is part of Channel Island National Park. p. 43.

Anaheim (34°N/118°W). City in Orange County. Eighth most populated city in the state. p. 56.

Antarctica. The earth's third smallest continent. p. 35.

Arctic Ocean. Large body of salt water north of the Arctic Circle. p. 35.

Asia. The earth's largest continent. p. 35.

Atlantic Ocean. Large body of salt water separating North America and South America from Europe and Africa. p. 35.

Australia. The earth's smallest continent. Also the name of the country that covers the whole continent. p. 35.

Baja California. Peninsula between the Gulf of Mexico and the Pacific Ocean. Part of Mexico. Also called Lower California. p. 95.

Bakersfield (35°N/119°W). County seat of Kern County. Located on the Kern River at the southern end of San Joaquin Valley. One of 26 cities in the state with more than 100,000 people. p. 56.

Benicia (38° N/122°W). City in Solano County. Located on Carquinez Strait about 20 miles (32 km) northeast of Oakland. Was the state capital from 1853 to 1854. p. 162.

Berkeley (38°N/122°W). City in Alameda County. Located on San Francisco Bay. One of 26 cities in the state with more than 100,000 people. p. 56.

Black Sea. Large sea located on the southern divide between Europe and Asia. p. 289.

Blue Canyon (39°N/121°W). Town about 70 miles (112 km) northeast of Sacramento. Located near western edge of the Sierra Nevada at an elevation of 5,280 ft (1,584 m). p. 64.

Bodega Bay. Part of the Pacific Ocean about 20 miles (32 km) west of Santa Rosa. The Russians built a settlement nearby in early 1800s. p. 129.

Boston (42°N/71°W). Capital of and most populated city in Massachusetts. Located on Massachusetts Bay. p. 291.

Cairo (30°N/31°E). Capital of Egypt. Most populated city in Africa. Located on the east side of the Nile River. p. 40.

California Current. A cold ocean current. It flows south along the west coast of North America from about 48°N latitude to about 23°N latitude, where it joins the North Equatorial Current. p. 66.

Cape Horn (56°S/67°W). Point of land jutting out from the southernmost part of South America. p. 145.

Caribbean Sea. Part of the Atlantic Ocean bounded by South America on the south; Central America on the west; and Cuba, Puerto Rico, and other islands on the north and east. p. 288.

Carmel (37°N/122°W). City in Monterey County. Located on Pacific Ocean south of Monterey Bay. Also known as Carmel-by-the-Sea. p. 292.

Carmel Bay. Small inlet of Pacific Ocean west of Carmel and south of Monterey Bay. p. 103.

Carpinteria (34°N/120°W). Community in Santa Barbara County. Named by members of the Portolá expedition in 1769. p. 103.

Cascade Range. Mountains that extend from Lassen Peak in northern California to Washington and into Canada. Highest peak, with an elevation of 14,408 ft (4,392 m), is Mt. Rainier in Washington. p. 292.

Central Valley. One of the most important farming areas in the United States. Located between the Sierra Nevada and the Coast Ranges. Made up of the Sacramento Valley in the north and the San Joaquin Valley in the south. p. 70.

Channel Islands National Park. Established in 1938 on Santa Barbara Islands. p. 43.

Clear Lake. Largest freshwater lake entirely within the state. Located in Lake County about 80 miles (128 km) north of San Francisco. Also the name of a large reservoir in Modoc County. p. 233.

Coast Ranges. Mountains along the Pacific coast of North America stretching from Alaska to California. p. 292.

Colorado River. Rises at the Continental Divide in Rocky Mountain National Park in northern Colorado and flows into the Gulf of California in Mexico. p. 129.

Concord (38°N/122°W). City in Contra Costa County. One of 26 cities in state with more than 100,000 people. p. 56.

Crescent City (42°N/124°W). County seat of Del Norte County. Located on coast in northern part of state. p. 233.

Death Valley. Very low valley located at the northern edge of the Mojave Desert. It is 282 ft (86 m) below sea level. p. 292.

Drake's Bay. Inlet of the Pacific Ocean located east of Point Reyes. Named after Sir Francis Drake, who first entered the bay in 1579. p. 95.

Eastern Hemisphere. The half of the earth east of the Prime Meridian. It includes Australia and most of Europe, Africa, and Asia. p. 41.

Equator. A line, drawn on maps, that circles the earth halfway between the two poles. It is labeled 0° latitude. p. 40.

Eureka (41°N/124°W). County seat of Humboldt County. Northernmost natural harbor in the state. Located on Humboldt Bay. p. 43.

Europe. The earth's second smallest continent. p. 35.

Feather River. Rises in Plumas County and flows southwest into Sacramento River near Sacramento. p. 234.

Fontana (34°N/117°W). City in San Bernardino County. Henry Kaiser built California's first complete steel mill here. p. 43.

Fort Ross (39°N/123°W). Site of fort built by the Russians in 1812. Located about 30 miles (48 km) west of Santa Rosa. p. 129.

Fresno (37° N/120° W). County seat of Fresno County. Located in San Joaquin Valley. Ninth most populated city in the state. p. 56.

Great Salt Lake. An inland saltwater lake with no streams flowing out of it. Located in Utah. p. 290.

Hollywood (34°N/118°W). Part of the city of Los Angeles. Center for making of movies and television shows. p. 261.

Hoover Dam (36°N/115°W). Dam on the Colorado River. It is 726 ft (218 m) high. It was completed in 1936. Formerly called Boulder Dam. p. 234.

Humboldt Bay. Part of the Pacific Ocean. Located on northern coast of state at about 41°N latitude. p. 292.

Huntington Beach (34°N/118°W). City in Orange County. Located along Pacific Ocean southeast of Long Beach. One of the state's biggest oil strikes was made here in 1920. p. 56.

Imperial Valley. Once part of the Colorado Desert. Today it is a fertile agricultural area in the southeastern part of the state. The change from desert to farmland is the result of irrigation. Today water for irrigation reaches the valley by the All-American Canal. p. 202.

Indian Ocean. Large body of salt water between Africa and Australia. p. 35.

Inglewood (34°N/118°W). City in Los Angeles County. Located southwest of Los Angeles. p. 261.

Isthmus of Panama. Narrow piece of land in Panama. The Pacific Ocean is on one side, and the Atlantic Ocean is on the other side. The Panama Canal was built across this isthmus. p. 145.

Kings Canyon National Park. National park in the Sierra Nevada. General Sherman, a giant sequoia tree, and other sequoias are in this park. General Sherman is 267 ft (81 m) tall. p. 43.

Klamath Mountains. Part of the Coast Ranges stretching from Siskiyou County into Oregon. The highest peak is Mt. Eddy, which has an elevation of 9,104 ft (2,759 m). p. 292.

Laguna (34°N/118°W). City in Orange County. Located southeast of Long Beach. Also known as Laguna Beach. p. 292.

Lassen Peak (40°N/122°W). Mountain peak at southern end of the Cascade Range in Shasta County. It has an elevation of 10,457 ft (3,137 m). p. 292.

Lassen Volcanic National Park. National park in the northern part of the state at the southern end of the Cascade Range. p. 43.

Leningrad (60°N/30°E). Second most populated city in the Soviet Union. Located on the Gulf of Finland. p. 40.

Long Beach (34°N/118°W). City in Los Angeles County. Located on San Pedro Bay south of Los Angeles. Fifth most populated city in the state. p. 56.

Los Angeles (34°N/118°W). County seat of Los Angeles County. One of six cities in the United States with more than 1,000,000 people. Most populated city in the state. p. 56.

Madrid (40°N/4°W). Capital of Spain. Second most populated city in Europe. p. 40.

Malibu (39°N/119°W). A community along the Pacific Ocean. Located near Santa Monica. Also called Malibu Beach. p. 292.

Mediterranean Sea. Large body of salt water surrounded by Europe, Africa, and Asia. It is the largest sea in the world. p. 289.

Missouri River. Longest river in the United States. Rises in western Montana and flows into the Mississippi River near St. Louis, Missouri. p. 291.

Modesto (38°N/121°W). County seat of Stanislaus County. Located on the Tuolumne River about 25 miles (40 km) southeast of Stockton. p. 56.

Mojave Desert. Desert located south of the Sierra Nevada. Joins the Colorado Desert in the southeastern part of state. It includes parts of San Bernardino, Los Angeles, and Kern counties. The chief towns in the Mojave Desert are Barstow and Mojave. p. 292.

Mojave River. Rises in the San Bernardino Mountains and flows into the Mojave Desert toward the city of Barstow. Part of the river flows underground. p. 292.

Monterey (37°N/122°W). City at the southern end of Monterey Bay. Portolá established a presido and Father Serra a mission here in 1770. p. 98.

Monterey Bay. Inlet of the Pacific Ocean along the coast of Santa Cruz and Monterey counties. The cities of Santa Cruz and Monterey are on Monterey Bay. p. 103.

Mount Diablo (38°N/122°W). Mountain peak at the northern end of the Diablo Range, which is part of the Coast Ranges. It has an elevation of 3,849 ft (1,173 m). p. 292.

Mount Shasta (41°N/122°W). Highest mountain peak in the Cascades. Has an elevation of 14,161 ft (4,316 m). Also the name of the town in Siskiyou County that is at the base of the peak. p. 43.

Mount Whitney (37°N/118°W). Highest mountain peak in the Sierra Nevada. It is also the second highest peak in the United States. It has an elevation of 14,495 ft (4,418 m). p. 43.

Newport Beach (34°N/118°W). City in Orange County. Located along Pacific Ocean southeast of Long Beach. p. 233.

New York City (41°N/74°W). Most populated city in the United States. Located at the mouth of the Hudson River in the state of New York. p. 291.

North America. The earth's third largest continent. Our country is in North America. p. 35.

Northern Hemisphere. The half of the earth that is north of the Equator. p. 40.

North Pole. The most northern place on the earth. p. 39.

Oakland (38°N/122°W). County seat of Alameda County. Sixth most populated city in the state. Located on the east side of San Francisco Bay. p. 56.

Omaha (41°N/96°W). City in Nebraska. Located on the Missouri River. p. 187.

Oroville (40°N/122°W). County seat of Butte County. Located on the Feather River about 65 miles (104 km) north of Sacramento. p. 202.

Oroville Dam (40°N/122°W). Located in Butte County across the Feather River. Highest dam in the United States. It is 771 ft (235 m) high. It was completed in 1968. p. 234.

Owens River. Rises in the Sierra Nevada in the western part of Mono County. Water from this river is brought to Los Angeles by the Los Angeles Aqueduct. p. 202.

Pacific Ocean. The earth's largest body of water. It stretches from the Arctic Circle to Antarctica and from the western coast of North America to the eastern coast of Asia. p. 35.

Palo Alto (37°N/122°W). City in Santa Clara County. Home of Stanford University. Named by members of the Portolá expedition in 1769. p. 103.

Panama Canal. Ship canal that crosses a narrow piece of land called the Isthmus of Panama. This canal connects the Pacific Ocean and the Atlantic Ocean. p. 288.

Panama City (9°N/79°W). Capital of the Republic of Panama. Located on the Pacific Ocean side of the Panama Canal. p. 145.

Pasadena (34°N/118°W). City in southern part of the state. Site of annual Rose Bowl parade and football game. One of 26 cities in the state with more than 100,000 people. p. 56.

Peking (40°N/116°E). Capital of China. Fourth most populated city in the world. p. 40.

Philadelphia (40°N/75°W). City in Pennsylvania. Located at point where Delaware and Schuylkill rivers join. One of six cities in the United States with more than 1,000,000 people. p. 291.

Point Reyes (38°N/123°W). Point at the southern end of a small peninsula in Marin County. It is one of the windiest and foggiest places in the United States. Point Reyes National Seashore is here. p. 95.

Prime Meridian. 0° line of longitude. It divides the earth into the Eastern Hemisphere and the Western Hemisphere. p. 41.

Promontory Point (41°N/112°W). Place near Ogden, Utah. It is near Promontory where tracks for the Central Pacific and the Union Pacific railroads were joined in 1869. p. 187.

Redwood National Park. National park near Crescent City. Some of the world's oldest and tallest trees are in this park. One tree grew to be 367 ft (112 m) high. p. 43.

Richmond (38°N/122°W). City in Contra Costa County on eastern shore of San Francisco Bay. p. 233.

Russian River. Rises in Mendocino County and flows south into Sonoma County, then west into the Pacific Ocean. p. 202.

Sacramento (38°N/121°W). Capital of California. Also the county seat for Sacramento County. Seventh most populated city in the state. The Sacramento and American rivers join in Sacramento. p. 56.

Sacramento River. Rises near Mt. Shasta in Siskiyou County. Flows into Suisun Bay, which is part of San Francisco Bay. p. 43.

St. Joseph (40°N/95°W). City in Missouri on the Missouri River. It was the eastern end of the Pony Express route. p. 187.

St. Louis (39°N/90°W). Most populated city in Missouri. Located on the Mississippi River near the point where it is joined by the Missouri River. p. 187.

Salt Lake City (41°N/112°W). Capital of and most populated city in Utah. Located near Great Salt Lake. p. 187.

Salton Sea. Lake in Riverside and Imperial counties. It is below sea level. At one point it had become a dried-up lake. But water from the Colorado River was channeled into it in 1905. p. 43.

San Andreas Fault. Fault line stretching along the western part of the state. It is about 750 miles (1,210 km) long. Earth movement along this line in 1906 caused the San Francisco earthquake. p. 195.

San Antonio de Padua (36°N/122°W). One of the nine missions started by Father Serra. p. 113.

San Bernardino (34°N/117°W). County seat of San Bernardino County. One of 26 cities in the state with more than 100,000 people. p. 56.

San Bernardino Mountains. Located in southern part of state. They border on the Mojave Desert. The highest point is San Gorgonio Mountain, which has an elevation of 11,502 ft (3,451 m). The Mojave River starts in these mountains. p. 292.

San Carlos Borromeo (37°N/122°W). Name of the second California mission, which was started by Father Serra in 1770. Its first location was Monterey. But Father Serra later moved it to just south of Carmel. p. 113.

San Clemente. An island located in the southwest part of Santa Barbara Islands. It is south of Santa Catalina Island. Part of Los Angeles County. Also the name of a city in Orange County. p. 292.

San Diego (33°N/117°W). Located on San Diego Bay. First of 21 Spanish missions was built here. Today it is the county seat for San Diego County. San Diego is the second most populated city in the state. It is the eighth most populated city in the United States. p. 56.

San Diego Bay. Natural harbor along which the city of San Diego grew. p. 292.

San Diego de Alcala (33°N/117°W). Name of the first California mission, which was started in San Diego in 1770 by Father Serra. p. 113.

San Francisco (38°N/122°W). County seat for San Francisco County. Third most populated city in the state, and the thirteenth most populated city in the United States. Located on San Francisco Bay. p. 56.

San Francisco Bay. Part of the Pacific Ocean. One of the world's best harbors. p. 292.

San Gabriel Arcángel (34°N/117°W). One of the nine missions started by Father Serra. Located near Los Angeles. p. 113.

San Gabriel Mountains. Located southwest of Mojave Desert. Highest point is San Antonio Peak, which has an elevation of 10,080 ft (3,024 m). p. 292.

San Joaquin River. Rises in the Sierra Nevada. Flows into the Sacramento River near San Francisco Bay. It is about 350 miles (560 km) long. p. 43.

San Jose (37°N/122°W). County seat for Santa Clara County. Fourth most populated city in the state, and the seventeenth most populated city in the

United States. Located on the Coyote and Guadalupe rivers. First state capital of California. p. 56.

San Lorenzo (38°N/122°W). Community in Alameda County. Named by members of the Portolá expedition in 1769. p. 103.

San Luis Obispo (35°N/121°W). County seat of San Luis Obispo County. Located about 10 miles (16 km) from the Pacific Ocean. San Simeon castle is nearby. Also the name of one of the nine missions started by Father Serra. p. 113.

San Miguel Island. Located in the Pacific Ocean at the northwest end of Santa Barbara Islands. Part of Channel Islands National Park. p. 95.

Santa Ana (34°N/118°W). County seat of Orange County. Tenth most populated city in the state. Located east of Long Beach. Named by members of the Portolá expedition in 1769. The first airplane made in the state was made here in 1907. p. 56.

Santa Barbara (34°N/120°W). County seat of Santa Barbara County. Located on Santa Barbara Channel about 80 miles (128 km) northwest of Los Angeles. p. 233.

Santa Barbara Channel. Narrow body of water between mainland of state and San Miguel, Santa Rosa, and Santa Cruz islands. p. 98.

Santa Barbara Islands. Chain of eight islands (San Miguel, Santa Rosa, Santa Cruz, Anacapa, San Nicolas, Santa Catalina, San Clemente, and Santa Barbara). These islands stretch for about 150 miles (240 km) along the southern coast from Point Conception to San Diego. p. 43.

Santa Catalina. Island in the Pacific Ocean. Part of Los Angeles County. p. 95.

Santa Cruz (37°N/122°W). County seat of Santa Cruz County. Located at mouth of San Lorenzo River on Monterey Bay. Also the name of an island located off the southern coast at about 34°N latitude. p. 233.

Santa Fe Springs (34°N/118°W). City in Los Angeles County. Located north of Long Beach. One of the state's biggest oil strikes was made here in 1921. p. 198.

Santa Lucia Range. Mountain range in Monterey and San Luis Obispo counties. One of the Coast Ranges. p. 103.

Santa Margarita (35°N/121°W). Small village in San Luis Obispo County. Named by members of the Portolá expedition in 1769. p. 103.

Santa Monica (34°N/118°W). City on Santa Monica Bay. p. 233.

Santa Rosa (38°N/123°W). County seat of Sonoma County. Located near San Francisco. p. 195.

Sequoia National Park. Established by Congress in 1890. Includes Mt. Whitney. p. 43.

Sierra Nevada. High mountain range in eastern part of state. Mt. Whitney, with an elevation of 14,495 ft (4,418 m), is in this range. Mt. Whitney is the highest peak in the United States outside of Alaska. p. 292.

Signal Hill (34°N/118°W). City in Los Angeles County about 20 miles (32 km) from Los Angeles. One of the state's biggest oil strikes was made here in 1921. p. 198.

Sonoma (38°N/122°W). City in Sonoma County. Located south of Santa Rosa. p. 292.

South America. The earth's fourth largest continent. p. 35.

Southern Hemisphere. The half of the earth that is south of the Equator. p. 40.

South Pole. The most southern place on the earth. p. 39.

Springfield (40°N/90°W). Capital of Illinois. Located on the Sangamon River. p. 291.

Stockton (38°N/121°W). County seat of San Joaquin County. One of 26 cities in the state with more than 100,000 people. Large port on the San Joaquin River. p. 56.

Tuolumne River. Rises in Yosemite National Park and flows into San Joaquin River in Stanislaus County. Hetch Hetchy Dam crosses this river. p. 202.

Vallejo (38°N/122°W). City in Solano County on San Pablo Bay about 20 miles (32 km) north of Oakland. Was the state capital from 1851 to 1853. p. 162.

Washington, D.C. (39°N/77°W). Capital of the United States. Located on the Potomac River. p. 291.

Western Hemisphere. The half of the earth west of the Prime Meridian. Includes all of North America and South America. p. 41.

Yosemite National Park. Located in the Sierra Nevada about 180 miles (288 km) east of San Francisco. p. 43.

GLOSSARY
The page references tell where each entry appears in the text.

acorn. The nut that grows on an oak tree. p. 84.

adobe. A mixture of wet clay and straw used as a building material. p. 112.

aerospace. Having to do with the production of all kinds of aircraft, such as airplanes and spacecraft. p. 231.

agriculture. The raising of crops or of livestock; farming. p. 179.

alcalde. The chief local official and judge of a Spanish or Mexican town. p. 158.

amendment. An addition or change, such as one made in a constitution or a body of laws. p. 244.

ancestor. A person from whom one is descended—for example, a father, mother, grandfather, grandmother, and so on. p. 237.

anchor. To hold in place; a heavy metal object attached to a rope or chain that is dropped in the water to hold a ship in place. p. 98.

aquarium. A tank or building used for showing collections of living fish, water animals, and water plants. p. 259.

aqueduct. A structure of pipes or a channel used to transport water over a distance. p. 202.

Assembly. The name given to a body or part of a legislative branch of government. The California Assembly is made up of 80 members who represent 80 districts of nearly equal population. p. 247.

astronaut. A pilot who travels in outer space. p. 34.

aviation. The art of flying aircraft. p. 199.

bargain. To come to an agreement; an agreement to make a trade or an exchange. p. 146.

battalion. A large group of soldiers. p. 132.

bay. A protected part of the ocean that reaches into land. p. 67.

bill. A possible law presented to a legislature to be voted upon. p. 247.

biplane. A plane that has two sets of wings on each side of the plane, one above the other. p. 199.

boom. To grow very fast. p. 186.

border. To touch; an outer edge or boundary. States and countries touch one another at their border. p. 37.

boundary. A line that separates one state or country from another; a border. p. 37.

boycott. An organized campaign in which people join together and refuse to have any dealings with a particular group or business. p. 237.

breakwater. A wall of rocks to protect a harbor or beach from strong waves. p. 68.

bribe. Something, such as money, given to a lawmaker or other public official for special favors. p. 164.

cannery. A food-processing factory. p. 265.

capital. City that serves as the seat of government of a country or state. p. 162.

capitol. A building in which state lawmakers meet. p. 163.

ceremony. A special act or an event that honors something important that has happened. p. 87.

Chicanos. A name some Mexican Americans call themselves. p. 236.

chief. The head of a group; the leader of an Indian village. p. 86.

citrus fruit. A fruit with a thick rind and pulpy, juicy insides, such as an orange, lime, lemon, or grapefruit. p. 181.

Civil War. In America the war between the states. Any war between citizens of the same country is called a civil war. p. 168.

climate. The kind of weather a place has over a long period of time, as shown by such things as temperature and precipitation. p. 62.

clipper ship. A fast sailing ship, long and narrow, with tall masts and many sails. p. 172.

coastline. The land along the edge of an ocean, or sea. p. 67.

commerce. The buying and selling of goods, especially in large amounts and shipped from place to place. p. 276.

commute. To travel back and forth regularly. p. 263.

compass rose. A drawing that shows where north, south, east, and west are on a map. p. 39.

computer. An electronic machine that can be programmed to do different tasks, such as solve problems or process and store information. p. 230.

Congress. The group of men and women who make the laws for the United States. p. 161.

congressional district. A part of a state that is represented in the United States House of Representatives by an elected person called a representative. p. 252.

conservation. The use of natural resources in such a way as to prevent their waste or complete destruction. p. 204.

constitution. A set of laws by which a state or country is governed. p. 158.

consumer. A person who uses anything that has been produced. p. 276.

continent. A very large body of land. There are seven continents: Asia, Africa, North America, South America, Europe, Australia, and Antarctica. p. 34.

contour line. A line on a map that shows a certain distance above sea level. All places along the same contour line are exactly the same distance above sea level. p. 70.

convenience food. A food that is partly prepared or cooked before it is sold in a store. p. 230.

county. The largest territorial division for local government within a state. p. 54.

county board of supervisors. The law-making body for a county. This board is also responsible for enforcing the law. p. 250.

county seat. The city, town, or place in a county that is the center of county government. p. 250.

cradle. A rocking device used in panning for gold. p. 149.

craft. A trade or type of work that requires special skill. p. 81.

crisis. A turning point; an important or deciding event. p. 202.

dam. A wall built across a river or other body of water to hold back the water. p. 203.

delegate. A person who has the right to act or speak for others. p. 158.

delta. Land that is formed by mud and sand at a river's mouth. p. 70.

depression. A period of time when business is very bad and large numbers of people are unemployed and have little money. p. 212.

desert. A region or place with very little rainfall and few plants. p. 67.

diverse. Having many differences or many different qualities. p. 252.

drought. A long period of dryness without rain. p. 181.

dugout canoe. A boat made by hollowing out a large log. p. 82.

Dust Bowl. Area, especially in the Great Plains in the United States, where soil erosion caused by poor farming methods and a long period of little rainfall resulted in severe dust storms. p. 214.

earthquake. A shaking or trembling of the earth, often leaving cracks in the earth's surface. This is caused by the shifting of layers of the earth far beneath the surface. p. 192.

east. A direction word. Facing north, east will be on one's right. West will be on one's left. p. 38.

economic. Having to do with the production and selling of goods and services. p. 279.

electronics. An area of study from which television, radio, computers, and other devices using electricity have developed. p. 230.

elevation. Distance or height above sea level. p. 70.

endangered species. A group of animals that are scarce and in danger of dying out completely. p. 260.

Equator. The imaginary line on the earth that is halfway between the North Pole and the South Pole. It is shown on a map or globe by the latitude line numbered 0°. p. 40.

eroding. Wearing away of the earth's surface by the action of water, wind, or ice. p. 149.

estimate. To judge or to figure out something, such as distance or location on a map or globe. p. 42.

ethnic. Having to do with a group of people who share the same language and customs and often the same religion and country of origin. p. 258.

event. Something that happens. People's actions make many events happen. p. 36.

executive branch. The branch of government responsible for carrying out the laws. p. 247.

expedition. A trip that is made for a special purpose, such as for exploration. p. 101.

explorer. A person who travels in search of something new. p. 92.

export. A product that is sent out of one country for sale in another country. p. 278.

exposition. A large fair or public show. p. 195.

fault. A break in the solid rock layer of the earth. p. 194.

fertile. Able to produce crops easily; rich. p. 71.

fiesta. An event held for religious holidays, weddings, births, or just for fun. p. 118.

fishing grounds. Special places on a river where Indian tribes fished. p. 83.

fog. Clouds that form near the ground. p. 66.

food processing. Freezing, canning, and packaging foods for the marketplace. p. 265.

foreign trade. Buying products from and selling products to other countries. p. 278.

forty-niners. Name given to gold seekers who came to California in the gold rush of 1849. p. 145.

free state. A state in the United States in which slavery was not permitted. p. 160.

freeway. An express highway with limited entrances and exits on which no tolls are charged. p. 263.

galleon. A large, tall sailing ship. p. 96.

geography. The study of the earth and how people use it. p. 36.

glider. An aircraft similar to an airplane but without a motor. p. 199.

globe. A model of the earth. A globe shows how the earth looks from space. p. 34.

government. The office, people, or act of ruling. The leaders who make the laws and carry them out. p. 122.

governor. The top elected official of a state or other political unit. p. 122.

graph. A special kind of drawing that uses pictures, circles, bars, and lines to give facts and compare things. p. 57.

greenbelt. A large open area of parks, farmland, or grassland that circles a city. p. 273.

grid. A system of crossing lines or boxes on a map or globe. Crossing latitude and longitude lines form a grid. p. 42.

harbor. A protected body of water deep enough for ships. p. 67.

hemisphere. Half of a sphere, or ball. Half of the earth. p. 40.

hemp. A tall plant whose strong, tough fibers are used to make rope or heavy string. p. 115.

history. The study of the past. History is filled with interesting stories about people and events. p. 36.

hydroelectric power. Electric power produced from falling water. p. 219.

hydroplane. A plane that can land on and take off from water. p. 199.

import. A product bought from a foreign country and brought into this country for sale or use. p. 278.

independence. Freedom from the control of another country or person. p. 116.

industry. A business or trade. p. 180.

invention. Something produced for the first time. p. 196.

irrigation. The bringing of water to crops, other plants, or an area of land by pipes, canals, or ditches. p. 115.

isthmus. A narrow strip of land connecting two larger pieces of land. p. 145.

judicial branch. The branch of government that interprets or explains the laws. p. 247.

key. The place on a map where symbols are explained. p. 44.

land grant. A gift of land. p. 118.

latitude. Distances north or south of the earth's Equator measured in degrees. The lines that measure latitude run east-west on a map or globe. p. 40.

legislative branch. The branch of government that makes the laws. p. 247.

legislature. A group of people or the part of government responsible for making the laws for a state or country. p. 239.

lieutenant governor. The person who takes over the duties of a governor when a governor is unable to do the job. p. 249.

livestock. Farm animals. p. 110.

local government. The elected people who make and enforce the laws and provide public services in a county, a city, or a town. p. 244.

longitude. Distance east or west of the Prime Meridian measured in degrees. Lines of longitude on a map or globe run from the North Pole to the South Pole. p. 41.

manufacture. To make something by hand or by machine. p. 276.

map. A special kind of drawing used to show what the earth or a part of the earth looks like if viewed from overhead. p. 37.

mayor. A person elected or appointed to act as chief officer of a city. p. 236.

merchant. A buyer and seller of goods and services. Merchants include storekeepers, hotelkeepers, bankers, and transporters. p. 151.

military governor. The person who governs, or rules, a state or region in the name of an army. p. 158.

mineral. A substance, found in the earth, that is neither plant nor animal. It can be mined and used for various purposes. p. 278.

mission. A settlement of a church and other buildings and land with the purpose of turning people into Christians. p. 101.

mountain. A piece of land that rises steeply and much higher than the land around it. p. 52.

national monument. A place or building that the national government preserves and keeps unchanged for all the people. p. 73.

national park. A park or scenic area that is set aside by the national government for use by all people. p. 60.

native Californian. One of any group of California Indians; person who is born in California. p. 78.

natural boundary. A boundary that exists in nature, such as a mountain range, river, or sea. p. 160.

natural resource. A thing made by nature that is useful to people. Natural resources are such things as forests, water, land, and minerals. p. 52.

nature. All the living and nonliving things that make up the world. p. 78.

navel orange. A large, juicy, sweet seedless orange imported into California from the country of Brazil. p. 182.

neutral. Not taking sides in a fight or an argument. p. 220.

New Deal. A term used to describe policies put forward by President Franklin D. Roosevelt to fight the depression. In the New Deal, the government created jobs and granted other types of aid to people. p. 217.

Nisei. A son or daughter of Japanese immigrants who grows up and goes to school in the United States. p. 224.

north. A direction word. North is the direction toward the North Pole. p. 38.

North Pole. The most northern place on earth. The northern end of the earth's axis. It is located in the Arctic Ocean. p. 38.

nuclear power. The power released from the nucleus, or core, of an atom, used to produce electricity. p. 283.

ocean. A large body of salt water. There are four oceans—the Atlantic, Pacific, Indian, and Arctic. p. 34.

ocean current. A steady flow of water in one direction in the ocean. p. 65.

oil refinery. An industrial plant where gasoline and other products are made from oil taken out of the ground. p. 221.

oil strike. The act of finding oil in a certain place. p. 198.

padre. The Spanish word for "father," used as the name for a religious leader. p. 110.

panning. Use of a shallow, round pan with slanted sides to separate gold or other metal from waste materials by washing. p. 149.

party. A group of people taking part together in some action. p. 128.

peninsula. A piece of land that has water on three sides and is connected to a larger body of land. p. 68.

petroleum. An oily liquid found in the earth from which gasoline and many other products are made. p. 52.

pirate. A person who attacks and robs ships at sea. p. 96.

pitch. A sticky substance from some evergreen trees. p. 81.

placer gold. Gold found in rivers or streams. Placer is mud and sand that contains gold or other minerals. p. 149.

plain. A large area of land that is almost level and is often treeless. p. 52.

planetarium. A building or room that has a cameralike machine that shows the movements of the planets and stars by projecting light on the inside of a dome. p. 263.

plaza. A public square in a town or city. p. 131.

pollution. The act of making any part of the earth's air, soil, or water dirty by putting waste materials in them. p. 282.

population density. The number of people per unit of area, as a square mile or square kilometer. p. 55.

precipitation. The moisture that falls on the earth's surface. It includes rain, snow, sleet, and hail. p. 63.

presidio. The Spanish word for a fort from which soldiers can defend a settlement. p. 101.

price war. A period in which rival businesses cut their prices to get customers. p. 186.

Prime Meridian. The line of longitude from which other lines of longitude are measured. The Prime Meridian is numbered 0°. It passes through England. p. 41.

producer. A person who makes movies. p. 206.

program. A plan undertaken toward a goal. p. 217.

prospector. One who explores an area in search of minerals such as gold. p. 142.

pueblo. The Spanish word for "town." p. 117.

pyrite. A common mineral that is made up of iron and sulfur. Because of its pale, shiny yellow color, it is often called "fool's gold." p. 140.

ranchero. The owner of a rancho. p. 118.

rancho. The Spanish word for "ranch." p. 117.

range. A long row of mountains. p. 68.

real estate. Property that includes houses and land. p. 186.

recreation. The activities that people choose for fun and rest. p. 60.

republic. A government in which the people elect representatives to run the country. p. 131.

reservation. An area of land set aside for use by the Indians. p. 167.

retail trade. Business selling a product in a small quantity directly to the consumer. p. 276.

revolt. The act of people rising up against their leaders. p. 131.

rodeo. A roundup of cattle. p. 118.

satellite. A kind of spacecraft created to circle the earth. p. 231.

sauna. A building or room used for taking steam baths. p. 80.

scale. A way of showing size or distance on a map. p. 44.

sculptor. A person who carves or molds a material such as wood or stone into a work of art. p. 208.

scurvy. A disease of the gums caused by not eating fresh vegetables or fruit. p. 96.

sea otter. An animal that lives along the Pacific coast and is hunted for its fur. p. 100.

season. A period or time of the year. Spring, summer, autumn, and winter are seasons of the year. So are wet and dry seasons. p. 63.

Senate. The name given to a body or part of a legislative branch of government. The California Senate has 40 members. p. 247.

senator. An elected member of a senate or legislative body. p. 247.

sequoia. A giant California pine tree that sometimes reaches heights of almost 300 feet (91 m). p. 61.

settlement. A new place where people build homes; small village. p. 100.

shellfish. A water animal that has a shell. p. 83.

silicon. A material found in nature. It is used in building computers. p. 276.

slave. A person owned by another person. A slave could be bought and sold. p. 160.

slogan. A saying that everybody knows. p. 186.

sluice box. A long, narrow, sloping box used in panning for gold. Gold-bearing sand and gravel were placed in the box and washed with water. The gold was caught behind cross boards lining the bottom of the box. p. 150.

smog. A mixture of smoke, gases, and fog that pollutes the air. p. 282.

social problem. Any problem having to do with people and how they relate to each other. p. 283.

south. A direction word. South is the direction toward the South Pole. p. 38.

South Pole. The most southern place on earth. The southern end of the earth's axis. It is located on the continent of Antarctica. p. 38.

sphere. An object that is round like a ball. The earth is a sphere. p. 34.

squatter. A person who lives on land without owning it or paying any rent. p. 166.

state government. The elected leaders who make and carry out the laws of a state. p. 244.

strike. An action in which workers stop working to try to get what they want from their employers. p. 237.

stucco. A material made of cement, sand, and lime. Stucco is used to cover walls. p. 258.

suburb. A smaller town or community near a large city. p. 187.

supreme court. The highest court in a country or state. p. 249.

surrender. To give up. p. 224.

sweathouse. A special house kept warm by rocks and stones that have been heated in a fire. Indians used these houses to take sweat baths. p. 80.

symbol. Something used on a map that stands for a real thing or place on the earth's surface. p. 44.

tailrace. A ditch used to carry off water from a mill or mine. p. 140.

talkie. A name given to a movie with sound. p. 206.

tallow. Fat from sheep or cows that is used to make candles. p. 115.

tannic acid. A substance found in acorns. p. 84.

tar. A sticky black substance often used as blacktop to pave streets. p. 81.

telegraph line. A way of sending coded messages long distances over wires by electricity. p. 175.

temperature. Degree of hot or cold, such as of the air. p. 64.

thermometer. An instrument that is used to measure temperature. p. 64.

tourist. A person who travels for pleasure. p. 212.

trading post. A store where goods are exchanged, bought, and sold. p. 122.

transcontinental. Going across a continent, such as a railroad or airline. p. 175.

transportation. The moving of people and goods from one place to another. p. 112.

trend. An idea that is put forth and accepted by many people. p. 281.

tribe. A group of people who are related and are tied together by geography or customs. p. 78.

tule balsa. A simple boat made by tying together plants called tules. p. 82.

tunnel. An underground passageway. p. 177.

union. A group formed within an industry to protect the interests of its members. p. 237.

United Nations. A group formed, following World War II, whose members try to have countries solve their differences peacefully. p. 225.

urban area. An area made up of a large city and its suburbs. p. 256.

valley. A long, low place between hills or mountains. p. 68.

vaquero. The Spanish word for "cowboy." p. 115.

veto. A decision of a governor or other elected official not to sign a bill passed by a legislature into law. p. 249.

vigilante. A member of a group that captures and punishes criminals without help from government leaders. p. 164.

vineyard. A place where grapes are grown. p. 181.

voyage. A trip made by water. p. 94.

wagon train. A group of wagons traveling together. p. 147.

waterwheel. A wheel turned by the movement of running water. p. 140.

weather. The way the air is at a certain time in a given place. p. 62.

west. A direction word. When facing north, west will be on one's left. East will be on one's right. p. 38.

GRAPH APPENDIX

THE FIVE MOST POPULATED STATES

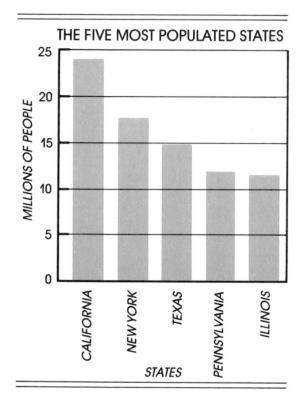

CALIFORNIA: FIVE MOST POPULATED COUNTIES

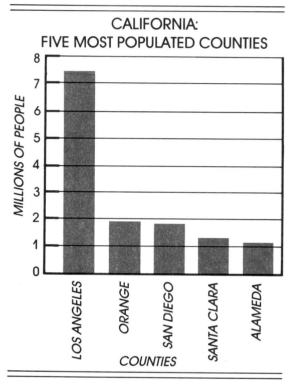

FARM INCOME BY LEADING STATES
(in dollars)

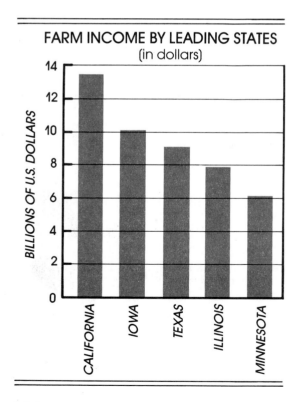

VEGETABLE PRODUCTION BY LEADING STATES

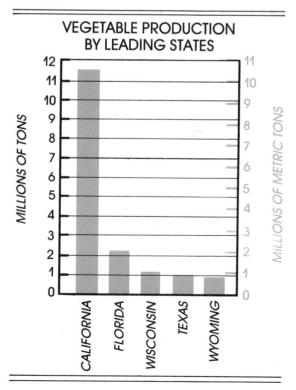

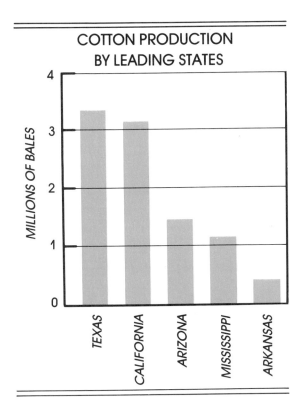

COTTON PRODUCTION BY LEADING STATES

MILLIONS OF BALES

4, 3, 2, 1, 0

TEXAS, CALIFORNIA, ARIZONA, MISSISSIPPI, ARKANSAS

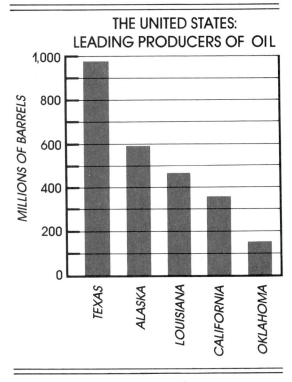

THE UNITED STATES: LEADING PRODUCERS OF OIL

MILLIONS OF BARRELS

1,000, 800, 600, 400, 200, 0

TEXAS, ALASKA, LOUISIANA, CALIFORNIA, OKLAHOMA

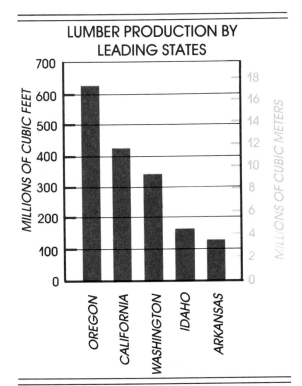

LUMBER PRODUCTION BY LEADING STATES

MILLIONS OF CUBIC FEET

700, 600, 500, 400, 300, 200, 100, 0

MILLIONS OF CUBIC METERS

18, 16, 14, 12, 10, 8, 6, 4, 2, 0

OREGON, CALIFORNIA, WASHINGTON, IDAHO, ARKANSAS

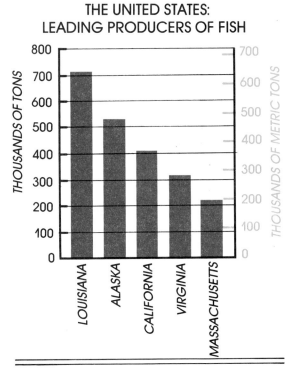

THE UNITED STATES: LEADING PRODUCERS OF FISH

THOUSANDS OF TONS

800, 700, 600, 500, 400, 300, 200, 100, 0

THOUSANDS OF METRIC TONS

700, 600, 500, 400, 300, 200, 100, 0

LOUISIANA, ALASKA, CALIFORNIA, VIRGINIA, MASSACHUSETTS

AVERAGE MONTHLY PRECIPITATION

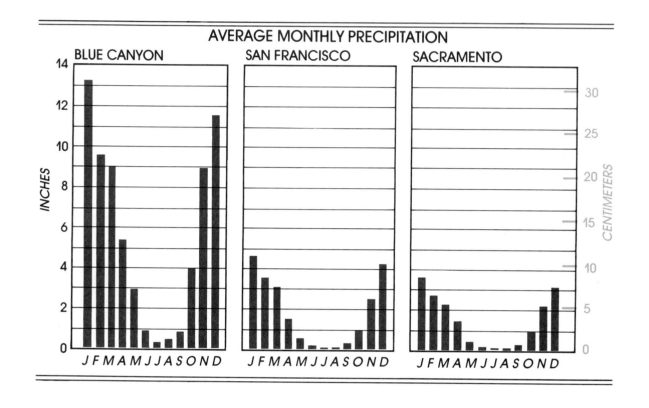

AVERAGE MONTHLY PRECIPITATION

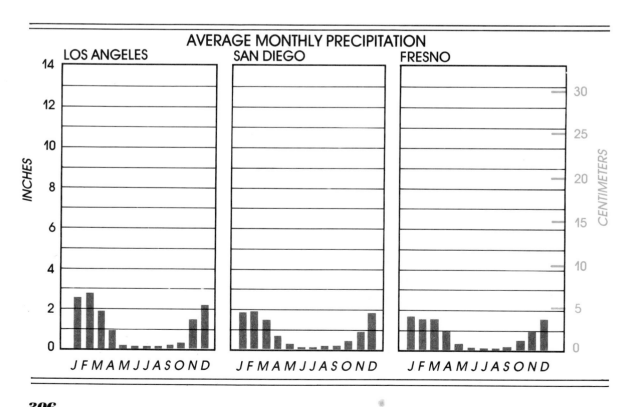

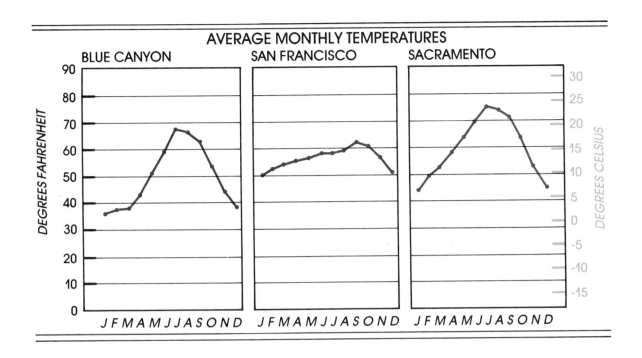

AVERAGE MONTHLY TEMPERATURES

BLUE CANYON   **SAN FRANCISCO**   **SACRAMENTO**

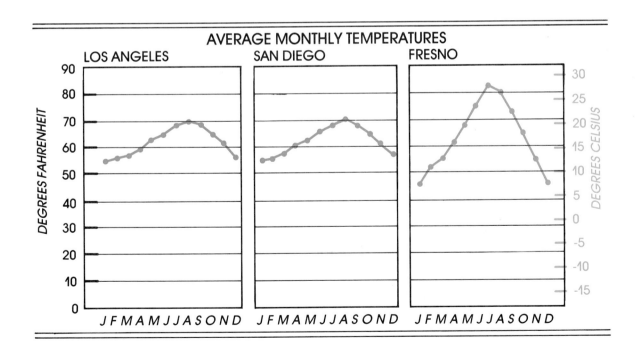

AVERAGE MONTHLY TEMPERATURES

LOS ANGELES   **SAN DIEGO**   **FRESNO**

FACTS ABOUT CALIFORNIA COUNTIES

County Name	County Seat	County Population	Population Rank	Area in Square Miles (Square Kilometers)	Area Rank	Largest Population Center
Alameda	Oakland	1,105,379	5	736 (1,907)	50	Oakland
Alpine	Markleeville	1,097	58	739 (1,913)	49	Markleeville
Amador	Jackson	19,314	48	589 (1,526)	54	Jackson
Butte	Oroville	143,851	25	1,646 (4,264)	28	Chico
Calaveras	San Andreas	20,710	47	1,021 (2,645)	40	Angeles
Colusa	Colusa	12,791	52	1,153 (2,985)	39	Colusa
Contra Costa	Martinez	656,380	10	730 (1,890)	51	Concord
Del Norte	Crescent City	18,217	49	1,007 (2,607)	42	Crescent City
El Dorado	Placerville	85,812	33	1,715 (4,443)	27	South Lake Tahoe
Fresno	Fresno	514,621	13	5,978 (15,483)	6	Fresno
Glenn	Willows	21,350	46	1,319 (3,417)	36	Willows
Humboldt	Eureka	108,514	30	3,579 (9,270)	14	Eureka
Imperial	El Centro	92,110	32	4,173 (10,808)	10	El Centro
Inyo	Independence	17,895	50	10,223 (26,478)	2	Bishop
Kern	Bakersfield	403,089	14	8,130 (21,056)	3	Bakersfield
Kings	Hanford	73,738	34	1,392 (3,605)	34	Hanford
Lake	Lakeport	36,366	42	1,262 (3,269)	38	Lakeport
Lassen	Susanville	21,661	45	4,553 (11,791)	8	Susanville
Los Angeles	Los Angeles	7,477,503	1	4,070 (10,542)	11	Los Angeles
Madera	Madera	63,116	36	2,145 (5,555)	24	Chowchilla
Marin	San Rafael	222,568	22	523 (1,354)	55	San Rafael
Mariposa	Mariposa	11,108	54	1,456 (3,771)	31	Mariposa
Mendocino	Ukiah	66,738	35	3,512 (9,096)	15	Ukiah
Merced	Merced	134,560	26	1,944 (5,036)	25	Merced
Modoc	Alturas	8,610	55	4,064 (10,527)	12	Alturas
Mono	Bridgeport	8,577	56	3,019 (7,818)	19	Bridgeport
Monterey	Salinas	290,444	18	3,303 (8,555)	17	Salinas
Napa	Napa	99,199	31	744 (1,927)	48	Napa
Nevada	Nevada	51,645	38	960 (2,487)	44	Grass Valley

FACTS ABOUT CALIFORNIA COUNTIES

County Name	County Seat	County Population	Population Rank	Area in Square Miles (Square Kilometers)	Area Rank	Largest Population Center
Orange	Santa Ana	1,932,709	2	798 (2,066)	47	Anaheim
Placer	Auburn	117,247	27	1,416 (3,668)	32	Roseville
Plumas	Quincy	17,340	51	2,573 (6,664)	22	Portola City
Riverside	Riverside	663,166	9	7,214 (18,684)	4	Riverside
Sacramento	Sacramento	783,381	7	971 (2,516)	43	Sacramento
San Benito	Hollister	25,005	44	1,388 (3,595)	35	Hollister
San Bernardino	San Bernardino	895,016	6	20,064 (51,967)	1	San Bernardino
San Diego	San Diego	1,861,846	3	4,212 (10,908)	9	San Diego
San Francisco	San Francisco	678,974	8	46 (120)	58	San Francisco
San Joaquin	Stockton	347,342	15	1,415 (3,665)	33	Stockton
San Luis Obispo	San Luis Obispo	155,435	24	3,308 (8,568)	16	San Luis Obispo
San Mateo	Redwood City	587,329	11	447 (1,157)	56	Daly City
Santa Barbara	Santa Barbara	298,694	17	2,748 (7,117)	21	Santa Barbara
Santa Clara	San Jose	1,295,071	4	1,293 (3,349)	37	San Jose
Santa Cruz	Santa Cruz	188,141	23	446 (1,156)	57	Santa Cruz
Shasta	Redding	115,715	28	3,786 (9,806)	13	Redding
Sierra	Downieville	3,073	57	959 (2,484)	45	Loyalton
Siskiyou	Yreka	39,732	40	6,281 (16,267)	5	Yreka
Solano	Fairfield	235,203	21	834 (2,161)	46	Vallejo
Sonoma	Santa Rosa	299,681	16	1,604 (4,154)	29	Santa Rosa
Stanislaus	Modesto	265,900	19	1,506 (3,901)	30	Modesto
Sutter	Yuba City	52,246	37	602 (1,559)	53	Yuba City
Tehama	Red Bluff	38,888	41	2,953 (7,649)	20	Red Bluff
Trinity	Weaverville	11,858	53	3,190 (8,261)	18	Weaverville
Tulare	Visalia	245,738	20	4,808 (12,454)	7	Visalia
Tuolumne	Sonora	33,928	43	2,234 (5,785)	23	Sonora
Ventura	Ventura	529,174	12	1,862 (4,823)	26	Oxnard
Yolo	Woodland	113,374	29	1,014 (2,627)	41	Davis
Yuba	Marysville	49,733	39	640 (1,658)	52	Marysville

100 MOST POPULATED CITIES IN CALIFORNIA

Cities	Official 1980 Census	Official 1980 Rank	Cities	Official 1980 Census	Official 1980 Rank
Los Angeles	2,966,850	1	Richmond	74,676	51
San Diego	875,538	2	Lakewood	74,654	52
San Francisco	678,974	3	Santa Barbara	74,414	53
San Jose	629,546	4	San Buenaventura	74,393	54
Long Beach	361,334	5	El Cajon	73,892	55
Oakland	339,337	6	Westminster	71,133	56
Sacramento	275,741	7	Whittier	69,717	57
Anaheim	219,494	8	South Gate	66,784	58
Fresno	217,289	9	Alhambra	64,615	59
Santa Ana	204,023	10	Escondido	64,355	60
Riverside	170,591	11	Buena Park	64,165	61
Huntington Beach	170,505	12	San Leandro	63,952	62
Stockton	149,779	13	Alameda	63,852	63
Glendale	139,060	14	Newport Beach	62,556	64
Fremont	131,945	15	Irvine	62,134	65
Torrance	129,881	16	Mountain View	58,655	66
Garden Grove	123,307	17	Fairfield	58,099	67
San Bernardino	118,794	18	Redondo Beach	57,102	68
Pasadena	118,072	19	Hawthorne	56,447	69
Oxnard	108,195	20	Rancho Cucamonga	55,250	70
Sunnyvale	106,618	21	Palo Alto	55,225	71
Modesto	106,602	22	Fountain Valley	55,080	72
Bakersfield	105,735	23	Redwood City	54,951	73
Berkeley	103,328	24	Monterey Park	54,338	74
Concord	103,255	25	Walnut Creek	53,643	75
Fullerton	102,034	26	Bellflower	53,441	76
Hayward	94,342	27	Pico Rivera	53,387	77
Inglewood	94,245	28	Cerritos	53,020	78
Pomona	92,742	29	Montebello	52,929	79
Orange	91,450	30	Napa	50,879	80
Ontario	88,820	31	Baldwin Park	50,554	81
Santa Monica	88,314	32	La Mesa	50,308	82
Santa Clara	87,700	33	Visalia	49,729	83
Norwalk	85,286	34	South San Francisco	49,393	84
Burbank	84,625	35	National City	48,772	85
Chula Vista	83,927	36	Lynwood	48,548	86
Santa Rosa	83,320	37	Livermore	48,349	87
Downey	82,602	38	Lancaster	48,027	88
Costa Mesa	82,562	39	Upland	47,647	89
Compton	81,286	40	Huntington Park	46,223	90
Carson	81,221	41	Arcadia	45,994	91
Salinas	80,479	42	La Habra	45,232	92
Vallejo	80,303	43	Gardena	45,165	93
West Covina	80,291	44	San Rafael	44,700	94
El Monte	79,494	45	Novato	43,916	95
Daly City	78,519	46	Redlands	43,619	96
San Mateo	77,640	47	Vacaville	43,367	97
Simi Valley	77,500	48	Antioch	42,683	98
Thousand Oaks	77,072	49	Rosemead	42,604	99
Oceanside	76,698	50	Redding	41,995	100

GOVERNORS OF CALIFORNIA

Spanish Governors	1. Gaspar de Portolá	1769-1770
	2. Felipe de Barri	1770-1775
	3. Felipe de Neve	1775-1782
	4. Pedro Fages	1782-1791
	5. José Romeu	1791-1792
	6. José Arrillaga	1792-1794
	7. Diego de Borica	1794-1800
	8. José Arrillaga	1800-1814
	9. José Argüello	1814-1815
	10. Pablo de Solá	1815-1822
Mexican Governors	1. Luis Argüello	1822-1825
	2. José Maria Echeandia	1825-1831
	3. Manuel Victoria	1831-1832
	4. Pío Pico	1832-1833
	5. José Figueroa	1833-1835
	6. José Castro	1835-1836
	7. Nicolás Gutiérrez	1836 (January to May)
	8. Mariano Chico	1836 (few months)
	9. Nicolás Gutiérrez	1836 (few months)
	10. Juan B. Alvarado	1836-1842
	11. Manuel Micheltorena	1842-1845
	12. Pío Pico	1846 (February 22 to August 10)
American Governors Under Military Rule	1. John D. Sloat	July 7, 1846
	2. Robert F. Stockton	July 29, 1846
	3. John C. Frémont	January 19, 1847
	4. Stephen W. Kearny	March 1, 1847
	5. Richard B. Mason	May 31, 1847
	6. Persifor F. Smith	February 28, 1849
	7. Bennet Riley	April 12, 1849
Governors of the State of California	1. Peter H. Burnett	1849-1851
	2. John McDougal	1851-1852
	3. John Bigler	1852-1856
	4. John Neely Johnson	1856-1858
	5. John B. Weller	1858-1860
	6. Milton S. Latham	1860
	7. John G. Downey	1860-1862
	8. Leland Stanford	1862-1863
	9. Frederick F. Low	1863-1867
	10. Henry H. Haight	1867-1871
	11. Newton Booth	1871-1875
	12. Romualdo Pacheco	1875
	13. William Irwin	1875-1880
	14. George C. Perkins	1880-1883
	15. George Stoneman	1883-1887
	16. Washington Bartlett	1887
	17. Robert W. Waterman	1887-1891
	18. Henry H. Markham	1891-1895
	19. James H. Budd	1895-1899
	20. Henry T. Gage	1899-1903
	21. George C. Pardee	1903-1907
	22. James N. Gillett	1907-1911
	23. Hiram W. Johnson	1911-1917
	24. William D. Stephens	1917-1923
	25. Friend W. Richardson	1923-1927
	26. Clement C. Young	1927-1931
	27. James Rolph, Jr.	1931-1934
	28. Frank F. Merriam	1934-1939
	29. Culbert L. Olson	1939-1943
	30. Earl Warren	1943-1953
	31. Goodwin J. Knight	1953-1959
	32. Edmund G. Brown	1959-1967
	33. Ronald Reagan	1967-1975
	34. Edmund G. Brown, Jr.	1975-1982
	35. George Deukmejian	1982-

IMPORTANT DATES IN CALIFORNIA HISTORY

1492	Christopher Columbus sails to America.
1535	Hernando Cortés reaches Lower California.
1542	Juan Rodríguez Cabrillo reaches Upper California.
1602	Sebastián Vizcaíno explores coast of California.
1769	Gálvez Expedition arrives in San Diego. Mission San Diego de Alcala is founded by Father Junípero Serra at San Diego. San Diego is founded.
1770	Mission San Carlos Borroméo is founded at Monterey.
1771	Mission San Antonio de Padua is founded. Mission San Gabriel Arcangel is founded.
1772	Mission San Luis Obispo is founded.
1776	Mission San Francisco de Asis is founded. Mission San Juan Capistrano is founded.
1777	Mission Santa Clara is founded.
1782	Mission San Buenaventura is founded.
1786	Mission Santa Barbara is founded.
1787	Mission La Purisima Concepcion is founded.
1791	Mission Santa Cruz is founded. Mission Nuestra Senora de la Soledad is founded.
1796	First ship from the United States (the *Otter*) arrives at Monterey.
1797	Mission San Jose de Guadalupe is founded. Mission San Juan Bautista is founded. Mission San Miguel Arcangel is founded. Mission San Fernando Rey de Espana is founded.
1798	Mission San Luis Rey de Francia is founded.
1804	Mission Santa Ines is founded.
1812	Russians build fort at Fort Ross.
1817	Mission San Rafael Arcangel is founded.
1821	Mexico gains its independence from Spain.
1823	Mission San Francisco de Solano is founded.
1826	Jedediah Smith party travels to California.
1841	John Bidwell party travels to California.
1842	Russians leave California.
1844	John Frémont enters California.
1846	California independence proclaimed during Bear Flag Revolt in Sonoma. Mexican-American War begins in Texas.
1848	Treaty of Guadalupe Hidalgo ends Mexican-American War. California becomes part of the United States. James Marshall discovers gold in the American River.
1849	State constitutional convention is held at Monterey. Peter H. Burnett is elected first governor of California.
1850	California becomes the thirty-first state.
1854	State capital is moved to Sacramento.
1861	Telegraph lines are completed between California and the East Coast. Civil War starts. First California oil well is drilled in Humboldt County.
1862	Congress passes the Pacific Railroad Bill.
1865	Civil War ends.
1869	Transcontinental railroad is completed.
1887	More than 200,000 people move to southern California.
1890	First Pasadena Tournament of Roses parade is held.
1906	San Francisco earthquake strikes.
1907	Movies first produced in California. First airplane is built in California.
1910	First United States air show is held in California.
1913	Owens Valley Aqueduct is completed. Webb Act passed to prevent Japanese from buying land in California.
1914	Panama Canal opens.
1917	United States enters World War I.
1920	Large oil strike is made at Huntington Beach.
1921	Large oil strikes are made at Santa Fe Springs and Signal Hill.
1927	First "talkie," *The Jazz Singer*, is produced in California.
1929	Depression begins.
1931	Hetch Hetchy Dam is completed.
1936	San Francisco-Oakland Bay Bridge and Golden Gate Bridge are completed.
1941	United States enters World War II. Japanese Americans forced to move to "relocation centers."
1945	World War II ends.
1962	Cesar Chavez starts union for farm workers.
1969	American astronauts land on the moon.
1972	State constitution is revised.
1980	Official census ranks California first in population among the 50 states.
1982	George Deukmejian is elected governor.

INDEX

The Key to Pronunciation above is reprinted from *The World Book Dictionary,*© 1981, by permission of J.G. Ferguson, Publishing Company, Chicago, IL 60601

CREDITS

4 5 6 7 8 9 10-RRD-91 90 89 88 87 86 85 84